DANCING IN PETERSBURG

H.S.H. *The Princess Romanovsky-Krassinsky*

DANCING IN PETERSBURG

THE MEMOIRS OF KSCHESSINSKA

Translated by
A R N O L D   H A S K E L L

LONDON
VICTOR GOLLANCZ LTD
1960

This book was originally published in French under the title
SOUVENIRS DE LA KSCHESSINSKA

© 1960 by Librairie Plon

© English translation 1960 by Victor Gollancz Ltd.

Printed in Great Britain by
The Camelot Press Ltd., London and Southampton

PREFACE

THESE MEMOIRS, which were practically completed several years ago, have been prevented from appearing until now by a series of painful circumstances.

When they were finished, I spoke of them to the Grand Duchess Marie, sister of the Grand Duke Dimitri Pavlovitch, who was kind enough to read them. Not only did she take the greatest interest in them, but she encouraged me warmly to publish them, and offered to translate them into English, which she knew perfectly, and to see to their publication. She wished also to write a foreword, in order, she said, to emphasise her friendship for me, and especially to show that the family did not look on me as a stranger.

For a year we worked together on the details, while she undertook the translation. But failing health slowed down her work, and finally she was forced to abandon it. In December 1958 death removed her from us, and she now lies with her brother Dimitri in the vault on the property of her son, Count Bernadotte, at Mainau in Germany.

I then started afresh with my husband, the Grand Duke André. But his strength failed during the last two years of his life, and we were unable to complete the task with our old diligence. On top of everything, in 1956 I suffered a fall, whose after-effects left me immobilised for more than six months. Then God took back my husband, and for a long time I was incapable of undertaking any task.

These memoirs were written in close collaboration with the Grand Duke, and all those who have read the Russian text have praised his work. I do not think that I could have completed them without him.

PRINCESS MARIE ROMANOVSKY-KRASSINSKY.

CONTENTS

LIST OF ILLUSTRATIONS

CHAPTER I

A DYNASTY OF ARTISTS

How often, during our childhood, did I hear my father tell us our family's history, whose origins go back to the Counts Krassinsky.[1] Nobody had ever thought of writing this story; with the help of my memories I shall try here to retrace the essential details.

The artistic dynasty of the Kschessinskys, whose sole representative I am today, came into being a century and a half before my birth.

The story which my father told us happened in Poland during the first half of the eighteenth century. My great-great-grandfather, as eldest son, had inherited a considerable fortune from his father, Count Krassinsky, while his only and younger brother received very little. Some time later my great-great-grandfather lost his loved wife and died of sorrow, after first entrusting his son Wojciech, my great-grandfather, to his French tutor. A twelve-year-old orphan was thus the head of the important inheritance of the Counts Krassinsky.

His uncle, wishing to have the fortune he considered himself cheated of, now determined to hire assassins to get rid of the boy. Fortunately one of these men was overcome by remorse and warned the tutor, who decided that the only way to save his charge was to flee with him from Poland. He hastily assembled a few documents, gathered everything that he could carry off without arousing the household's attention, and took young Wojciech with him into France, where he put him in the Krassinsky family house at Neuilly. As a further precaution he registered the child under his mother's name of Krzesinsky (Kschesinsky). This took place in 1748.

After his tutor's death young Wojciech stayed in Paris, where, in 1763, he married Anna Ziomkowska, a Polish émigrée, by whom he had a son, Jan, born in 1770. Later when my great-grandfather returned to Warsaw with his son, thinking all danger past, he had the unpleasant surprise of discovering that during his fifty years' absence his uncle had proclaimed him dead and seized all his property. His efforts to obtain restitution were of no avail: in his headlong flight his tutor had forgotten to take certain documents. In addition many archives,

---

[1] The names "Krassinsky" and "Kschessinsky" have been spelt with two "s's" instead of one, in order to give a more exact rendering of Russian pronunciation.

particularly those of the churches, had disappeared during the wars and disturbances which had ravaged Poland. Though unable to have his rights recognised, my great-grandfather nevertheless kept a great many papers locked in a box which on his death he bequeathed to Jan, who in turn passed it on to my father, warning him to keep it carefully. "Your future depends on it," he said. Alas, my father, taken in by some dishonest relative, one day lent him the box, which he was destined never to see again. The only evidence he now had left to support his claims was a ring with the arms of the Counts Krassinsky.[1]

In 1798, shortly after his return to Warsaw, my grandfather married Felicité Petronelli-Derengowska, by whom he had three children: my Uncle Stanislas, born in 1800, my Aunt Mathilde and my father, born in 1821.

My grandfather had devoted himself to music from childhood; as a virtuoso violinist he is reputed to have played at Nicolo Paganini's concerts. Nature had also endowed him with a magnificent voice through which he became principal tenor at the Warsaw Opera and was called "my *slowik*" (nightingale) by the King of Poland. He was to lose his beautiful voice but, far from being discouraged, he turned to drama, and very soon acquired a reputation as a superb actor.

This was the man my father had to follow. Initiated into the art of dancing at eight years old under the direction of Maurice Piona the maître de ballet, he began with classical dances but later devoted himself entirely to character dances and mimed roles.

In 1835, at the age of fourteen, he danced for the first time in the presence of the Tsar, at Kalisz, at the time of the meeting between Frederick William III of Prussia and Tsar Nicholas I. The Emperor had wanted this important political event to be marked by particularly brilliant displays. As well as lavish manœuvres and military parades on the outskirts of the town, balls, shows and spectacular receptions were organised in the town itself in honour of the King of Prussia; a theatre was built for these festivities and the best artists in Warsaw were called

[1] These arms can be found in the Polish armorial: "On a blue azure background a silver horseshoe crowned with a gold cross, on this cross a crow holding in its beak a gold ring; on the shield, a count's crown, a noble's helmet and crown under the same black crow: azure and silver fillet." My father also clearly remembered going several times, as a child, to the palace of the Krassinskys with my grandfather; he also recalled that my grandfather received a certain sum of money every month. These memories may be taken as indirect evidence of our origins.

upon. My father enjoyed recalling these days, which also had some influence on his artistic career.

The emperor Nicholas I stayed in Warsaw several times. An informed balletomane, he appreciated Polish national dances and was particularly delighted by the mazurka.[1] St. Petersburg had not yet seen these dances, and, in 1851, the Tsar decided to transfer five male and five female dancers from Warsaw to the Russian capital where they could interpret his favourite dance.

My father was one of the five male dancers invited to St. Petersburg. He was seriously hurt in the hand, however, during the performance, in Warsaw, of the ballet *Catherina*, and was forced to abandon the move. It was only later that he reached the capital where, on January 30th 1853, he appeared on the stage of the Alexandre Theatre in *Les Noces Paysannes*, dancing the krakowiak, the mazurka and a *pas-de-trois* with Snietkowa and Parkatcheva. From this time he settled in St. Petersburg, which he was not to leave till his death.

The public of the Maryinsky Theatre gave him unfailing success. His interpretation of the mazurka was considered exemplary; he was even rated higher than the famous Warsaw dancer Popel. For many years afterwards balletomanes spoke of his dazzling successes in the mazurka which he composed for the ballet *Laquelle des Trois*, danced with Marie Petipa, Liadova II and Kocheva. Here is one record among many, that of A. Plestscheev,[2] who had seen him at the height of his glory: "It is difficult to imagine a prouder, livelier or more fiery performance of this national dance. Kschessinsky gave it a stamp of grandeur and nobility. It was due to him, or as it has been said, to his lightness of leg, that the mazurka first received the overwhelming popularity which it was to enjoy in our capital's high society. Felix Kschessinsky gave mazurka classes, and the dance thus became one of the chief ballroom dances throughout Russia."

[1] On the 11th July 1851, when a gala performance was to be given in the Peterhof Gardens to honour the Grand Duchess Olga's birthday, the Emperor came on stage in person during the dress rehearsal and expressed a wish to see the mazurka performed. As the dancers had no Polish costumes, he told them to dance in their Neapolitan fishermen costumes. Luckily the conductor, A. N. Liadov, had had the forethought to bring the music! This amusing incident was related by an eye-witness, General G. . . ., in his book, *Description de Peterhof.*

[2] Alexander Plestscheev was one of the leading Russian theatre critics, and more especially of the ballet.

CHAPTER II

YEARS OF CHILDHOOD

I HAD A VERY happy childhood. My parents adored us and lived only for us. I owe them the marvellous enchanted atmosphere which will remain for ever in my mind as the most precious memory of my early years.

After finishing her studies at the Imperial Theatre School my mother remained for several years in the Ballet Company. Then she gave up the stage on marrying the French dancer Lédé. Widowed, she remarried, her second husband being Adam-Felix Kschessinsky, my father. She had thirteen children in all, of whom I was the youngest.

I was born on August 19th 1872 (September 1st according to the Gregorian calendar)[1] at Ligovo, a small town on the road to Peterhof, about nine miles from St. Petersburg. My parents used to rent a villa there at that time, in order to allow the children to enjoy themselves in the fresh air, far from the capital's dusty and overheated atmosphere.

For several years in succession we spent the summer months there. Not far from the house where I was born was the famous Cabaret Rouge where the Empress Catherine II had spent a night in 1762 when, clad in the uniform of the Preobrajensky Regiment, she was on her way to St. Petersburg at the head of her regiments of the Guard. She was proclaimed Empress on June 23rd 1762.

I was my father's favourite child. Guessing my gifts and my artistic vocation, he hoped that I might carry on our family's glorious tradition on the stage where he himself and his father before him had shone. Already when only three years old I liked to dance, and my father used to take me to the Grand Theatre where ballets and operas were performed. This was a great delight to me. I can remember a curious incident that took place during one of these matinées.

That day the ballet *Le Petit Cheval Bossu* was being performed. First presented on December 3rd 1864 by Saint-Léon at Mouravieva's benefit performance, this charming ballet was within the grasp of a little girl just starting to adore the theatre. My father had the mimed role of the *khan*; it was one of the best in his repertoire. And so he put

[1] Dates will be given by the "Russian" calendar until the exile (the Gregorian calendar was introduced into Russia on February 16th 1918). For outstanding events both dates will be given.

1a. Felix Kschessinsky, my father.

1b. Julie Kschessinska, my mother.

2.   Myself aged eight.

me, all alone, backstage in one of the special artists' balcony boxes, and hurried off to get ready.

These boxes had a special charm: they were backstage and gave one a view not only of the performance but also of the scene changing in the interval, a sight which naturally thrilled me. How can I forget the wonder of the ballet, the concentration with which I followed the dancing and my father's acting, the ever-renewed enchantment of décors and lights. On stage it was day, then night and moonlight, the wind, storm and thunder, all of which transported me and seemed wonderful, mysterious and enchanting.

When the performance was over I quietly waited for my father to return, knowing that he needed time to change and remove his make-up. But seeing nobody come I silently slipped from my seat and hid behind it, convinced that I would thus be able to remain invisible in the box until the evening performance which was to start in a few hours. In the meantime, hidden in my corner, I could watch the fascinating process of erecting new décor.

Meanwhile my father, who had removed his make-up, had calmly left the theatre to return home, happy and well content, thinking only of the ballet and his acting, and forgetting everything else including his daughter. He only remembered when he heard my mother cry out in horror: "Where is Mala?"

"My God!" said my father. "She's at the theatre," and he ran back to fetch me.

Meanwhile, still comfortably settled behind the seat, I was not losing a scrap of what was going on on the stage. When I heard my father's hurried footsteps I immediately slipped under the seat in the hope of avoiding his eye and, in spite of everything, attending the evening performance. Alas, pitilessly dragged from my hiding-place I was brought back home without further delay.

The Grand Theatre no longer exists. It was demolished at the end of the nineteenth century, and a conservatoire, with a small theatre, built on the same site. But my earliest memories and artistic impressions belong there: it was there that my vocation took shape, there that I first appeared on the stage, and in the same place—the Conservatoire Theatre—that in 1917 I was to dance for the last time in Russia.

My mother had four children of her marriage to my father. One died young, the other three devoted their lives to dancing. Julie, my elder sister, was very beautiful. Unsurpassed in character dances, she appeared under the name Kschessinska I. She was considered an adornment to the stage, and always received the best positions. Iouzia, my brother, was a very talented dancer, resembling my father in every respect. He was as good-looking, tall, and slim as my father, and he worshipped his art, that art which my father considered life's most precious gift.

Having had the opportunity, during my long life, of seeing many admirable artists, I often think of my father and of Virginia Zucchi, and I believe that today, in spite of all the changes in taste, technique and the requirements of dancing, they would both still have the same success as before and would be considered artists of the first rank, serving as examples to all whose acting is exaggerated and uninspired.

On February 8th 1898 the Press, celebrating my father's sixty years of artistic life, stressed the impossibility of naming all the roles he had interpreted, all the ballets in which he had appeared. "While ballerinas, maîtres de ballet, stage managers, directors and conductors constantly succeeded one another, he was always there, faithfully at his post, steadfast and irreplaceable."[1]

However the ballets I loved the most, of all this countless number, were the ones where I danced at his side—*Paquita*, *La Fille de Pharaon*, *Esmeralda*. His acting inspired me. With him I no longer felt I was simply a dancer acting before an audience, but the actual character I was playing.

Nobody, as I have said, ever danced the mazurka like my father. He bequeathed to me this dance into which he put all his temperament. Through his interpretation and Nicholas I's fondness for the dance, the mazurka established itself first in the theatre and next in the ballroom under a simplified form more easily mastered by amateurs. There was stiff competition to take private lessons with him; everywhere he was fêted and received as a friend. Many were the times when I accompanied him to his children's classes, and took delight in sweeping up his little pupils into the frenzied whirls of a fiery mazurka.

We were not rich, but the stage and classes brought my father enough to allow us to enjoy comfort and ease. Our apartment was always large and was situated in the smartest part of town; there was always a huge room where pupils came for their classes. How I adored these lessons! When I was still a child I tried my hardest to dance in the next room to the strains of mazurkas and waltzes coming from the classroom.

My father liked to spend his spare time in manual work, and he was

[1] The weekly *Niva*, 1898.

as much a master in this craft as in his art. I remember that one day he built a very elaborate aquarium, with its bottom decorated with stone ornaments. But his real masterpiece was the model of the St. Petersburg Grand Theatre. Everything was there: the scenery went up and down as in a real theatre, the lighting was a system of tiny oil lamps, and by turning a handle one could have a complete change of scene— he also painted the décor for a ballet. After his death this model was placed in the Bakhouchin Museum in Moscow.[1]

My father loved entertaining and he knew how to feast his guests. Christmas and Easter were the times especially when he showed off his culinary talents! By an ancient custom, carefully observed in our family, a wide assortment of dishes covered the table.

At Easter my father prepared the *koulitchs* himself. With a white apron round him he kneaded the dough, always in a brand new wooden bowl. Following tradition he made twelve *koulitchs*, one for each of the Apostles. The effigy of a lamb decorated with a flag was placed on the table. On Easter Saturday the parish priest came to bless our Easter table.

Christmas Eve we celebrated very solemnly *en famille*. Only intimate friends were invited; among them I remember M. Rache, my brother Iouzia's tutor. We celebrated the feast according to Polish traditions. Until six o'clock in the evening, when the first star appeared, we had to observe the strictest fast. But at supper, the great day's main event, my father's culinary gifts reached their climax. Tradition called for thirteen fish dishes—fasting dishes—each of which had a symbolical significance (later my father limited the number to seven). First two fish soups were brought in, which my mother served herself, one Russian style, the other Polish style with cream. I liked the latter best, and although I have never tasted it except at my parent's house I have not forgotten it; my father, so it seemed, was the only one who knew its secret recipe. When the meal was over, we lit the candles on the Christmas tree, at the foot of which the presents for the guests were arranged. This custom of the Christmas tree was one which I was to keep up all my life, and even today I know no greater joy than lighting the candles and giving everybody their presents.

I should like to describe everything about this happy childhood with

[1] This was the museum to which I gave my first Polish costume, a real doll's costume, which was made for me when I was four years old, as well as the child's shoes which I had worn on the Grand Theatre stage in *Le Petit Cheval Bossu*, in which I appeared in the tableau of the underwater kingdom.

its seasonal colours, like those summers in the country, on our Krassnitzy estate, near Siverskaia Station, forty miles from St. Petersburg, which my father had bought from General Gaussmann. Our house, built of wood and situated on the heights overlooking the river Orlinka had only two storeys. Surrounding it, valleys and fields extended as far as the eye could see. My father had arranged the estate in his own way and made several changes, among them in the old dining-room, which was too small to hold our whole family as well as the many visitors who came in constant streams. A huge bath house had also been installed on the river. Not far from the house were a large orchard and a vegetable garden: and beyond was the vast forest where I often went, early in the morning, to pick mushrooms. The estate included a farm—a real dairy establishment—and wonderful meadows. Haymaking was for us children the best time of summer. The haymakers were by tradition invited to lunch before the work began. We were on excellent terms with the peasants of the region who loved and respected my father for his fairness and cordiality. The peasants' children were our companions in play, and every Sunday we invited them to tea.

Our day began very early. My father rose at five, to supervise the work and make sure that his instructions were followed. We ourselves rose just before breakfast, which was served at eight o'clock, and was every bit as substantial and varied as lunch, tea and dinner. But even so this did not stop us running to the orchard to gorge ourselves on fruit and berries. Sports, walks and games also kept up our appetites: for easier climbing of trees and hiding in the bushes I wore a grey boy's suit. And, as is best in the country, we went to bed early. Such a way of life made us as plump as anything. Besides, it must be confessed, I was greedy, a failing which was later to draw from our maître de ballet Leon Ivanov the cutting remark: "It is heartrending to see such a gifted artist become so fat!"

My father had turned the nineteenth of August, my birthday, into the summer's most delightful holiday, in which villages, hamlets, and the surrounding villas and estates all shared.

Early in the morning the peasants from the neighbouring villages came, with their families, to congratulate me and bring me presents: a basket of eggs, fruit, mushrooms, white cheese, napkins embroidered with little crosses. These gifts moved me greatly.

Friends never stopped pouring in, particularly on Saturdays and Sundays; but it was most of all on my birthday that the house overflowed with guests from the capital and the neighbouring estates. We fitted up these guests wherever there might be space, and those who could not have a room slept in the hay-loft. I remember that one day we moved the ladder from the loft where one of our guests was taking a siesta. He did not appreciate the joke when he awoke.

In the evening the grounds about the house were lit up by lamps made and arranged by my father. Then there was a wonderful firework display, likewise prepared by my father, which people flocked to see from all parts. One year we even had the amazing sight of a torchlight procession galloping up from one of the nearby estates.

Needless to say these celebrations were followed by a supper that was as tasty as it was lavish, always washed down with hot Swedish punch, which my father knew how to make. He thought of countless things to amuse me and make me happy on those days. Once he hung on the dining-room ceiling a wreath of fresh flowers which automatically descended on my head during supper. But another year when he wanted to repeat this effect, the wreath accidentally descended on my neighbour's head, a rather simple boy, who provided a general laugh.

At fourteen I had a flirtation with a very elegant young Englishman named Macpherson. Not that I was particularly in love with him, but this innocent little love affair entertained me. On my birthday Macpherson arrived with his fiancée. Could I put up with such an insult? I planned vengeance! When we were all together, his fiancée sitting beside him, I said, assuming an air of perfect indifference, that I adored going picking mushrooms in the morning. Whereupon the young Englishman politely asked leave to accompany me. I replied that I saw nothing to stop him, provided, of course, that his fiancée agreed. As all this took place before all the guests she could only agree, inwardly raging, and the following day young Macpherson and I went picking mushrooms through the forest. It was there that he gave me a beautiful ivory purse, decorated with forget-me-nots, an ideal present for a girl of my age. By the end of the walk I thought that Macpherson had completely forgotten his fiancée. That walk through the woods won me many love-letters and flowers from him! But I soon grew tired of the idyll; my young squire did not interest me. But his marriage was permanently compromised. That was the first time I suffered remorse!

CHAPTER III

THE IMPERIAL THEATRE SCHOOL

Behind the Imperial Alexandre Theatre stretched the wide but short Theatre Street, leading to the Tchernichev Bridge. This yellow-and-white ensemble in St. Petersburg Empire style was one of the finest in the capital. In Theatre Street there were none but official buildings. Starting from the Alexandre Theatre on the right was the Ministry, where the Lord Chamberlain exercised his functions; on the left the whole street was filled by the magnificent Imperial Theatre School, whose walls were decorated with reliefs.

The Alexandre Theatre's façade, its roof surmounted by three bronze horses, faced the Nevsky Prospect. Theatre Street was always very quiet. At most a coach carrying future dancers to rehearsals or performances sometimes passed through the large gateway. Even for such a short journey, at all times of the year, the School's pupils only went out in these vast, old-fashioned vehicles, hermetically sealed, which never ceased to excite the curiosity of passers-by anxious to catch a glimpse of the pretty faces hidden behind the windows.

Every autumn, after a medical inspection and a strict test of their dancing aptitudes, children aged from nine to eleven were admitted to the School whose full strength was sixty to seventy girls and forty to fifty boys, all bound by the boarding school's rules.

When they had finished their studies at the Ballet School, the pupils of both sexes, now seventeen to eighteen years old, passed into the Imperial Theatre Company where they remained for twenty years, after which they could either retire, safe with a pension, or be re-engaged by contract. The Ballet School taught not only ballet but also general subjects, like an ordinary school. The curriculum covered seven years, but there were only five classes, two of which lasted for two consecutive years.

Although the Schools and Companies in St. Petersburg and Moscow were separate, they were considered to be a single ensemble depending on the Ministry of the Imperial Court and run by the Administration of the Imperial Theatres. The artists of the Imperial Theatres, both those of St. Petersburg and Moscow, appeared in the theatres of both capitals.

The School rules demanded that the pupils should be boarders, but certain pupils were sometimes allowed to live with their families while they took the classes at the School. My brother, sister and I were among these rare exceptions. As a rule parents preferred their children to enter as boarders at the State's expense. But our parents preferred the other solution, wanting to keep us by their side and to look after our general instruction. They felt that family life was essential to our education. Their decision meant extra work for us, with daily lessons at home on top of those at school; but we were glad not to be separated from our parents like "the *pépinières*" as the boarders were called.

My sister Julie, six years older than I, entered the School first, followed by my brother Iouzia,[1] four years older than myself. At last, in the autumn of 1880, when I was just eight, I passed into the Imperial Theatre School.

The girls lived on the first floor of the School, the boys on the second. Each floor consisted of huge dormitories and rehearsal rooms with high ceilings and enormous windows. The first floor also contained the little School theatre, very well arranged, with only a few rows of seats. This was where the graduation performances took place, which were later moved to the Michel Theatre; and it was there, as will be seen, that my fate and my future were decided.

My first teacher at the Theatre School was Leon Ivanov, that admirable maître de ballet, some of whose arrangements—the second act of *Swan Lake* and the ballet *Casse-Noisette* to Tchaikovsky's music —were never surpassed, while among single dances, his czardas to Liszt's music remains unforgettable.

Leon Ivanov accompanied our dances himself on the violin, a violin which he seemed to love even better than his pupils. His gifts never reached a full flowering, partly owing to his innate indolence, partly to circumstances, for the all-powerful Petipa, chief maître de ballet, could at will lightly retouch any one of his creations, which passed henceforth from his fatherhood. Leon Ivanov taught the beginning exercises, what might be called the alphabet of ballet, in which I did not take much interest, having already learnt them at home before entering the School. I sometimes had the impression that Ivanov limited himself to telling us the movements and to routine observations. In a lazy voice he would tell us: "*Pliez!*" or "*Genoux en dehors!*" but he never stopped us, made no corrections, did not interrupt the class to point out a pupil's wrong movement. I also felt that he was not creative, that he lacked inspiration, and that instead of putting life into us he was content to teach us in a routine manner.

[1] Short for Joseph.

Later, when I was a dancer and he used to come to watch me, I discovered that he had another passion, besides his violin: like many artists, Ivanov liked food; undoing his napkin with a singular delight, he proclaimed, in inimitable fashion, "Now we are going to enjoy our food!"

I stayed three years in his class, and, when I was eleven, moved into that taken by Catherine Vazem, ballerina of the Imperial Theatres, where less simple movements were already accomplished. Not only were the exercises taught with a care to their right execution, but gracefulness was also demanded. Catherine Vazem's class began with exercises at the barre, followed by adagios and allegros in the middle of the studio. The steps were not complicated: attitudes, arabesques, leaps, *pointes*, *pas de bourrée*, *sauts de basque*, all the basic steps, in fact, which modern technique has preserved. Vazem saw that we adopted the correct position of the foot *sur les pointes*—a very important matter —and also that our *en dehors* was satisfactory. Her class was a kind of transition, preparing us for that of Johanson, a real school of virtuosity. Vazem carefully followed the pupils and did not hesitate to interrupt them if she thought the execution of steps incorrect or lacking grace. She was satisfied with me, and all she said, not unkindly, was "Kschessinska! Don't frown or you'll grow old before your time!" But her lessons also seemed to be lacking in inspiration. I had learnt all these movements a long time ago, and my enthusiasm suffered accordingly.

It was quite another matter in Johanson's class, which I entered when I was fifteen: so much so that later, as an artist, I was to go on working with him. Johanson, a Swede by birth, had nevertheless had time to become Russian in St. Petersburg. He was not only an excellent teacher, but a poet, an artist and inspired creator. He knew how to think, and he knew how to observe, and his pertinent remarks were highly valued by us. His art was noble because it was simple, and the man himself was as simple as he was sincere. Every movement he made had meaning, expressed a thought, reflected a state of soul, which he strove to pass on to us. I owe my career, in a large part, to him.

The part of the building where the girls lived was strictly separated from the boys' quarters. On the first floor were the girls' dormitories and classroom, and the rehearsal rooms, two large and one small. A wide corridor led from here to the School theatre on the same floor. A small staircase led to the floor above, a copy of the one below, holding the boys' rooms and the inspector's office. Following the

3*a*. The *datcha* at Ligovo (at the back of picture) where I was born.

3*b*. The small stage at the Theatre School.

4*a*. The Theatre at Krasnoïe Selo.

4*b*. Auditorium of the Maryinsky Theatre, St. Petersburg.

corridor which passed in front of this office and the classrooms, one arrived at a small but very lovely church, flooded in light, sparkling with the jewels encrusted in the icons which the artists had presented to the School. There were services on Saturday evening, Sunday morning and holidays. When the girls went to church accompanied by their teachers wearing their long uniform dresses with little white hoods, their hair strictly smoothed down and plaited, they used the wide main staircase.

Since all communication between boys and girls was strictly forbidden, many were the dodges which had to be used for an innocent exchange of looks, smiles or words. Naturally, the teachers did not let us out of their sight during rehearsals and dancing classes; however, despite our sentinels, we always managed to snatch a few seconds' flirtation, for these gatherings provided us with our only opportunities! These secret intrigues were part of the School's traditions, and each girl had her own particular boy-friend. But these meetings, these short idylls were most naïve and innocent. Sometimes, however, rather more serious flirtations took place and occasionally attained disquieting proportions, approaching, if not actually reaching, true love.

Learning caused me little difficulty, for I also studied at home and prepared my lessons in advance. Furthermore, although I was by nature high-spirited and lively, my behaviour in class was exemplary, which won me the liking of the Headmistress and the teachers. But I was very coquettish, and I can still remember my shame when our young, attractive geography master, Pavlovsky, asked me to take the place at the blackboard of a pupil who did not know the answers. It was a day when I was sure I would not be asked, for questions went in turns, and I had come to class in winter boots with laces and thick check stockings. In my confusion I got up and stammered that I knew my lesson, but would he be kind enough to let me answer from my seat. The teacher consented, though rather at a loss; but when the lesson was over he demanded to know the reason for my attitude. Blushing and embarrassed, I ended by confessing that I had not wanted to show myself before all the class in such an inelegant outfit. Far from being angry, Pavlovsky was most understanding and bestowed on me a charming smile.

A year after I entered the School, on August 30th 1881, I danced for the first time on the boards of the Grand Theatre, in the ballet *Don Quixote*, with an older pupil, Anderson, who was the same height as myself despite the difference in age. We played two marionettes, controlled by a thread in the hands of a giant, and performed our dance on points. I was not at all afraid, merely immensely happy at appearing on stage.

Accustomed to the stage from our earliest years, we took part in ballets and could see our greatest dancers at work. As age and experience helped us, we found it easier to appraise them, to observe their qualities and faults, to sum up their respective talents and even the general level of our ballet.

At the time when I was studying, the St. Petersburg Theatre ballet was already beginning to totter. The former generation's stars— Sokolova, Vazem, Gorchenkova—could no longer serve us as an example; and so my fervour for ballet began to wane.

I was fourteen when the famous Virginia Zucchi arrived in St. Petersburg. I was already receiving small roles which I strove to interpret to the best of my powers and which even won me praises. But I had no faith in what was being done in our company, and my dancing yielded me no deep satisfaction. I was seized with doubts: had I chosen the career which suited me? I cannot imagine where all that might have led me, had it not been for Virginia Zucchi's arrival, who, immediately, and radically, altered my state of mind, revealing to me the true meaning of our art. Virginia Zucchi was no longer young, but her exceptional gifts had lost none of their vigour. I felt an overwhelming, unforgettable sensation when I watched her. I felt that I was beginning to understand, for the first time, how one should dance in order to deserve the title of a great dancer. Virginia Zucchi had a wonderful gift for mime. She gave all the movements of classical ballet extraordinary charm and astonishing beauty of expression, filling the audience with enthusiasm whenever she danced.

Her acting henceforth became true art for me, and I understood that the essence of such art does not lie exclusively in virtuosity and technique. I realised that technique, far from being an end, is only a means.

Zucchi's movements, the line of the arms and back, were wonderfully expressive, and I wanted to seize them, to make a mental photograph of them, greedily following her acting with my childish eyes: later people were to say that I attained Zucchi's perfection in these movements. When, in my later career, I danced *Esmeralda*, I was inspired by memories of her interpretation which, in this ballet, had reached the most sublime dramatic expression. For me Zucchi was the genius of dancing, a genius which had inspired and directed me in the true way at a time when I was still on the verge of adolescence and about to begin my career: I have vowed her eternal gratitude!

The inspiration was like a crack of the whip and I understood what I must now try to attain. I knew to what I was called. Zucchi for her part understood my adoration, and for a long time I kept in a glass vase full of alcohol the flower which she one day gave me: a treasured memento which I had to leave in Russia when I departed to France.

From the day that Zucchi appeared on our stage I began to work with fire, energy and application: my one dream was to emulate her.

The result was that when I left the School I had already a complete mastery of technique. Thus I was able to shine at the graduation exam, which was attended for the first time, if I am not mistaken, by almost all the members of the Imperial Family.

This exam, without my knowing it, was to decide my destiny.

The graduation exam was a kind of grand climax to our work at the School. The future and a career stretched before us. It was an unforgettable day.

The arrangement was that the pupils graded first were allowed to choose their dance. My choice was the *pas-de-deux* from *La Fille Mal Gardée*, to the music of the Italian song *Stella Confidenta*, in which Virginia Zucchi, partnered by Paul Guerdt, had just achieved a phenomenal success. She had even kissed Guerdt on the stage, a gesture described by all the Press as quite without precedent. For this expressive and delightful dance, full of high-spirited coquetry, I wore a blue costume, decorated with little forget-me-not buds, and I was partnered by Rachmanov, who was graduating at the same time.

The School's management had always been friendly towards me, singling me out on several occasions. But the graduation exam required that the star should be not a day girl, but one of the boarders, "the *pépinières*". The pupils placed first that year were Rychliakova, a classical dancer of great virtuosity, and Skorsiouk, a character dancer with a style of her own and a powerful personality.

As well as the ballet section, the drama section of the School took part in the performance.

There is no need to describe our excitement on the eve of the day, or how happy we felt at the thought of being allowed to dance in the presence of the Imperial Family! Our young hearts beat with anxiety and hope. . . .

At last the longed-for day arrived. Assembled on stage behind the still-lowered curtain we knew, we felt that the Imperial Family was there, in our little theatre, waiting to see us dance.

Everything went wonderfully well. Each one of us strove his hardest to maintain the School's reputation; each received a share of applause.

After the performance the pupils from the drama and ballet groups assembled, without changing, in the great rehearsal room, where they found the members of the Administration, the schoolmistresses, teachers and management of the Imperial Theatres Administration, headed by I. A. Vselvolojsky.

The rehearsal room was linked to the School theatre by a long, broad corridor, where the classrooms were. And so we saw the Imperial Family emerge from the theatre and slowly come towards us. Leading them, towering over the others, came Tsar Alexander III, escorting the Empress Maria Feodorovna, who was smiling. Next came Nicholas Alexandrovitch, the heir to the throne, a young man, with the Emperor's four brothers: the Grand Duke Wladimir Alexandrovitch with his wife, the Grand Duchess Marie Pavlovna, the Grand Duke Alexis Alexandrovitch in Admiral of the Fleet's uniform, the Grand Duke Serge Alexandrovitch with his beautiful wife, the Grand Duchess Elisabeth Feodorovna, and the Grand Duke Paul Alexandrovitch with his young wife, the Grand Duchess Alexandra Gueorguievna, who had just married and was expecting her first child, Marie Pavlovna, born on April 6th 1890. Finally, behind these could be seen Field-Marshal the Grand Duke Michel Nicolaievitch with his four sons.

Tradition had it that boarders were presented before day pupils. But no sooner had the Tsar entered the room than he asked in his powerful voice: "Where is Kschessinska?"

I was standing on one side, having scarcely foreseen such a blow to tradition. The Headmistress and teachers, who were already about to present the two top pupils, Rychliakova and Skorsiouk, seemed put out and did not know what to do. But they soon recovered themselves and brought me to the Emperor. I curtsied according to custom. The Tsar then held out his hand to me and said, "Be the glory and the adornment of our ballet!"

I curtsied again, and vowed myself, in the depths of my heart, to deserve my Emperor's generous words. Then, as etiquette demanded, I kissed the Empress's hand.

Overwhelmed by what had just happened, I was hardly aware of what was going on around me. I felt the Emperor's words as a command. To be the glory and adornment of Russian ballet! No need to say how this excited my imagination! To be worthy of the Emperor's confidence, such would henceforward be my task, a task to which I determined to devote all my power.

When all the pupils had been presented in turn to the Emperor and Empress, and warmed by the kindest words, we passed on into the girls' dining-room, where supper was served on three tables arranged as a horse-shoe.

"Where are you sitting?" the Tsar asked me as soon as we came in.

"I have no special place, Your Majesty," I answered. "I am a day girl."

The Emperor then sat at one of the long side-tables. On his right sat the boarder who was to say grace before the meal. Another boarder was to sit on his left, but the Emperor gently moved her aside and said to me, "Sit next to me."

Then he turned to the Tsarevitch, told him to sit in the next place, adding on our behalf with a smile, "Careful now! Not too much flirting!"

A plain white glass stood in each place. The Tsarevitch looked at it for a moment, then said: "I am sure you don't use glasses like that at home?"

I was never to forget this prosaic, insignificant question. God knows what we spoke of afterwards: but I fell in love with the Tsarevitch on the spot! I can still see his magnificent eyes, his tender, kind expression. Almost from his very first words he was something more to me than the Tsarevitch, heir to the throne. It was like a dream.

These are the few words which the future Emperor Nicholas II wrote in his *Journal*, on March 23rd 1890, about that evening:

> We went to see the performance at the Theatre School. Saw a short play and a ballet. Delightful. Supper with the pupils.

Years later, reading these lines, I became aware of the impression which our first meeting had left on the Tsarevitch.

After keeping us company for some time, the Emperor rose to move on to the next table. His place was then occupied in turn by the Grand Duke Michel Nicolaievitch and by the other older members of the Imperial Family. Their kindly attention was thus fairly distributed among us all.

The Tsarevitch spent the whole evening with me. When we finally parted, we saw each other in a new light. In both our hearts an attraction had been born impelling us irresistibly towards each other.

How happy I was that night! How joyful at seeing my parents so pleased and proud of their daughter! The prey of the strongest exaltation, turning over and over in my mind the events I had just lived through, I did not sleep a wink the whole night.

The following morning I had to go early to school. We had a little carriage drawn by two ponies called the Fairies Carabosse because the carriage reminded us of the ballet *The Sleeping Beauty*, in which the Fairy Carabosse is drawn in a carriage by rats. Riding through the streets in this outfit I was certain that nobody had eyes except for me, that I was famous, that nobody could fail to know my happiness!

Two days later as I was driving with my sister in Great Morskaia Street and we were approaching Palace Square, the Tsarevitch suddenly passed before us in his carriage. He recognised me, turned round and gave me a long look. This meeting, as happy as it was unexpected, was not the only one. When I was walking along the Nevsky Prospect and passing Anitchkov Palace, where Alexander III then lived, I saw the Tsarevitch and his sister, the Grand Duchess Xenia Alexandrovna. They were watching the passers-by through the high stone balustrade which surrounded garden and palace. Fortune was giving me everything: my young heart wanted nothing more.

On May 6th, the Tsarevitch's birthday, I decorated my room with little flags. A childish game, of course, but that day the whole town was decked in his honour.

Shortly after the performance which I have just described, but before my official graduation from the school, I made my début on the stage, on April 22nd 1890, at the farewell performance for Papkov, the conductor. This time I was partnered not by a pupil, but by an experienced dancer, Nicolas Legat, which increased my confidence.

The famous critic A. Plestscheev, who often noted my first appearances, wrote on this occasion: "The chief attraction in Papkov's farewell performance was the début of three daughters of Terpsichore's large family: Mlles. Kschessinska, Skorsiouk, and Rychliakova.

"In the *pas-de-deux* from *La Fille Mal Gardée* Mlle. Kschessinska was a true delight. Pretty, graceful, her face lit up with a happy childlike smile, she revealed genuine balletic gifts of a mature nature: Mlle. Kschessinska has strong points, which enable her to execute the fashionable *doubles tours* with the assurance worthy of an experienced dancer. I was once again impressed by this young beginner's irreproachable accuracy as well as by the beauty of her style. M. Legat showed himself the ideal partner for Mlle. Kschessinska II. The *pas-de-deux* was an enormous success, although it had only recently been performed by Mlle. Zucchi and M. Guerdt."

A week later I appeared in the *divertissement* and M. Plestscheev gave me more praise:

"After a week Mlle. Kschessinska II has distinguished herself once again, this time in the *divertissement*. It is now some years since as a child she danced the famous mazurka from *Paquita*, and from that moment the balletomanes' club had predicted a brilliant future for her."

Still on my début, Shalkovsky, a very well-known critic, compared me to Virginia Zucchi! He also rated me highly, and never failed to draw attention to me in his articles.

After such happiness and excitement I still had to think of the graduation exams. I did my dancing exercises during the day at school, and prepared the other subjects by night at home, keeping myself awake with coffee while the household slept. It was spring, I remember, the white nights of St. Petersburg, nights when the sun scarcely ever sets.

I left School with the first prize, the *Complete Works* of Lermontov. I was almost eighteen: nobody in the world, I thought, was happier than I!

CHAPTER IV

MY DÉBUT

SCHOOL FINISHED, I left with my parents for our small estate at Krassnitzy. In the immediate future I was to appear in the season at Krasnoïe Selo, but I was attracted most of all by the certainty of seeing the Tsarevitch, who was serving with the Hussars that year and was to spend the summer on manœuvres.

For some years past the whole Imperial Guard of the St. Petersburg district and the provincial regiments assembled for summer manœuvres at Krasnoïe Selo camp, about fifteen miles from the capital, and connected to it by the Baltic Railway.

During the 'sixties, when the Grand Duke Nicolas Nicolaievitch—Commander of the Danube army during the Russo-Turkish War of 1877-1878 and father of the Grand Duke Nicholas, Commander-in-Chief of the Russian armies at the beginning of the First World War—was Commander-in-Chief of St. Petersburg military district, a wooden theatre had been built at Krasnoïe Selo for the entertainment of the officers in camp during the manœuvres. Performances were given twice a week during the whole of July and the first fortnight of August, the period which the Grand Duke spent in camp. The programme included a comedy and a ballet *divertissement*.

On finishing my studies I was attached, from June 1st 1890, to the Imperial Theatre Ballet Company, and so was to take part in these performances.

My first performance of the season took place the day the camp was inspected by the Commander-in-Chief, the Grand Duke Wladimir Alexandrovitch, Alexander III's favourite brother.

I awaited that day, almost fainting, seized by extreme impatience and some anxiety. I had only one dream, to see the Tsarevitch during the performance and perhaps even to meet him. For by an old custom the Emperor, accompanied by the Grand Dukes, mounted the stage during the interval before the ballet *divertissement*, and chatted with the performers.

My dream came true! Not only on the first day, but during every performance, the Tsarevitch came and talked to me! Ever since the memorable graduation performance at School, I had had but one desire, to see him again, even from afar; and now I was granted the realisation of my dream beyond all hope.

One evening, before the divertissement, as I ran happily on to the stage, I almost bumped into the Emperor. However, I was able to pull myself up in time and to greet him. "Ah!" he said to me, frowning, but with his eyes smiling, "you must have been flirting!"

The Emperor and the Imperial Family occupied the left-hand box as you looked from the stage. When there was no room left in the box, some of the family sat in the first row of the stalls. But the Emperor always sat in the box, close to the stage, between two pillars.

By an old tradition, the last performance of the Krasnoïe Selo summer season ended with a general galop—called the infernal galop —danced by all the artists who had taken part in the spectacle. We were on the point of starting the rehearsal when the Grand Duke Nicholas Nicolaievitch *père*, who had long ago retired, unexpectedly arrived at the theatre.[1]

The Grand Duke sat in the Imperial Box and the rehearsal of the galop began. Suddenly he stopped the dance and began impetuously to show Ivanov that his arrangement was wrong. Leon Ivanov answered back, whereupon the Grand Duke, hastening on to the stage, undertook to show us how to set about it. For he was passionately fond of ballet and was on intimate terms with Ivanov and my father, often receiving them with complete informality.

Thus, far too fast for my liking, those happy days at Krasnoïe Selo went by, blissful days of hope untroubled by care.

As soon as the manœuvres were over the Emperor returned to Peterhof, where he usually spent the end of the summer. And for a long time I was not able to see the Tsarevitch again. He was to go on a journey round the world, a journey to last nine interminable months.

The feelings I had experienced towards him at our first meeting had now invaded my heart and my thoughts. I thought that, without being in love with me, he did feel a certain affection towards me, and I gave myself up to my dreams. For we had never had the chance to be alone together, and I knew nothing of his feelings for me.

Now that I am separated from those exciting days by more than sixty years, I have finally been able to read, in the Emperor Nicholas II's

---

[1] The Grand Duke had fallen in love with the dancer Tchislova, by whom he had two sons, who received the name Nicolaiev and later served in the Horse Grenadiers of the Guard, and two daughters, of whom one, a great beauty, married Prince Cantacuzène. She was one of our great friends.

Journal, which appeared after the Revolution, the few lines referring to that far-off summer of 1890, at Krasnoïe Selo, to a time when he was still Tsarevitch. We could not meet alone at the time, but my heart had not deceived me about his feelings. Here are those few lines:

July 10th, Tuesday: Watched the performance at the theatre. Went on stage.

July 17th, Tuesday: I like Kschessinska II very much.

July 30th, Monday: Gossipped at her window[1] with little Kschessinska.

July 31st, Tuesday: After lunch went, for the last time, to the dear little theatre at Krasnoïe Selo. Said goodbye to Kschessinska.

August 1st, Wednesday: Blessing of the colours at noon. Those minutes spent in front of the theatre tantalised my memory.

Towards the end of that wonderful summer I went to Peterhof to stay with Maroussia Poiré, and spent my days there in the hope, not to be fulfilled alas! of meeting the Tsarevitch in one of the walks.

The hussar Eugene Volkoff, whom I knew well, was the Tsarevitch's brother officer and was to accompany him on his journey round the world. He was very intimate with Tatiana Nicolaieva, one of the dancers. I learnt from her that the Tsarevitch had expressed to Volkoff his desire to see me before he left, asking him to arrange a meeting. But I was living with my parents then and he hesitated to visit me at home. Meeting elsewhere was a difficult business. So there was no further meeting and the Tsarevitch then asked me to send him a photograph. But I had only one, and what was more I thought it dreadful. So I did not sent it to him.

At last the sad day of his departure arrived.

On October 23rd (November 4th) 1890 he left Gatchina with his brother, the Grand Duke George Alexandrovitch, arriving first in Athens. After visiting the town, they embarked together on the cruiser *Souvenir d'Azov*, together with Prince George of Greece.

Thanks to the Press, I was able to follow daily the stages of their journey: Cairo, Bombay, Calcutta, Ceylon, Singapore, Nagasaki, Kyoto . . . and, in my dreams, to share in it. I followed him; I called his appearance to mind. Although I had never done any drawing before, I set to work with spirit and succeeded in making a pencil copy of an engraving of him. I even managed to do his portrait in naval officer's uniform from a photograph.

[1] This was my dressing-room window, on the ground floor of the theatre and opening on to the Imperial Family's private entrance.

Suddenly we learnt that on April 29th (May 11th) 1891, at Otsa, a Japanese fanatic had given the Tsarevitch a sabre thrust in the head. Thanks to the presence of mind of Prince George of Greece, who had time to deflect the terrible blow, the wound was not fatal. But the Tsarevitch was to keep the mark for his whole life and often complained of headaches near the scar.

We were informed of the attack at once, but without further details, remaining several days without news of the Tsarevitch's health. My torments of anxiety and the no less profound joy which succeeded them when we finally received reassuring news can easily be imagined.

The Emperor gave the order to break off the journey across Japan and return at once. Via Vladivostok, crossing the whole of Siberia by carriage, the Tsarevitch thus reached St. Petersburg, and, without halting in the capital, arrived on August 4th/16th 1891 at Krasnoïe Selo, where the Emperor and Empress were then living. That very evening he went to the theatre, and I was at last able to see him again after his long absence. Alas, he went away again soon afterwards, to Denmark, accompanying his parents, and he was only to return to St. Petersburg at the end of the year.

If during my first season on the Imperial stage I was still not given whole ballets, I was nevertheless entrusted with roles where I could show my capacities. In *The Sleeping Beauty*, for instance, I had a number of parts: the fairy Candide in the first act, the Marchioness in the Second Act, and Little Red Riding Hood in the third. This was the dance that the Tsarevitch liked best. In addition, like all the other young ballet dancers, I took part in the opera performances which called for dancing.[1]

As I was eager to attain the Italian school's virtuosity, much admired then by the public, I began to take classes with Enrico Cecchetti, still keeping up my private lessons with Christian Johanson, whom I liked greatly. But my classes with the Italian teacher annoyed Johanson, who told me one day: "If you don't like my teaching, I can stop giving you lessons altogether." I was so ashamed and hurt that I gave up Cecchetti's classes and studied Italian technique on my own.

My sister and I still lived with our parents, who only allowed us to go out—and then with a chaperone!—to visit our closest friends. However, we always found a way to elude their vigilance, bringing up, for instance, as pretext an invitation to people whom we were allowed

[1] *The Imperial Theatres Annual* for the year 1890-1891 listed my appearance in twenty-two ballets and twenty-one operas.

to visit. If we had to wear evening dress, we covered it with a coat before going to say goodbye to our parents; and as soon as we came in we went to wish them good night, but not without first taking off our ball dresses and putting on nightdresses! In fact, we played *La Fille Mal Gardée*! All this was very romantic and gave spice to our secret outings. But in fact the escapades were very innocent.

At the end of the 1890-1891 season my godfather and close friend of my parents, Strakatch, invited me to accompany him on a journey abroad, as a reward for having so successfully finished my studies.

We went to Biarritz, London, and thence to Italy, where we visited Rome, Milan—not forgetting to go to La Scala—and many picturesque places in that country. Paris was our last stop before St. Petersburg. I had no idea, on returning to the capital, how my life was to change.

CHAPTER V

HAPPY DAYS

THE TSAREVITCH returned from Denmark in the autumn of 1891. From that time I only saw him by chance in the streets of the capital. Once, however, on January 4th 1892, at the dress rehearsal of the opera *Esclarmonde*, in which the beautiful Swedish singer Sanderson had a triumph, fortune granted us a fleeting encounter.

The Emperor and the Tsarevitch were sitting in the front row, while the Empress and Grand Duchesses were in the Imperial box in the middle of the Grand Tier. I was also in the Grand Tier. Leaving my box in the interval, I went downstairs, and ran into the Tsarevitch, who was on his way up, going to the Imperial box. He could hardly stop, for we were surrounded by too many people; but I was overwhelmed by the mere fact of having been able to come so near him.

I adored driving out alone, every day, with a Russian coachman, and often, as I went along the river bank, I would meet the Tsarevitch, coming out at the same time as myself. These were meetings at a distance. Yet nothing would have made me give them up. And when I developed a nasty boil on my eyelid, soon followed by another on my leg, provided with a magnificent bandage over my eye, I stoically maintained my daily outings . . . until the day when the boils became bad enough to make me stay at home. Neither bandage nor my absence had escaped the Tsarevitch's notice.

At the time my sister and I had a small bedroom of our own in our parent's house and a sitting-room prettily decorated. One evening, sitting alone at home quietly in my room, my eye still bandaged, I heard the front-door bell ring. The maid opened the door and came and told me that the hussar officer Eugene Volkoff wanted to see me. I asked her to show him into the sitting-room. This room had two doors, one leading to the hall, the other to the drawing-room, and it was through this one that I saw not Volkoff but the Tsarevitch himself appear.

I could not believe my eyes, or rather my eye, and was so overjoyed with this unexpected meeting that I was never to forget it. It was his first visit, a brief one, but we were alone, we could chat in perfect freedom! I had dreamed so often of such a meeting alone.

Next morning I received a note from him: "I hope your little eye

and leg are better. Since our meeting I have been in the clouds! I shall
try to come back as soon as possible. Niki."

My first letter from him! It made an enormous impression on me!
I too was in the clouds.

I read and re-read that first letter until I knew it by heart. Later he
wrote to me often, scattering charming allusions through his letters,
like the quotation from Hermann's song in *La Dame de Pique*: "Forgive
me, divine creature, for having disturbed your rest!" Indeed, the
Tsarevitch liked seeing me very much in this opera, in which, dressed
as a shepherdess with a white wig, I danced the pastorale in the first act.
We acted Saxony statuettes and porcelain in Louis XV style. We were
pushed out of the wings in twos on platforms with little wheels. Once
on the stage, we jumped off and began to dance while the choir sang
"Mon cher petit ami, l'aimable et gentil berger". As soon as the pastorale
was finished we leaped back on to our platforms and were whisked
back into the wings. He adored this scene.

Another time in his letter he mentioned André's love for the
"Pannotchka"[1] in Gogol's *Tarass Boulba*, a love which made the hero
forget everything, even his father and his country. I did not then
understand the implicit meaning in those words, "Think of Tarass
Boulba and of what André did for love of a young Polish girl!"

From then on the Tsarevitch often came to see me, always in the
evening, and often with the "Michailovitchs", as we called George,
Alexander and Serge, the sons of the Grand Duke Michel Nicolaïevitch. These evenings had a charming intimacy about them. The
Michailovitchs sang Georgian songs which they had learnt during their
stay in the Caucasus, where their father had been Viceroy for more
than twenty years. My sister often joined us. As we were in our
parents' home I could not offer my guests a meal, but I sometimes
managed to serve them champagne! I can still remember the evening
when the Tsarevitch undertook to perform my Red Riding Hood
dance from *The Sleeping Beauty*. He took a basket, tied a little hand-
kerchief in his hair and, in the sitting-room bathed in shadow, danced
the roles of Red Riding Hood and the wolf. It also happened that one
evening the maid announced the Prefect of Police of St. Petersburg:
the Emperor had learnt that his son had left the Palace, and the Prefect
had thought it his duty to inform the Tsarevitch without delay.

The Tsarevitch often brought me presents. At first I would not
accept them, but this gave him such sorrow that I had to change my

[1] Young Polish noblewoman.

mind. These small gifts were very beautiful. On the first of them, a gold bracelet adorned with a large sapphire and diamonds, I had engraved two dates that were dear to me, that of our first meeting at the Theatre School and that of his first visit—1890-1892.

On Sundays, when I went to the Michel Riding School to watch the horse-races (my box was just opposite the Imperial box), the Tsarevitch never failed to send me flowers by two hussars, his regimental comrades, Prince Peter Pavlovitch Golitzin, whom we called Pika, and Pepa Kotliarevsky. These two officers were known as my "aides-de-camp"; they called me their "angel". When the races were over I returned home in my little single-seat carriage, proceeding slowly along Karavannaia Street towards Anitchkov Palace with the secret design of being overtaken by the Tsarevitch's carriage and having thus another opportunity of seeing him. For love feeds on such silent conversations. On the day of the Annunciation, for instance, which was the Horse Guards' anniversary, I attended the parade in one of the public's reserved boxes; the Emperor, with his suite, reviewed the regiment, but the Tsarevitch, who followed his father, had eyes for nobody but me, and I for him.

Happiness does not come without terrible awakenings. During an evening which we spent together the Tsarevitch told me of an imminent journey he had to make abroad so that he could meet Princess Alice of Hesse, to whom he was to be engaged. He had already on a previous occasion read me the passages from his *Journal* in which he described his feelings for the Princess and those for me. Everything drew him towards me. At that time he had only a fairly vague feeling for Princess Alice and saw the engagement as an unavoidable necessity. But whatever his feelings he was required by his destiny to marry a princess, and of all possible fiancées he liked Princess Alice best.

It was my first great sorrow. When he left me I remained there, powerless to move, as if made of stone, unable to sleep the whole night. The next days were terrible. My ignorance of the future in store for me plunged me into unbearable despair.

But his journey was short, and led to nothing: Princess Alice refused to change religion and to become Orthodox. Her conversion was one of the fundamental conditions of the projected marriage. There was no engagement.

When he returned we resumed our evenings, as before. The Tsarevitch was gay, full of high spirits. We were each other's own once more. My happiness can be imagined, as well as my determination to think no more of the future.

The winter season came to an end. Summer arrived, and we were
ready to leave, I for my parents' estate, he for Krasnoïe Selo. The
summer season promised to be a particularly happy one. It was.

Rehearsals for the summer season at Krasnoïe Selo Theatre took
place at the Theatre School. My sister and I, to attend them, left our
estate at Krassnitzy and returned to St. Petersburg. As soon as I entered
our apartment I rushed to the piano, where the servants used to leave
the letters which arrived while we were away. Sure enough, I found
the precious letter which I had been expecting. Our servants stayed in
the flat during the summer; and so we could play mistress of the house
and receive guests: Baron Zeddeler, my sister's future husband, the two
hussars whom I have mentioned, Prince Pika Golytzin and Pepa
Kotliarevsky, and finally Volodia Svetschin, whom I had met when he
was studying at Law School. He was then an officer in the Preobrajensky Regiment, where he had served for some time with the Tsarevitch, whom he adored and tried to imitate in every respect. He wore
a beard exactly like his; like him, he rode alone in a carriage driven
by a plump coachman; and like him he wore his *bachly* (a sort of hood)
thrown back and tried to cross his arms exactly like his model. He was
so successful that he did resemble the Heir Apparent and was often
taken for him: nothing delighted him more than to be given an impeccable "eyes right". Volodia Svetchin was spending the summer at
Serguievo, near Strelna, where he had a villa and sometimes gave very
agreeable dinner parties in honour of myself and my sister, whom he
was courting.

On the days when there were performances at Krasnoïe Selo the
artists caught the train at the Baltic Station and usually arrived in time
for lunch, which we ate in the restaurant, opposite the theatre.

It was during this season that I was finally given the best dressing-
room, whose two windows opened on to the Imperial Family's
private entrance. I tried to decorate it as prettily and intimately as
possible, with furniture in light wood, the walls hung with cretonne,
and always with an abundance of flowers.

The Grand Duke Wladimir Alexandrovitch liked to attend rehearsals. He would come and sit in my dressing-room and gossip with
me, greatly regretting, he added with a smile, that he was no longer
young. One day he gave me his photograph with these charming
words, "*Bonjour, douchka*".[1] He was full of kindness and we remained
the best of friends until his death.

[1] A term of endearment equivalent to "little darling".

5a. The Open-air Theatre at Peterhof.

5b. A performance in honour of Kaiser Wilhelm II.

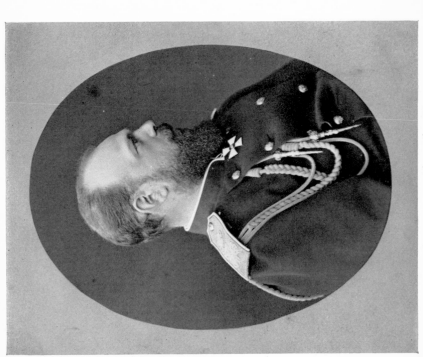

6a. The Emperor Alexander III.

6b. The Grand Duke Wladimir Alexandrovitch.

The Tsarevitch also often attended rehearsals. Knowing the time he would arrive, I watched out for him through the window, from which I could see him coming a long way off, across the park, from the Palace to the theatre. He came on horse-back, dismounted nimbly and at once came to my dressing-room, where we could chat freely until the rehearsal began. Then he sat in the Imperial box between the pillars, almost on a level with the stage, insisting that I should come and sit on the edge of the box, so that we could continue our confidences. He only returned to the Palace when the rehearsal came to an end and it was time for dinner.

In the evening, when the Tsar and Tsarina were to attend the performance, all the artists stood at the windows overlooking the door of honour. The Imperial landau drawn by three magnificent horses, with a Cossack sitting next to the coachman, at last appeared and we greeted the Emperor, who replied with a military salute, while the Empress gave us her most charming smile. The Tsarevitch next appeared in his own *troika*.

How many faces remain linked to these happy days! In the intervals the young Grand Dukes came to see me in my dressing-room, as did their elders: the Grand Duke Wladimir Alexandrovitch, Prince Christian, the Empress's nephew and future King of Denmark, the Grand Duke Mecklemburg-Schwerin, husband of the Grand Duchess Anastasia Mikhailovna, a man of great charm with whom I was to have a deep friendship. And how many unforgettable evenings, made to delight a twenty-year-old's heart, evenings as full of fun and games as youth itself! One evening we agreed with the Tsarevitch that he should return to sup at the Palace after the show, but afterwards come back to the theatre in his *troika* and take me to Baron Zeddeler's, at the Preobrajensky Regiment's camp, where my sister was also to go. I was to wait for him in the park, near the theatre.

All the theatre lights were already out. The alley, dark and deserted, stretched into nothingness before me. I did not dare venture there alone, and I asked a theatre attendant to accompany me. At last I heard the bells of the *troika*, furiously driven, saw the lanterns dancing, and the Tsarevitch appeared. It was a wonderful night, and we decided to go for a *troika* ride across Krasnoïe Selo. Like an arrow we drove through empty streets and avenues, carried away by the drumming of the horses' hooves, our blood lashed by the wind and our eyes filled with fleeting shadows in a star-studded sky.

At last we went to supper. Baron Zeddeler shared quarters with his friend, Schlitter. My sister was in love with Zeddeler, and I with the

Tsarevitch; poor Schlitter, with no woman as his companion, had to play the solitary squire, and comforted himself with this sally: "No candle for God and no poker for the devil!" There was never such a gay supper, and the Tsarevitch stayed with us until dawn: he did not want to leave!

The last performance of the summer season ended, as usual, with a spectacular galop. I was terribly sad at the thought that these wonderful months were now over, when I had been able to meet the Tsarevitch so freely. The end of the season coincided with the end of the manœuvres: The Tsarevitch was preparing to accompany the Tsar to Denmark, from where I received warm, moving letters.

We were more and more drawn to each other, and I was thinking more and more of having a place of my own. Moreover, though he did not openly mention it, I guessed that the Tsarevitch shared this wish. I was living with my parents who, in view of my age, naturally still saw me as a child, and I longed for greater independence.

But this wish had its rub: I thought above all of the great grief I would cause my parents by leaving them. I dreaded the moment when I would have to inform them of my intentions. As a woman, my mother would doubtless understand me, but my father . . .? It was all the more painful to approach him because I was his favourite. He was a man of principles, and his daughter's departure in such conditions was bound to be a terrible moral blow to him. I knew indeed that this was one of the things that "just is not done", but I adored the Tsarevitch, I thought only of him and of my happiness, however brief and transitory it might be.

I can still see, as I write these lines, the evening when I finally decided to speak to my father. He was sitting at the table in his study, and I waited by the door, afraid to enter. Then my sister came to my aid: she went in first and told him everything. My father was shattered: he tried to let none of his feelings appear, but I could not but feel it. He listened to my account and merely asked me if I realised that I could never marry the Tsarevitch and that our idyll would be short. I replied that I fully understood, but that I loved him with all my heart, that I did not care what happened in the future. I wanted to take advantage of the happiness open to me, even if it proved of short duration.

My father imposed one single condition: that my sister should come and live with me.

As I had foreseen, it was a great grief for my father to agree to my leaving, and I was no less grieved to cause him pain. But, whatever the cost to me, I felt relieved at having tackled that ordeal with complete frankness.

I soon found a charming little house, No. 18 in the English Prospect. The house, which belonged to Rimsky-Korsakov, had been built by the Grand Duke Constantin Nicolaïevitch for the dancer Kouznetsova. There was a story that the Grand Duke, fearing an attempt on his life, had installed iron shutters on his study windows on the ground floor. There was a secret safe in one of the walls. The house was well furnished and consisted of basement, ground floor, and one upper floor. Behind the house was a first garden leading into a second larger one, at the bottom of which were the outhouses. There was also a stable and a barn, and the party wall separated it from the Grand Duke Alexis Alexandrovitch's home. There was no private electricity at the time; the house was lit by a multitude of oil lamps of all styles and sizes. When I moved in the only change I had made was in the bedroom on the first floor, next to which was a delightful dressing-room. So I took possession of my new house: I was at last on my own and free! With a beating heart I awaited the Tsarevitch's return.

CHAPTER VI

EARLY SUCCESSES

ALTHOUGH I WAS STILL tormented by my parent's grief, I had every reason to be happy. I was at last on my own and the winter season promised to be an exceptionally fine one. I was going to be given the lead in the best ballets—no longer to dance small isolated roles, but whole ballets like a true *première danseuse*!

The house was at last ready: the only thing lacking was a cook. So we had to have dinner and supper sent in from neighbouring restaurants. But this did not spoil our happiness.

There was a house-warming to celebrate my move and the beginning of my independence. The guests showered me with presents and the Tsarevitch gave me a vodka service, eight little gold glasses studded with precious stones, and his photograph inscribed "To my dear Panni", as he called me.

The days passed by uneventfully. The Tsarevitch was naturally kept very busy with his many duties. Also, as heir to the throne, he was not his own master. So we led a "quiet", retiring life.

The Tsarevitch usually came for supper. I knew the approximate time, and I stood by the window, waiting for the regular gallop of his magnificent charger, which rang out from afar on the roadway. He was often accompanied by his young uncles, the Grand Dukes George, Alexander and Serge Mikhailovitch, who were of the same age as he. Sometimes also Count André Chouvalov came, with Vera Legat, the dancer, whom he was later to marry. Nicholas Nicolaievitch Figner, tenor at the Maryinsky Theatre, whom the Tsarevitch was particularly fond of, was among our constant visitors. After supper we talked or played baccarat for very modest stakes. It was an intimate and delightful atmosphere.

I was very keen to dance the ballet *Esmeralda*, in which Virginia Zucchi had surpassed herself. So I went and asked this favour of Marius Petipa, the famous and all-powerful maître de ballet.

Petipa always spoke Russian, which he knew very poorly, despite a long stay in Russia. He called everybody "*tu*". He usually arrived at the theatre whistling, wrapped in a check plaid. He prepared his programme beforehand, and never improvised during rehearsals.

Without even looking at us, he merely showed us the movements and steps, accompanying his gestures with words spoken in indescribable Russian: "You on me, me on you; you on mine, me on yours." Which meant that we had to move from our corner ("you") to "me", where he was! To make his meaning clearer, he tapped his chest every time he said "me". But we understood his mime and vocabulary perfectly, and knew what he wanted us to do.

I told him that I should like to dance *Esmeralda*. He listened carefully and asked me point-blank in his jargon, "You love?"

Confused, I answered that I was indeed in love, that I did love.

Whereupon he continued, "You suffer?"

I thought it a strange question, and immediately replied, "Certainly not!"

Then he explained to me—a fact which I was to remember later—that only artists who had known the sufferings of love could understand and interpret the role of Esmeralda. Yes, I was to recall his profound words later when I won the right to dance *Esmeralda*, a right which suffering alone could bring—when Esmeralda became my best role.

During the 1892-1893 season I received my first ballet, *Calcabrino*, a three-act ballet by Marius Petipa to Modeste Tchaikovsky's book and music by Minkus, the recognised purveyor of ballet scores at the time.

I worked diligently with Cecchetti, anxious to make myself ready for such an important role, and striving fully to attain the virtuosity which the Italian dancers were then demonstrating on the Russian stage. Italian technique called for abrupt, precise, clear-cut movements, while Russian and French techniques are more lyrical, softer, more expressive, even in steps most marked with brio and virtuosity. It was only later that I was to return to our own technique, realising its grace and beauty.

I danced *Calcabrino* on November 1st 1892, succeeding Carlotta Brianza, who had just left our theatre. I had a great success. Critics and balletomanes showered me with praise. I was partnered by Enrico Cecchetti, my teacher; following the examples of Virginia Zucchi and Guerdt, I kissed him on the stage.

This is what A. Plestscheev wrote about my first appearance in a leading role: "M. F. Kschessinska took Carlotta Brianza's place on November 1st 1892 in *Calcabrino*, in which she danced the roles of Mariette and Dragonianza. She gave a youthful and highly talented interpretation, which bore the marks of hard work and stubborn determination. Can it be so long ago that Mlle. Kschessinska first appeared on the stage? Is it not just recently that we read of her début? And here she is already deciding to be Mlle. Brianza's successor! This pleasing young dancer deserves to be congratulated for her courage and self-confidence alone. She executed *doubles tours* without the slightest mistake, and she astonished the balletomanes by her *jetés en tournant* in the second act variation. But in fact, in spite of technical difficulties, Mlle. Kschessinska very successfully repeated all the dances which the Italian ballerina had so admirably performed. The influence of Cecchetti, her teacher, has undoubtedly greatly contributed to this young dancer's triumph; and Mlle. Kschessinska knew this, for she covered Cecchetti with kisses in front of the audience."

At the same time another ballet critic wrote:

"Mlle. Kschessinska II made her début, eagerly awaited by all who are interested in the future of Russian ballet, on Sunday, November 1st 1892, in the ballet *Calcabrino*. The talented young dancer scored a complete triumph. Although the dances in this ballet arranged for Carlotta Brianza are full of difficulties in which we may see the last word in modern technique, the young dancer brilliantly accomplished her task and delighted the spectators. Every seat in the Maryinsky Theatre was filled, and a large public acclaimed Mlle. Kschessinska II, who won all hearts with her first entry on the stage. Our ballerina performed the long scene in the first act, the difficult adagio in the second, in fact the many dances in this ballet, with rare aplomb and true artistic brio, with the finish which can hardly be demanded of an artist who has just left the Theatre School. Mlle. Kschessinska owes these brilliant results equally to our model School and to her present teacher, Cecchetti. Let me repeat that her début may be considered a landmark in the history of our ballet."[1]

There was also a favourable notice in the Western European Press. Thus *Le Monde Artiste* in Paris wrote:

"A new star, Mlle. Kschessinska, making her début as *première danseuse*, scored a brilliant success. This success is all the more pleasing to the Russians because it was won by a pupil from their national school whose only loan from the Italian school was the indispensable element needed to modernise the classical ballet. This young prima ballerina has everything on her side: a charming physique, faultless technique, polished execution and perfect lightness. Once she has

---

[1] Both these criticisms were reproduced in the *Critical and Biographical Outline*, which appeared in 1900 on the tenth anniversary of my entry into the company.

caught up a little in the way of mime she will be an accomplished artist."

What gave me special pleasure was to see the critics note my successful efforts to overcome technical problems which, by common consent, only the Italian dancers had hitherto been able to surmount.

On November 18th 1892, for the fiftieth performance of *The Sleeping Beauty*, a ceremony took place behind the lowered curtain in honour of Tchaikovsky who was presented with a crown. I was to dance one of the fairies.

When Tchaikovsky reached the theatre I brought him on to the stage, then disappeared for a moment to go and chat with the Tsarevitch and the Grand Dukes who had come to see me back-stage. This made me rather late, and everybody noticed my absence when the various delegates made their speeches and the crown was presented to the composer. This little incident was related in an article by George Bakhrouchev in the book, *Tchaikovsky and the Theatre*.

Tchaikovsky was a delightful man. Before the first performance of *The Sleeping Beauty* he often came to rehearsals and accompanied us himself at the piano; we were very fond of him.

On January 4th 1893 I took the Italian ballerina Dell'Era's place as the Sugar Plum fairy in *Casse-Noisette*, in which I danced a delightful and effective *pas-de-deux*.

But the greatest thing that happened to me was my appearance, on January 17th 1893, as Aurora in *The Sleeping Beauty*. Of all the praise I received that which meant most to me was Tchaikovsky's, who came and congratulated me in my dressing-room and expressed his desire to compose a ballet for me.

Alas, Fate decided otherwise, for the famous composer was to die of cholera before the end of the year, on October 25th 1893.

CHAPTER VII

THE INEVITABLE

I COULD FEEL THAT the Tsarevitch was less and less his own master. And doubts began to assail me. Had not the eternal question of his engagement and marriage to Princess Alice been raised once again?

My torments grew when the Tsarevitch had to go to London in order to attend the marriage, on June 24th (July 6th) 1893, of his cousin the Duke of York, George V to be, to Princess Mary. For he would again meet Princess Alice, who was then staying with Queen Victoria. But the question of the engagement remained open this time too, and nothing came of it.

I wanted to spend the summer at Krasnoïe Selo or near it in order to be closer to the Tsarevitch, who could not often leave camp to visit me in St. Petersburg. I had even found a charming little villa by the Duderhof Lake. The Tsarevitch was in no way opposed to my plans, but I was advised not to settle so near the camp so as not to arouse undesirable rumours and gossip. So I decided to rent a villa at Koerevo, a large residential house, built in Catherine II's reign and of an unusual triangular design. The story went that the Empress, when crossing Koerevo forest one day, had herself chosen this site for a house. When asked how she wanted it built, she seized the three-cornered hat of one of the courtiers who surrounded her and said, "This is the plan of the house!" And so the architect had shaped the building like a triangle. Entering the estate, one found an avenue at the end of which stood a colonnaded house with an imposing flight of steps. On the right were some more modern lodges. The angle opposite the façade of this strange, triangular construction receded into a shabby park stretching almost as far as the Volkhonsky high road, which linked Tsarskoïe Selo to Peterhof.

By day everything on this estate seemed intimate and wonderful, but in the evening, and especially at night, this enormous, forsaken ensemble had something sinister and fearsome about it. The large building and the lodges seemed lost in a thick, endless forest, far from all human life. So my sister came and slept in my room, and, for greater security, we decided that our manservant and his wife, who

7. The Tsarevitch, the future Emperor Nicholas II.

8.   In the ballet *La Fille mal Gardée*.

lived at the other end of the house, should henceforward sleep in a room next to ours.

It was a very sad summer. The Tsarevitch seldom visited me in my new house. It had become very difficult for him to leave camp and do what he wanted.

The performances at Krasnoïe Selo no longer had the same carefree joy for me which had lit up the previous season. My heart was gripped with heavy foreboding. Yes, something was going to happen, something for which I must be always ready, but which I tried to put out of mind.

On August 10th 1893 the Tsarevitch and Emperor left for Libava, and then for Denmark. The Tsarevitch did not return to St. Petersburg until the autumn, on October 8th 1893.

The winter season began, as usual, at the beginning of September. My repertoire already included three ballets; on February 20th 1894 a fourth was added—*Paquita*, a three-act ballet by Mazillier and Fescher, to music by Delvèze and Minkus, and choreography by Frederiks and M. Petipa. But if I was happy at that time on the stage, it was quite another matter in my private life. My heart was heavy and constrained, and I had a foreboding of some terrible, imminent sorrow.

The 12th of January 1894 saw the announcement, already long foreseen, of the engagement between the Grand Duchess Xenia Alexandrovna and the Grand Duke Alexander Mikhailovitch. This union had always been encouraged by the Tsar and Tsarina, who looked upon it with the utmost favour. We also celebrated the event at home, with the Tsarevitch. My sister and Baron Zeddeler were with us. We sat on the ground and drank champagne, in, God knows why, my sister's bedroom.

Then came another event, something which I could not celebrate as I should have liked and ought to have done as a Russian, for all it brought to me, to my heart, was desolation and despair. On April 7th 1894 was announced the engagement of the Heir Apparent and Princess Alice of Hessen-Darmstadt. It was something which I had foreseen, expected, known must happen. Nevertheless it brought me inconsolable sorrow.

At the beginning of this same year, 1894, alarming rumours had begun to circulate about the Emperor's state of health. The famous Professor Zacharyn had been summoned in consultation from Moscow. Nobody knew just how serious was the Tsar's illness, but everybody felt that his life was in danger. And this, I realised, could only hasten the Tsarevitch's engagement to Princess Alice.[1]

The Tsarevitch and I had often spoken of his imminent marriage leading to our inevitable separation. He had not concealed from me that, aware of his duty which called upon him to marry, he considered Princess Alice the most likely of all the fiancées proposed to him, and that he felt a growing attraction to her.

He won her consent during his stay at Coburg, where he attended the marriage of the Grand Duke Ernest of Hesse to Princess Victoria-Melita of Saxe-Coburg-Gotha, who later (in 1905) married the Grand Duke Cyril Wladimirovitch and became the Grand Duchess Victoria Feodorovna.

The marriage took place in the presence of a great many representatives of both families, including Queen Victoria, surrounded by her grand-daughters, Princesses Victoria and Maud, the German Emperor Wilhelm II, the Grand Duchess Marie Alexandrovna, the Grand Duke Wladimir Alexandrovitch, the Grand Duchess Marie Pavlovna.

On his arrival at Coburg the Tsarevitch once again asked for the hand of Princess Alice. For two days the Princess refused to give her consent. She only accepted on the third day, yielding to the entreaties of all her family.

Opinions may differ as to the role played by the Tsarina during her husband's reign, but I must say that the Tsarevitch, in choosing Princess Alice, found in her a wife deeply imbued with the principles underlying the Tsars' authority: a woman of high moral worth who was his faithful companion in times of trial, who was able to support and console him, and to face, with incomparable dignity, a martyr's captivity and death.

After his return from Coburg the Tsarevitch no longer visited me, but we went on exchanging letters. The last time I wrote to him was to ask his permission to continue using "*tu*" to him and to come to him in case of necessity.

[1] In his edition of *The Letters of Tsar Nicholas II and the Empress Marie* (London, 1937), Edward Bing writes, p. 73:

"For five years already Nicholas had been in love with Princess Alice of Hesse, although his father, Alexander III, had opposed the marriage when the project was first discussed in 1891. Both Helen of Orléans and Margaret of Prussia, approached by Alexander's emissaries, refused to marry the Tsarevitch on the ground that they could not give up their faith to become Greek Orthodox. At last, in 1894, when the Tsar, gravely ill, felt that the end was near, he granted his son's most ardent desire and Nicholas was permitted to go to Darmstadt to propose to 'Alix'."

He replied in these moving lines, which I shall never forget:

"Whatever happens to my life, my days spent with you will ever remain the happiest memories of my youth."

He also assured me that I could always go straight to him and call him "*tu*" as in the past. He kept his promise: whenever circumstances made me ask him for help, he received my request favourably and never said no to me.

My conversations with the Tsarevitch and the trust he always showed me remain among the most precious memories of my life.

He had an incomparable knowledge of the Russian language and its subtleties, and found the greatest pleasure in reading the Russian classics. In addition to being erudite and speaking several languages perfectly he was aided in his reading by an extraordinary memory. He was also an excellent physiognomist.

The Tsarevitch possessed a markedly high sense of duty and dignity. Self-mastery was one of his characteristics. He could control himself and conceal his inner feelings, maintaining this calm confidence in the most critical hour. This was not due to coldness, for in his relations he was kind, simple and charming. All who knew him, captivated by his gentle and beautiful expression, came under his spell.

By nature a mystic and fatalist, he had the highest conception of his mission. He considered it his duty to remain in Russia, even and especially after the Revolution, and would never leave his native land: he thus paid with his own life and the lives of his family for his faith in the Russian people.

But I saw quite clearly that the Tsarevitch did not have the qualities needed to be a ruler. Not that he lacked character and will-power, but he did not have the gift of making his opinion prevail, and he often gave in to others though his first impulses had been right. But if I sometimes told him that with such a character he was scarcely made to reign, Heaven knows that I never entertained the idea of suggesting that he should renounce being Tsar.

After his engagement the Tsarevitch begged me to fix a time and place for our last meeting. We agreed to meet on the Volkhonsky highway, near the barn and some way off the road.

I came from the town by carriage; he rode there from the camp. As always when there is too much to say, tears tighten one's throat and stop one finding the words one would like to utter. What is there to say when the last moments arrive, those terrible, inexorable minutes of farewell . . .?

When the Tsarevitch departed for camp I remained by the barn and watched him go until he was no longer in sight. He kept on turning back. I did not weep, I was profoundly unhappy, torn, and my pain went on increasing as Niki drew farther away.

Then I returned home, to the house which seemed so empty. I felt that my life was over, that no more happiness would ever come to me, that henceforth I would know nothing but sorrow, great sorrow.

I knew that some would pity me, but others would derive pleasure from my grief. I did not want compassion, but it would need courage to face the others. But all that only occurred to me later. For the moment there was nothing but terrible boundless suffering, the wrench of losing my Niki! No words can describe what I felt later when I knew that he was with his fiancée. My youth's happy springtime was over. A new life was beginning, the painful life of a woman with a prematurely broken heart!

For the summer I rented the first floor of a villa at Strelna, where I settled with my sister. I lived there like a hermit, isolated from the outside world, with neither the wish nor the energy to see anyone at all. The only thing I wanted was to be left alone.

But I had to pull myself together to be in a fit state to appear during the summer season at Krasnoïe Selo. At least I should have the consolation of seeing my loved Niki, even from a distance. . . . I saw him again! I danced Perrot's little ballet, *La Naïade et le Pêcheur*, with music by Pugni, and other works whose names I have forgotten. But it was an unhappy, painful time.

On July 28th a gala performance was arranged at the Peterhof Palace Theatre for the marriage of the Grand Duchess Xenia Alexandrovna to the Grand Duke Alexander Mikhailovitch. Marius Petipa had arranged a one-act ballet, *Le Réveil de Flore*, in which Flora, the leading role, was given to me.

The Peterhof Palace Theatre, built in 1745 in the reign of the Empress Elisabeth Petrovna, in place of an old riding school, had been rebuilt in 1857. For the gala performance it was completely restored, enlarged by means of outside annexes and fitted with electric light. It was also splendidly decorated.

Among the high-ranking foreigners who attended the marriage were Queen Olga of Greece, Grand Duchess of Russia and aunt of Tsar Nicholas II, Princess Alexandra of Wales, later to be Queen, with her two daughters, Victoria and Maud, childhood friends of the Tsarevitch, and Prince Christian of Denmark.

Apart from the ballet *Le Réveil de Flore* the programme of the gala included the second act of the opera *Romeo and Juliet,* with N. N. Figner and his wife, Medea Figner.

Those who have never attended a gala performance in Russia cannot imagine the splendour and richness devised by the Court ministry for such solemn occasions. All the streets and roads leading to the theatre had been lit up and decorated with incomparable magnificence.

After the celebration of the marriage the young couple left for the Château de Ropcha, near St. Petersburg, where the inhabitants gave them such a warm and loud welcome that the horses were frightened and bolted, throwing the newly married couple into a ditch. Fortunately, they got away with a scare. This gala marked the end of the summer season, and I withdrew to Strelna.

I was not alone in my grief and trouble. The Grand Duke Serge Mikhailovitch, with whom I had formed a deep friendship from the day when the Tsarevitch had brought him home, remained with me to console and protect me. I never felt for him anything approaching my love for the Tsarevitch, but he won my heart by his affection and devotion. And he remained the faithful friend he had shown himself from the beginning all his life, both in times of happiness and in the most painful moments and the hardships of the Revolution.

I found out later that the Tsarevitch begged Serge Mikhailovitch to watch over me as well as to keep him informed about my life and to tell him if his assistance was needed. For he knew that I would have painful days to endure and that, without his support, I risked becoming the prey of many intrigues. I knew and felt for my part during my whole life that he was protecting me: indeed, his powerful protection was evident every time ill-wishers tried to pull me down or to do me harm.

I was especially touched by the Tsarevitch's wish that I should always inhabit that house where we had spent so many unforgettable hours together. He gave it to me as a present, and I was deeply moved.

For the whole of that summer I went for long walks in the shady alleys in the park which stretched from the sea to the magnificent palace of the Grand Duke Constantin Nicolaïevitch.[1] This was how one day I came to see a charming *datcha* in the middle of a huge garden which extended to the sea. This large deserted villa was for sale. I thought it delightfully situated. Seeing how much I liked it, the Grand

[1] Strelna Palace was built in 1711 by Leblond, and rebuilt in 1804 in Gothic style by Russko. It later passed into the hands of the Grand Duke Constantin Pavlovitch.

Duke Serge Mikhailovitch bought it in my name, and I was able to spend the following summer there.

The Emperor's state of health, though causing some anxiety, was not alarming. Such at least was the general opinion. At any rate the Tsar attended the manœuvres at Krasnoïe Selo as usual, after which, for the hunting season, he left with his family for Skernevitsy, where Professor Leyden, the famous German physician, was called into consultation. This specialist diagnosed chronic nephritis. It was therefore decided that the Emperor should go straight to the Crimea in the hope of recuperating in a milder climate and with a quieter and more regular life. But alas, the expected improvement did not take place. On the contrary, the Emperor's health deteriorated to the point where it was thought wise to call his closest relatives to his bedside. At the same moment Princess Alice, the Tsarevitch's fiancée, was also sent for, and arrived a few days before the Tsar's death. He passed away on October 20th 1894, in his fiftieth year, the fourteenth of his reign, mourned by all Russia. During so short a reign he had succeeded in increasing and enhancing the glory and might of the Russian Empire, in raising it to an unprecedented level and assuring his country many years of peace, which justly earned him the title of "Peacemaker". I was heartbroken, for I had truly adored him, and the few words he had spoken to me at the graduation performance had become permanently engraved in me like a rule which I was to follow all my life.

On the day after Alexander III's death—that is to say, on the day the Emperor Nicholas II succeeded to the throne—Princess Alice was converted to the Orthodox religion and took the name of the Grand Duchess Alexandra Feodorovna. The Emperor's earthly remains were brought from Livadia to St. Petersburg and placed in the Peter and Paul Fortress, where for several days an enormous crowd passed in front of the still-open coffin.

A week after the funeral the marriage of Nicholas II was celebrated in the Winter Palace. Mourning, prescribed for a year, was naturally lifted for that one day.

All these events—the arrival of the Imperial fiancée in Russia and the marriage itself—which ought to have been marked with joy and happiness thus took place in a time of general affliction, a fact which many interpreted as an evil omen.

My feelings on the day of the Emperor's marriage can only be understood by those really capable of loving, of loving with all their heart and soul, those who sincerely believe in the existence of true love. Hour by hour, in my thoughts, I followed the events of that fatal day. I suffered terribly, and tried my hardest to keep the wound which this painful blow had recently opened hidden in the depths of my being. I wanted to regard the woman who was stealing my loved Niki from me by marrying him as my sovereign, and nothing else.

In February 1895, making a break with solitude, I left for Monte Carlo on the invitation of Raoul Guinsbourg. My brother Iouzia, Olga Preobrajenska, Bekeffi and Kiakcht came too. I have found, among other cuttings, a review of these performances:

"Europe made its first acquaintance, in the spring of 1895, with Mlle. Kschessinska II, Raoul Guinsberg having invited her for four performances at the Casino Theatre. She was greeted with unqualified enthusiasm. Her performance of character dances in particular raised frenzied applause. Newspapers and reviews carried the warmest praises in honour of our dear artist. Delighted with her talent, the famous French critic Francisque Sarcey devoted his column in *Le Temps* to her."

On returning from Monte Carlo I danced the first act of *Calcabrino*, *The Sleeping Beauty* and *Le Réveil de Flore*, but the season was not an exciting one, for the Imperial Court was still in mourning.

In June I went to Warsaw to dance with my father, Bekeffi and Legat. Perhaps I may be allowed to quote here a passage from A. Plestcheev's book, *Our Ballet*:

"The appearance of Felix Ivanovitch Kschessinsky and his daughter in the mazurka was greeted with thunderous applause and a real deluge of flowers. The Warsaw newspapers devoted very complimentary articles to this mazurka. Our dancers gave four performances in Warsaw and the theatre was full each time, despite the great heat. Mlle. Kschessinska literally dumbfounded the people of Warsaw by her classical dances, which were of a quality they had not seen for a long time. Felix Kschessinsky told me that in Warsaw he met a number of former partners from his young days; and these crippled, bent old ladies would not believe that they were seeing the same Kschessinsky, still upright, strong, fresh and able to hold the stage!"

Warsaw gave me a welcome such as I had never known, even in St. Petersburg. Each of my appearances in the Polish capital during the following years ended triumphantly.

The Warsaw ballet critics also attested their approval. On June 4th 1895 the *Gazeta Polska* wrote:

"Mlle. Kschessinska, star of the ballet of St. Petersburg, appeared in

Pan Twardowski on the stage of the Grand Theatre. She fully justified
her renown. Her dancing is as varied as the sheen on a diamond.
Sometimes she is all lightness and softness, at others fire and passion.
But she is always graceful and the spectator is carried away by the
extraordinary harmony of all her movements. We have never seen
such a marvellous performance of the czardas as Mlle. Kschessinska's.
The public was charmed and conquered, and showed its feelings by
the warmest ovations in honour of the great dancer."

I spent the summer of 1895 in my new villa at Strelna, hastily
furnished. I had completely transformed my bedroom: the walls
were covered in cretonne, the furniture ordered from Meltzer in St.
Petersburg, the best manufacturer in the city. I also had time to re-
decorate a little round boudoir with charming light wood furniture
from Buchner.

Summer passed by in the purest calm. The Krasnoïe Selo season had
been cancelled owing to mourning. Besides, I was ill, and I took
advantage of this to put off my appearance on stage until the end of
November.

The Grand Duke Serge Mikhailovitch spoilt me, doing his best to
comfort and entertain me, to anticipate my smallest wishes. He had
given me the *datcha* at Strelna. I had everything, but neither that nor
even the Grand Duke's friendship and affection could make up for my
lost happiness. And although, in company, I tried hard to appear
carefree and gay, when I was alone I could not help weeping as I
remembered my first love. . . .

CHAPTER VIII

TRIUMPHS AND PLOTS

THE STAGE NO LONGER tempted me: I did little work and danced my old roles, *Paquita*, *Coppélia*, *The Sleeping Beauty*, in a completely uninspired way. The famous Italian dancer Legnani, known for her virtuosity, was appearing on our stage at the time and was naturally given the best roles. She appeared in St. Petersburg, in *Cinderella*, and was the first dancer in the Russian capital to execute thirty-two *fouettés*, which were later introduced into *Swan Lake*. La Legnani had a great success. I found the 1895-1896 season a sad one. My heart was taking a long time to heal. All my thoughts were of Niki.

The Coronation, arranged for May 1896, was drawing near. Everybody was in a fever of preparation, and roles were being distributed in the Imperial Theatre for the gala performance which was to take place in Moscow. Two companies, from St. Petersburg and from Moscow, were to be joined for this extraordinary performance.

I was to dance *Le Réveil de Flore*, during an ordinary season at Moscow. But I was not given a part in the gala performance, for which a new ballet, *La Perle*, with music by Drigo, was being prepared; rehearsals had already started and the leading role had been given to la Legnani. Thus, although I already had my own repertoire and the title of ballerina, I was being deprived of any share in the gala! This was an insult, witnessed by the whole company, and I could not tolerate it! Seized with the deepest despair, I ran to the Grand Duke Wladimir Alexandrovitch, Alexander III's favourite brother and the Tsar's eldest uncle, who had always shown me friendship and kindness. He alone could intercede for me and would understand the shocking injustice with which I had been treated. Exactly what the Grand Duke did and how he set about it, I do not know, but the result was swift and decisive. The Administration of the Imperial Theatres received orders to allow me to participate in the Coronation gala in Moscow.

My honour was saved, and more than this, I was filled with happiness to see Niki intervene thus on my behalf. The Administration would never otherwise have agreed to alter its decision.

Two years after his marriage, two years after our parting, he had kept his promise. This showed me that he had not taken our meeting as a simple little love affair, and that he would always keep me a small place reserved in his heart!

When the Administration received the order from the Imperial Court, rehearsals for *La Perle* were already over, and all the roles distributed. In order that I should have a part in the ballet, Drigo had to compose additional music, and Petipa arranged a *pas-de-deux* specially for me in which I danced the Yellow Pearl (there were already white, black and pink pearls in the ballet).

In the general atmosphere of gaiety surrounding the Coronation I tried to suppress my grief, to receive many friends at the Dresden Hotel, where I was staying—in fact, to appear carefree; but I was living a terrible torment! It was agonising to watch the Tsar pass the platform where I was sitting, the Tsar who was still "Niki" to me, one I adored and who could not, could never belong to me! There I was, alone, torn by two conflicting feelings—my joy in sharing in the patriotic joy of all Russia, and the stifled, solitary cry of my love.

The Coronation celebrations began with the Tsar's solemn entry into Moscow.

He arrived on May 6th. But, following an ancient custom, he spent the days preceding the Coronation not in Moscow itself, but in the Petrovsky Castle, about four miles from the Kremlin. The official entry did not take place until May 9th/21st.

From the windows of my hotel I was able to watch the imposing ceremony which began at two in the afternoon and finished at about four. Troops lined the whole route. The procession was enormous. Besides detachments from the various cavalry regiments of the Guard, there were representatives of the Asian tribes from the Russian Empire in their national dress. There were delegations of Cossacks, members of the high nobility led by the Marshal of the Nobles of the Moscow district, all on horseback, followed by the Court orchestra and the Imperial Hunt in their rich uniforms, headed by His Majesty's Master of the Horse and Master of the Hounds.

Next, still on horseback, came the dignitaries of the Imperial Court. Other dignitaries followed in carriages.

Finally, the Tsar appeared, riding a white horse whose horseshoes had silver nails.[1] He was followed by the members of the Imperial Family and by the foreign princes who had come to Moscow to attend the Coronation.

[1] The Emperor's horse's shoes and the silver nails were later carefully preserved in the Arms Museum.

Behind the foreign princes came the Empress Marie Feodorovna and the Grand Duchess Olga Alexandrovna, in a gold carriage with a crown above it, drawn by eight white horses. Two small pages sat on the traces.

In the gold carriage which followed the Tsarina Alexandra Feodorovna sat, all alone. Behind her in other gold carriages came the Grand Duchesses. The weather was magnificent, and the Tsar's entry to Moscow took place under the most favourable conditions.

On the evening of the Coronation the entire town was lit up. At ten o'clock the Emperor and Empress appeared on the balcony of the Palace facing the left bank of the river Moskowa. A bouquet of flowers was then presented to the Tsarina on a gold salver with a hidden electric switch; as soon as the Empress had taken the bouquet, this switch gave a prearranged signal to the Moscow power station. At once the huge steeple of John-the-Great glowed with hundreds of little electric lights and the illuminations started up everywhere. I tried to go and see this, but soon had to give up, for it was impossible to find a way through the enormous crowd which had invaded the streets. But I was able to admire the main part of the illuminations on the Palace of the Kremlin.

When the Coronation festivities were over, the Tsar and Tsarina went to the home of the Grand Duke Serge Alexandrovitch on his estate near Moscow, inherited from his mother, the Empress Marie Alexandrovna. Five officers of the Preobrajensky Regiment were also invited to the party. They had served at the same time as the Tsar when he was still Heir Apparent and when the regiment had been commanded by the Grand Duke Serge Alexandrovitch. These officers included Baron Zeddeler, my sister Julie's future husband, Alexander Sevastianovitch Etter, Schlittler and others whose names I have forgotten.

Apart from the gala performance, I also appeared in Moscow in normal performances, which won me unqualified success and a great number of flowers, as well as a very pretty silver basket.

After all this I returned to St. Petersburg. Gradually I began to live once more. I took part in the Krasnoïe Selo season, which was gayer and more animated than the previous season. A dancer from Moscow, Djouri, who was very kind and nice, was also there. When there were several consecutive performances we spent the night at the theatre, in our dressing-rooms, to avoid having to go back home. On those nights, after the performance, we all went to sup at the restaurant

opposite the theatre. Once the Grand Dukes Cyril and Boris Wladimirovitch, whom I often saw in Moscow, remained and had supper
with us. After which we all returned to the theatre and danced on the
stage while the Grand Duke Boris Wladimirovitch, installing himself
in the conductor's stand, brilliantly conducted a silent and imaginary
orchestra.

I started the 1896-1897 season at the Michel Theatre, where, for the
first time in my life, I danced *La Fille Mal Gardée*, a three-act ballet by
Dauberval, with music by Guertel and choreography by M. Petipa
and L. Ivanov. Hitherto I had only danced the first act of this ballet, at
Krasnoïe Selo. But I liked the role of Lise, which suited me, and I
danced it with brio.

"Mlle. Kschessinska II had taken great pains in preparing herself for
this role," wrote A. Plestcheev, "which she interpreted most thoughtfully and carefully. Lise's passage from tears to joy, her high spirits and
tricks, her fear and trembling as she stands crestfallen before her mother—
all this was conveyed in the most expressive way and received the greatest
success. But Mlle. Kschessinska II was equally distinguished in the
purely dancing part of *La Fille Mal Gardée*; she was equally fine in the
demi-caractère dances and in the classical *pas-de-deux* performed with
M. Kiatcht. The adagio in this last dance was particularly successful,
and the final group brought loud and repeated applause."[1]

Later *La Fille Mal Gardée* became my favourite ballet.

On September 25th, also for the first time, I danced *Mlada*, a ballet
entirely transformed by M. Petipa—another performance which the
critics greeted as "an outstanding success".[2]

Finally, on December 8th 1896 came the benefit performance for the
maître de ballet, Marius Petipa, to mark the fiftieth anniversary of his
entering the service of the Imperial Theatres. For this occasion a new
ballet-féerie in three acts and seven tableaux entitled *Bluebeard* was put
on, with music by P. P. Schenk and choreography by Petipa himself.
I took the role of Venus, in the last act, which Petipa called "an
astronomic ballet" and where, according to A. Plestscheev, I represented "the choreographic dessert". "Ballet lovers," he wrote, "and
all those who appreciate ballet must be delighted as they admire dances
such as these. Mlle. Kschessinska dances like a true artist, with astonishing accuracy, always full of beauty and fire, a fire which belongs to
her alone. . . ."

The curtain went up after the first tableau of the third act, and
Legnani and I dragged Petipa on to the stage, where he was presented

[1] A. Plestcheev, *Our Ballet*, p. 424.   [2] Ibid., p. 425.

9b. Strelna: The verandah.

9a. The *datcha* at Strelna.

10b. In the ballet *Esmeralda*.

10a. The Grand Duke Serge Mikhailovitch.

with flowers, and speeches were made in his honour by various delegations.

During the previous season the stage had not tempted me: I worked little, and my dancing suffered. But this season, having resolved to take hold of myself, I started working with application: the Tsar might come to the theatre, and I was determined not to disappoint him.[1]

During the 1896-1897 season the Tsar and Tsarina came to the ballet almost every Sunday; but the Administration made me always dance on a Wednesday, the day when the Emperor never came. At first I thought this a mere coincidence, but I soon realised the truth, and felt it both as an injustice and an insult. This happened several Sundays in succession. At last the Administration gave me a Sunday: I was to dance *The Sleeping Beauty*. I was absolutely sure the Emperor would attend this performance. Imagine my surprise and distress on learning—for news travels very fast in the theatre—that the Administration had persuaded the Tsar to go to the Michel Theatre that night, where a French play, which the Emperor had been unable to see the previous Saturday, was being performed. It was clear that the Director of the Theatres had done his best to stop the Tsar seeing me. This injustice passed all bounds; and so, for the first time, I had recourse to the authorisation which the Tsar had given me once to apply directly to him. I wrote to him, telling him everything that was going on in the theatre, adding that I was finding it impossible, under such conditions, to remain on the Imperial stage. My letter was delivered to His Majesty in person by the Grand Duke Serge Mikhailovitch. Receiving no reply, I did not know whether the Emperor would follow the Director's wishes and go to the Michel Theatre or attend the ballet. At last Sunday arrived. There was an atmosphere of bitter disillusionment among the artists: there were murmurs that the Tsar never came to the ballet when Kschessinska was dancing, and that through me everybody would be deprived of his presence. True enough, the Imperial box was empty. The Director and all his staff had gone to the Michel Theatre and were preparing to greet the Emperor. Even the public seemed infected, and the atmosphere among the audience was very different from that of other Sundays. Everything seemed to

[1] During this season four Grand Dukes—Michel Nicolaievitch, Wladimir Alexandrovitch, Alexis Alexandrovitch and Paul Alexandrovitch—showed me a moving attention by giving me a brooch in the form of a ring, studded with diamonds and four large sapphires, in a case with a plaque engraved with their names.

indicate that the Emperor had indeed decided to go to the Michel Theatre, and I felt great distress in beginning the ballet in these conditions. The orchestra was already assembled, the musicians were tuning their instruments. Nothing but the last signal was awaited to raise the curtain and begin the performance. Suddenly there was an indescribable uproar. Everybody began to run, to gesticulate, to exclaim, "The Tsar is here! The Tsar is here!" . . . Since nobody had expected him, his sudden arrival caused a complete upheaval! The Director had to be immediately informed by telephone, and everybody leaped to do it! As for me, I was exultant. The whole company recovered its spirits and the performance took place in an unforgettable atmosphere of animation, excitement and gladness. After the show I told the artists that I knew about the Tsar's coming, but had remained silent on purpose. . . . My enemies, who had plotted this conspiracy and had at first been delighted at the Emperor's absence, did not conceal their vexation!

I cannot accuse the Director of the Imperial Theatres, I. A. Vsevolojsky, of causing the difficulties I suffered. He had always been considerate to me, and thought highly of me. But he was powerless against the influence of certain groups who flattered him without ceasing.

Before being given important ballets I had danced many of lesser importance, such as *Les Sylphides*—the old version—*Les Espiègleries d'Amour*, *Acis et Galatée*, *La Halte de Cavalerie*; later, with my consent, these ballets were given to other dancers. I was also given responsible roles in almost all the great ballets, before I even received the title of ballerina. For instance, in *Le Roi Candaule*, I had performed the dance of the three Graces, and my variation had always been greeted with enormous success. One day as I was dancing it I happened to slip and fall, but I managed to get up in time, and this earned me a real ovation. Later Nelidova, from Moscow, appeared in the same ballet while I danced the *"pas de Diane"* in the first act.[1]

I next received the principal role in *Le Roi Candaule*, an eminently dramatic part, especially in the mad scene, which enabled me to show my ability as a mime.

[1] The following is a passage devoted by A. Plestscheev to this ballet: "Mlle. Kschessinska II, our ballerina, had a resounding success. She received an ovation after her '*pas de Diane*' which she performed to perfection; she was worthily partnered by MM. Kiakcht and Legat II. She does indeed dance excellently. The public particularly liked the added variation borrowed from the ballet *La Perle Magnifique*" (*Our Ballet*, p. 433, February 9th 1897).

At the gala performance organised on April 16th 1897 at the Mary-insky Theatre in honour of the Emperor Francis-Joseph of Austria, who was on a state visit to Russia, I was given the first two acts of *The Sleeping Beauty* to dance.

During the summer of that same year, while I was living in my villa at Strelna, the Emperor informed me through the Grand Duke Serge Mikhailovitch that he would ride past my villa on a certain day at a certain hour with the Empress; he also informed me that I must with-out fail be in my garden at the appointed hour. So I chose a bench from which it would be easy to see me. He did in fact pass by, with the Empress, at the arranged time. I rose as they approached, and made a deep curtsy, to which they replied with a kind and gracious gesture. With characteristic grace the Tsar was bent on showing—but with complete tact—each time the opportunity arose, his care for me. And for me, who still loved him, this was an enormous consolation.

During the summer I became very keen on bicycling, and Countess Torbi, the wife of the Grand Duke Michel Mikhailovitch, gave me a skirt designed especially for this sport. I particularly liked riding in the park, on the lower road, which linked Strelna to Peterhof by way of Mikhailovka, the estate of the Grand Duke Mikhail Nicolaïevitch, and, beyond that, by way of Znamenka, which belonged to the Grand Duke Nicholas Nicolaïevitch. At Mikhailovka I often met either the Grand Duke Mikhail Nicolaïevitch, who was insistent that I should execute figure eights with my bicycle, an achievement in which I was not always successful, or the Grand Duke George Mikhailovitch, with whom I was on terms of close friendship.

That same summer I took part in three galas. At the first of these performances arranged at Peterhof on July 23rd 1897 in honour of the King of Siam, Samdetch-Fra-Paraminder-Maga-Tchula-Longkorn, I danced the first two acts of *Coppélia*. New décors and costumes had been specially created for the occasion.

The second gala, the most brilliant of the three, was danced on July 28th in honour of the German Emperor, Wilhelm II, not at the Peterhof Theatre, but on Olga Island, in the middle of the upper lake. Stands for the spectators had been arranged all round on the island itself, while the stage had been raised on piles above the water; the orchestra played in an enormous iron stand, below the level of the lake. The stage only had side scenery and wings: the magnificent view over the distant hills of Babigon served as a back-cloth. Not far from the stage was a little island, decorated with rocks and a grotto, in which I positioned myself at the very beginning of the performance. The

programme for this gala was the one-act ballet *Thétis et Pélée*, arranged
by Petipa to music by Delibes and Minkus. The guests reached the
island in little boats. The whole scene was bathed in electric light and
the ensemble had a truly fairy-like appearance. The ballet started with
the opening of the grotto in which I was hidden: I then stepped on to a
mirror, which began to slide towards the stage. This gave the audience
the impression that I was walking on the water.

The spectacle ended with the lighting up of the pavilions and far-off
hills beyond the stage. This display was favoured with exceptionally
fine weather, although there had been fears of rain in the morning
(but all plans had been made, if the worst came to the worst, to transfer
the show to the Peterhof Theatre; stage hands, carpenters and elec-
tricians were all standing by). Everybody gave deserved credit to the
Administration of the Imperial Theatres for having arranged this gala
performance with so much magnificence and taste. The organisation
had called for two months' intense and difficult work. The electrical
arrangements alone had cost a fabulous price.

A day or two later the Director I. A. Vsevolojsky sent for me to
give me an invitation from the Emperor of Germany to dance in
Berlin during the coming season. Although I was very flattered by the
Emperor's attention, I declined his invitation, for I preferred to stay in
St. Petersburg. If the truth be told, I have never much enjoyed dancing
abroad, especially when long periods were involved.

The third and last gala performance was given at Peterhof on
August 11th in honour of Felix Faure, the President of the French
Republic. This time the gala took place in the theatre. I danced the
polonaise and mazurka from the second act of the opera *La Vie pour le
Tsar*, accompanied by the opera chorus and two orchestras. Later I
appeared in the ballet *A Midsummer Night's Dream*, with music by
Mendelssohn-Bartholdi and Minkus.

CHAPTER IX

LA FILLE DU PHARAON

I OPENED THE season on September 10th 1897 with *The Sleeping Beauty*. But Legnani fell seriously ill, and I was charged with the whole repertoire until almost the end of the year. My efforts were rewarded with consistent success. "The ballerina is especially admirable in *Paquita*, *Mlada* and *La Fille Mal Gardée*," wrote A. Plestscheev, who added, referring to *Mlada* which I danced on September 21st: "The ballerina, whose *doubles tours* in this variation are always performed with absolute perfection, does not appear until the first tableau of the third act. In the third tableau of the same act Mlle. Kschessinska II danced, in incomparable fashion, the delicate variation *sur les pointes* to the sounds of the harp. At the public's request she had to give an encore of this number."[1]

On February 8th 1898 there was a benefit performance for my father, who had just completed his sixtieth year of artistic life, a life spent successively in Warsaw and St. Petersburg. This was a magnificent occasion, and when my father appeared on the stage the public gave him an enthusiastic welcome.

I danced the second act, rearranged, of Saint-Léon's *Fiametta*. I adored this ballet which the Tsar loved: in his *Journal* he mentions a performance where I danced this ballet. After this I took part in the third act of *Bluebeard*, in which my father and I danced Konsky's mazurka. This dance was so successful that we had to repeat it.[2]

Following tradition, my father's benefit performance began after the ballet, *La Halte de Cavalerie*, the curtain remaining raised. M. I. Petipa, the maître de ballet, greeted my father on behalf of the ballet company and MM. Ivanov, Guerdt and Oblakov gave him an illuminated address and a token, a diamond lyre. The baritones Iakolev and Tchernov now congratulated him on behalf of the Opera, and the

---

[1] A. Plestscheev, *op. cit.*, p. 437.

[2] This is Plestscheev's account of it (*op, cit.*, p. 446): "In this mazurka, lightly spiced with pantomime, the old man gaily twirls his moustache, shows first of all that it is difficult for him to be the young dancer's squire, then springs like a whirlwind, filling the whole audience with enthusiasm. Kschessinsky performs his national dance with beauty, nobility and pride. Mlle. Kschessinska danced with spendid grace and ardour; she was adorable in her magnificent costume."

former, after a brief address, presented him with a wreath. The drama company was represented by Mlle. Glinskaia and MM. Medvedev and Korovin-Krioukovsky. Then the delegate of the French company, M. Valbel, presented my father with a garland and proceeded to recall the successes which he had won in Warsaw, Paris and St. Petersburg. Meanwhile, case after case of presents was being passed up from the orchestra, including a chest full of silver which was so heavy that M. Drigo, the conductor, was unable to lift it!

A week later, on February 15th, the same performance with a few minor modifications was presented. At the stage door the public gave me an extraordinary ovation, covering me in flowers.[1]

On April 19th, at a performance which included several ballets, I again danced the second act of *Fiametta*. "Mlle. Kschessinska II," wrote A. Plestscheev, "danced *La Charmeuse* and *La Chanson à Boire* with her own particular fire and bravura. The talented ballerina moved the whole audience to transports of excitement. There were ceaseless cries of '*Bis*' and applause. Those who witnessed this unanimous admiration could not help calling to mind the words of the poet Nekrassov who says so truly that in raving over ballet a peaceful citizen forgets his age, his social position and his occupation."[2]

That summer I did not dance in the Krasnoïe Selo season, and rested in my country house. I only made one stage appearance, on July 18th 1898, at Peterhof, for the State visit of the King of Roumania. The ballet *La Perle*, already seen in 1896 in Moscow for the Coronation, was performed. But this time the principal role, that of the White Pearl, was taken not by Legnani, but by myself. Like the previous year's spectacle in honour of the Kaiser the ballet did not take place in the theatre, but on Olga Island. A small artificial island held a large shell in which the White Pearl was concealed. The performance enjoyed lovely weather and scored a great success.

Three of the friends who came to visit me at Strelna in the summer were to remain friends over many years: Prince Nikita Troubetzkoy, Prince Dimitri Djambakouriany-Orbeliany and Boris Gartmann. They were all three pages in the Imperial household at the time and commissioned as officers on August 8th 1898. To celebrate this occasion two of them—Prince Nikita Troubetzkoy and Prince Orbeliany—instead of supping in town with their comrades, came to celebrate at Strelna, where they spent the night. I remember sending champagne up to their room, so that they might go on celebrating their promotion. Nearly half a century has passed and on August 8th 1948 I received

---

[1] A. Plestscheev, *op. cit.*, p. 448.   [2] Ibid., pp. 450-1.

from Prince Nikita Troubetzkoy a most moving letter recalling that
distant occasion:

Petit-Clamart,
August 8th/21st 1948.

Dear Maletchka,

It is just after eight. Liouba and I are reliving our memories. I am
telling her how fifty years ago, at this very time, the late Mitia
Orbeliany (Djamba) and I were sitting at your sumptuous table, at
dear Strelna, and how touchingly warmly you celebrated his promotion and mine! We went to bed very late, then, and next morning
drank not tea but champagne, warm pink champagne. Yes, all that
is really very far away now, but to the eyes of memory it still seems
close! I thank you sincerely for the friendship you have always
shown me during half a century. I kiss your hands. Liouba sends her
love.

Your devoted
Nikita.

After his promotion Prince N. S. Troubetzkoy—or, more simply,
Nikita, as we always call him—was seconded to the Nijegorodsky
Dragoons. He later became aide-de-camp to the Grand Duke Nicolas
Mikhailovitch, and married Lioubov Nikolaievna Egorova. They
both now live in Paris, where Lioubov Egorova gives excellent ballet
classes. We have remained close friends.

Prince D. I. Orbeliany was first of all seconded to the Pskov Dragoons, and later to the Horse Guard. The Pskov regimental cap had a
pink headband, which earned Mitia Orbeliany the pleasant nickname
"pink monkey". He later became aide-de-camp to the Grand Duke
Alexander Nicolaievitch, and after the latter's death to the Grand
Duke Alexander Mikhailovitch.

Boris Gueorguievitch Gartmann, the third of my friends, was
seconded to the Horse Guard, where a brilliant career awaited him.
During the war he became their commanding officer. He lived in Belgium during the emigration, which meant that we could seldom meet. I
saw him last when he was making a short stay in Paris, on his way to
Menton, where he suddenly died. He was married to Marie Constantinovna, Prince Bielosselsky's youngest daughter. They were living
at Kislovodsk during the revolution. His wife, while still young, had
been stricken with paralysis. I can still see her when we fled from
Kislovodsk, lying on a waggon, never losing heart even in the most

dangerous moments: neither torrential rain nor the Red artillery fire undermined her indomitable courage. She died in Belgium in 1931.

After a long and well-earned rest, I danced *The Sleeping Beauty* on September 20th 1898. The best description of that occasion comes from A. Plestscheev:[1]

"Mlle. Kschessinska II scored her customary remarkable success in *The Sleeping Beauty*. She danced her variations with lightness and her own particular brilliance and polish: in spite of the audience's demands, for instance in the last act, she did not dance an encore. Mlle. Kschessinska II has many personal qualities which set her off among other dancers. Full of vitality, fire and ardour in her dancing, she lights up the stage by her appearance and her smile which never vanishes, even when her legs have to perform movements whose boldness risks, if not a fatal accident, at least a sprain. These difficulties of movement, which every dancer in our time has to face, were undreamed of by the dancers of Diderot's age!"

At last I was given a long and splendid ballet, *La Fille du Pharaon*, revived for me, in which I could show off my miming and dancing talents. It was my favourite ballet after *La Fille Mal Gardée*.

I danced it for the first time on October 21st 1899 at a benefit performance for Johanson's daughter.

La Fille du Pharaon is a ballet in four acts and nine tableaux, with a prologue and epilogue, with choreography by Saint-Georges and Petipa, and music by Pugni.

In this ballet, wrote A. Plestscheev, "Mlle. Kschessinska II, in a splendid costume, with the spotlight on her, soon wins the audience's attention. During the whole ballet, a long one, she never leaves the stage. Aspitchia's narrative in mime alternates with dances which have received occasional finishing touches from the talented Petipa, who has adapted them to modern technique, more demanding than in Rosatti's time. These mimed sequences whose subject is extremely dramatic move us greatly as Mlle. Kschessinska II performs them: her acting is never extravagant or exaggerated, but shows an instinctive sense of proportion. As a well known writer says, Mlle. Kschessinska II is full of tender naïve grace. She acts with spirit, in the fisherman's hut for instance, and mimes the story of the chase so clearly that one feels one is actually there. She is even better in the last tableau, where she begs for mercy for a man she loves, then burns with a blaze of gratitude when the father gives his consent to the marriage of Aspitchia

[1] Op. cit.

11*a*. In Spanish costume.

11*b*. In the ballet *Esmeralda*.

12b. In the ballet *La Fille du Pharaon.*

12a. In the ballet *La Fille du Pharaon.*

and Taon. This performance does not possess the realism and power of a Virginia Zucchi, but is none the less full of charm and brio.

"All this talented ballerina's dances are lovely, from the first act variation (of which she gave an encore) the huntresses' dance and the *grand pas d'action*, to the oriental variation and the variation on points in the vision scene. All these were performed by Mlle. Kschessinska II with impeccable ease. She is equally successful in the original Easter variation which she dances with pride, casting on her followers arrogant glances full of true Oriental seductiveness. The variation on points in the second tableau of the third act, a perfect piece of choreography, was danced in highly artistic fashion. It remains for me to mention her varied and tasteful costumes, which suit her delightfully. Mlle. Kschessinska II's success in such a hard, responsible role is undeniably deserved. The audience's reaction was unanimous: critics and connoisseurs were allied in their approval. This success finally convinces me that Mlle. Kschessinska II is the best Russian dancer of our time; in the three years which have passed since this book's first edition she has shown off her delightful talent in varied and startling fashion. She has now become such an outstanding artist that foreign dancers must reckon with her. She received many bouquets."

In spite of his age—he was almost seventy-seven—my father had the role of the King of Nubia in this ballet. To the music of a triumphal march, he appeared at the head of the procession, but his movement, so far from simply following the normal rhythm, reflected the melody's syncopation; his walk, which seemed so straightforward, was in fact extremely difficult. Many years later in my studio in Paris Prince S. M. Volkhonsky, speaking of Dalcrose, mentioned this entry of my father as an example of complicated rhythmical movements.

During the summer of 1898 I had been to Warsaw with Kiakcht and Bekeffi, and received as enthusaistic a welcome from public and Press as on my first visit. I loved these visits to Warsaw, where I always had the greatest success, both on stage and in society, and spent a very happy time. My numerous relations and friends vied with each other in their attentions to me: on waking I invariably found my room full of flowers sent by my admirers as soon as morning came.

With the theatre closed during Lent I took advantage of two weeks' holiday to visit my beloved Italy with Mme. Paule-Marie, my godmother, and to pass through Warsaw, where I spent a whole evening; then I took the night train to Czenstokow, which I reached at four o'clock, at the very moment when with great solemnity and to the music of the organ the curtain concealing the miraculous image of the Holy Virgin of Czenstokov was being raised. This image is venerated throughout Poland, and the ceremony takes place every day.

At the end of the 1898-1899 season Jean Alexandrovitch Vsevolojsky[1] retired from his position of Director of the Imperial Theatres, which he had filled for almost twenty years with great efficiency, love and zeal. Under him the Imperial Theatre progressed greatly in the artistic sphere. He brought Russian ballet and opera to a hitherto unknown height. The libretti of almost all the ballets and operas were either written by him or following his directions. He was also an excellent draughtsman with a profound knowledge of styles, and designed all the costumes most successfully. The décors were also prepared under his instructions, and thousands of his designs were preserved in the archives of the Imperial Theatres. His name remains closely linked to the history of the Russian theatre, to whose success he greatly contributed.

It was under Vsevolojsky's direction that I entered the Ballet School, graduated and embarked upon my dancing career; so my tribute to him is heartfelt. One could not have wished for a better director.

Of all the productions which took place under him *The Sleeping Beauty* undoubtedly remains his masterpiece. He wrote the book himself, Tschaikowsky composing the music and M. I. Petipa the choreography. He drew every one of the costumes himself. He was wholly bent, in his production of *The Sleeping Beauty*, on astonishing everybody with the music and the unprecedented luxury of the costumes and decor designed for this fairy-tale ballet.

J. A. Vsevolojsky was succeeded by Prince Serge Mikhailovitch Volkhonsky, appointed Director of the Imperial Theatres on July 22nd 1899. A highly cultured man and accomplished musician, Prince Volkhonsky was an excellent pianist. He was also an admirable actor who often appeared on the amateur stage. His appointment was warmly greeted by all connoisseurs and promoters of art. Although he was at that time almost a stranger to me, I felt a liking for him which was to be strengthened years later during the emigration, when I got to know and understand him better. He always behaved like a man of the world, irreproachably educated, with delicate manners and without the slightest affectation.

[1] J. A. Vsevolojsky was appointed Director of the Imperial Theatres on September 3rd 1881.

CHAPTER X

TEN YEARS ON THE STAGE

IN THE AUTUMN of 1899 I arrived in the capital to witness the first appearance as Swanilda in *Coppélia* of the Italian dancer Henrietta Grimaldi, who had been invited by the Administration of the Imperial Theatres for a few performances. This ballet was no longer in my repertoire, and I had passed on the role to Olga Preobrajenska.

During the variation on points at the end of the first act Grimaldi was forced to leave the stage, her eyes full of tears. As soon as the curtain went down M. Aistow, the stage manager, rushed into my box and begged me to take Grimaldi's place: she had just sprained her leg and could not go on dancing. At first I naturally refused to appear impromptu on the stage. I had no costume, no make-up with me. Also it was a long time since I had danced the part, and, most cogent of all, I was totally unprepared, having done no work the whole summer. But, confronted with the stage manager's confusion and wishing to relieve the Administration who would otherwise have been compelled to interrupt the performance, I finally agreed, not without alarm, to take Grimaldi's place. This is the notice which the performance later received:

"Although she was quite unprepared for the part which she had not danced for a very long time, Mlle. Kschessinska was only hesitant at the beginning: soon she recovered herself completely and gave a perfect rendering of the whole doll scene, both as regards technique and mime, not making a single mistake or leaving out a step. This is eloquent proof indeed of her great and brilliant gifts. It is hardly necessary to add that the public rewarded the artist with the loudest ovations. In an order of the day published the following day the Administration of the Imperial Theatres expressed its deep gratitude to Mlle. Kschessinska whose kindness allowed the performance to go on."[1]

At the beginning of the season I started to rehearse *Esmeralda*, which I had at last been given. The ballet was revived for me, and Prince

---

[1] Jubilee edition, 1900, p. 16, where we also read that "on September 9th 1898 the role of Swanilda was given to Olga Preobrajenska, after which date Mlle. Kschessinska did not appear in *Coppélia*".

Volkhonsky often attended rehearsals, supervising all the preparations
from close quarters. The Prince was extremely kind and pleasant to me,
which convinced me that we would always get on very well. But
apparently he had been warned, as soon as he was made Director, that
he would not find it at all easy to work with me! To which he replied
that he would soon gain the upper hand and would pay no attention to
my wishes. He was unfortunately not aware of the situation and of the
responsibilities of the leading dancers, who were loaded, not to say
overloaded, with an enormous repertoire. His lack of awareness was
soon to cause a clash which could easily have been avoided.

In spite of my still recent gesture (had I not in fact saved the Administration by taking Grimaldi's place when she was unable to go on?),
a gesture for which he had wanted to thank me personally, Prince
Volkhonsky decided to give Grimaldi, who had only recently been
invited as guest artist, my favourite ballet, *La Fille Mal Gardée*. Whereupon I went to him and begged him to reconsider his decision. I was
to appear in this work in the autumn; the ballets in one dancer's
repertoire cannot, without her consent, be given to another. Although
I framed my request politely, even with deference, he refused to do
what I asked. Things could obviously not rest there, and I took my own
steps. A few days later the Director received an order from the Court
Minister telling him to leave the ballet in question to me. I owed this
new favour to the Tsar, who intervened on my behalf, although he
was then at Darmstadt. As for Prince Volkhonsky, he continued his
pleasant and considerate behaviour towards me, as if nothing had
happened.

At about the same time as Prince Volkhonsky's appointment a man
of particular gifts and talents was appointed to the Administration
of the Imperial Theatres as official in charge of special services. This was
Serge Pavlovitch Diaghilev, who was exactly my age. I liked him from
the first, both for his intelligence and culture. I enjoyed talking with
him, and he showed me kindliness and consideration. Diaghilev had a
rich head of hair, with a greying lock in front, which earned him the
nickname "Chinchilla". When he entered the Administration's box
while I was dancing the waltz from *Esmeralda*, my stage companions
began to hum under their breath:

> "I've just heard
> That 'Chinchilla' is in his box,
> And I'm terribly afraid
> To make a mistake!"

S. P. Diaghilev nearly always accompanied me home after the performance. Curiously, I have always been successful with men in whom I expected least of all to awake admiration! And yet there was nothing boyish about me. This makes me think of an amusing incident: one evening I was at the Alexandre Theatre where a benefit performance for M. A. Pototzky was in progress. Before the show was over I decided to go to the Maryinsky Theatre, where *Faust* was being performed, and where I expected to find S. P. Diaghilev in his official seat in the second row. The seat next to his belonged to the Office Manager, Baron V. A. Koussov, whom I asked to give me his place. I had arrived just before the end of the opera, and without being seen I slipped down the passage and furtively sat next to Diaghilev, who was astounded when he happened to turn round and saw me instead of Koussov!

In February 1900, the first winter after his appointment, Prince Volkhonsky threw a brilliant reception in the Administration's luxurious rooms in honour of the famous Italian actor, Tomaso Salvini. He had just arrived in St. Petersburg for several performances—by special permission—of *Othello* at the Alexandre Theatre with our drama company. Salvini acted in Italian and the others in Russian. But his gestures and acting were so eloquent that nobody took any notice of the difference in language!

I attended the reception to which Prince Volkhonsky had invited St. Petersburg society and some of the leading artists from the Alexandre Theatre and the Maryinsky. There were also some of the Imperial Family; the reception was very successful and afforded matter for the gossip columns for a long time.

When I appeared on the stage nothing was more inspiring to me than to know that I had admirers in the audience. An artist must throw out a challenge to the spectators, inform them that she is there for them. She must attract them, carry them with her and gain their undivided attention. In my opinion, it was indispensable to charm the audience from the first; and the audience never failed to respond to my challenge with a roar of applause. The very success of the performance depended on this immediate contact. People agreed that nobody could bewitch the audience from the very beginning as I could.

This opinion was shared by the famous ballet critic, A. Volynsky, in his book, *The Maryinsky Theatre*. And recently (January 17th 1952) M. Adamovitch mentioned this in the lecture which he gave on *Ballet before Diaghilev*:

"In all fairness it is impossible not to call up first of all the name of Mathilde Kschessinska who for a quarter of a century was the image, the very prototype of the great star, the *prima ballerina assoluta* of the Imperial Ballet. She was an artist of outstanding technique with the special gift of gaining hold of the audience from her very first entry on to the stage. Volynsky used to say, 'A star can be recognised by her appearance. She owes it to herself to eclipse everybody else.' And he claimed that Kschessinska, with her brilliant triumphal quality, was incomparable in this respect. 'She was like a sudden flash of light,' he exclaimed. I remember that Isadora Duncan has also spoken, in her *Memoirs*, of the impression made by Kschessinska's magical appearance on the stage. She was indeed magical, so much so that one was always aware of a kind of fever gripping the audience as they waited for her appearance, a fever which only abated when the curtain fell. *Esmeralda*, in which Zucchi once shone, appears to have been Kschessinska's favourite ballet, and we have it from the lips of one of the highest Soviet critics that none of the many stars who succeeded her in this heavy role was able to eclipse her memory."

After *La Fille du Pharaon*, which I often danced during that season, I was given *Esmeralda* which I had long dreamed about and which I could now tackle without fear.

I had indeed steeped myself in the part ever since Virginia Zucchi gave her wonderful interpretation on the stage of the Maryinsky Theatre. I had made a note then of all her gestures, her miming and her attitudes. But I had been too young then; I had needed first to love and suffer in order to understand poor Esmeralda's emotions through my own experience. Petipa's valuable advice helped greatly to prepare me for this difficult role.

The first performance of *Esmeralda* was on November 21st 1899, and I scored a great success. I was satisfied with my own interpretation, knowing that I had overcome the difficulties of the role and created the Esmeralda that I had always imagined. No other dancer took the part until my retirement from the stage. I may be allowed to quote the words of the anthology devoted to me on my tenth anniversary:

"Mlle. Kschessinska's gifts cannot be described without mentioning her appearance on November 21st 1899 in *Esmeralda* at N. I. Kistov's benefit performance. In all the ballets she had hitherto danced Mlle. Kschessinska the dancer dominated Mlle. Kschessinska the mime. But in *Esmeralda*, where we have dramatic scenes alternating with dancing, and where mime is predominant, Mlle. Kschessinska gives an ideal interpretation. With admirable strength and realism she conveys the soul's most subtle transports; the spectator is astonished by her eloquent and expressive acting. She was also incomparable in the powerful jealousy scene, where Esmeralda dances before her rival, and in the march to the scaffold, where the intense drama revealed her sustained and thoughtful preparation. In this ballet as in all the others her technique was impeccable, full of life and personality. On the eve of the twentieth century our ballet can be proud of prospering thanks to national talent which no longer looks to the foreign dancer as the ideal."

In the jealousy scene, in which I see Phoebus with his fiancée and have to dance a *pas-de-deux* before my rival, I express my despair, in the final coda, like a wounded bird. It so happened that the dancer who was playing Phoebus' fiancée murmured quite loud: "Her knees aren't turned out." It was not even annoying! It was simply . . . stupid!

Such a remark gives an only too clear picture of the way in which certain dancers think of ballet technique. I was not one of those who dance themselves silly and think of nothing but details of execution, of turning out their knees, who are hypnotised by technique at the expense of acting. Where there is no mime technique must obviously be followed; but in scenes of powerful drama, where everything rests on the emotion, one can safely forget one's knees! The dancer who made this remark had not the slightest conception of what a dramatic interpretation should be.

The tenth anniversary of my career on the Imperial stage was drawing near. An artist generally received a benefit performance either after twenty years' service or on retirement, in which case it was a farewell performance. However, I decided to ask for this favour after only ten years on the stage. I needed special permission, so I framed my request, not to the Director of the Imperial Theatres, but straight to the Minister of the Imperial Court, a position then held by Baron Frederiks, a kind man, who had always shown himself most pleasant towards me.[1]

The Minister granted me an audience, for which I chose my clothes with the greatest care: a light grey woollen dress, very well fitted, and a triangular hat of the same colour. I was young and, as the newspapers of the time said, "graceful and slim". But there was no harm in helping nature and appearing in the best possible light! In fact, Baron Frederiks paid me countless compliments on my toilette. Emboldened by this,

[1] Baron (later Count) Vladimir Borissovitch Frederiks was Minister of the Imperial Court from 1896 until the Revolution (1917). The Imperial Theatres came directly under him, and in all questions of the theatre he alone could make personal reports to the Emperor.

I presented my request, which he immediately agreed to submit to the Tsar, the only person who could grant a benefit performance not covered by the regulations. Then, seeing him well disposed towards me, I told him that I owed my capacity to perform thirty-two *fouettés* without flaw to him.

"I am delighted," he said, a little confused, "but I do not quite see . . ."

Obviously he did not see at all, and did not understand how such a responsibility was his.

"It's very simple," I resumed. "To dance *fouettés* in one spot one has to have a clearly visible mark ahead every time one turns. You always sit in the middle of the front row of the stalls, and when it's dark your decorations glitter in the footlights!"

My explanation delighted him and he again assured me that I had no need to worry about the outcome of my petition.

Of course I *was* allowed my benefit performance, once again thanks to the Emperor! I chose Sunday, February 13th 1900, as my date, because it was a number which always brought me luck.

Before my benefit I danced at two performances at the little Hermitage Theatre, which was linked by a bridge to the Hermitage Museum and the Winter Palace. The theatre, the work of the Italian architect, Guarengui, had been built in Catherine II's reign, in 1783, on the site of the former palace where Peter the Great died; it took the place of the old theatre, which was demolished when the Winter Palace was reconstructed. During the winter seasons it was used for Court performances, attended only by guests of the Imperial Court.

On February 7th, at the Hermitage, I danced *Les Quatre Saisons*, a ballet with music by Glazounov and choreography by Petipa. On February 10th I appeared in *Les Millions d'Arlequin*, also by Petipa, but with music by Drigo. This ballet was full of beautiful melodies and had been perfectly produced; but the dances did not interest me at all. I only accepted it because it was new, and later handed it on to other dancers.

At last Sunday, February 13th, arrived, the day of the performance marking the tenth anniversary of my life on the Imperial stage.

On the day of their benefit performances dancers usually received from His Majesty's Cabinet what was known as "the Imperial present". In most cases it consisted of a jewel in gold or silver, enriched sometimes with precious stones according to the class of gift, and always bearing a crown or Imperial eagle. Male dancers usually received a gold watch. On the whole these gifts were not particularly beautiful, and I was not looking forward to receiving a present which I would not like wearing. So I begged the Grand Duke Serge Mikhailovitch to intervene and do his best to spare me such a gift. So on the day of the performance Prince Volkhonsky, Director of the Imperial Theatres, came into my dressing-room and gave me a magnificent brooch, a kind of serpent in diamonds coiled into rings and bearing in the middle a large cabochon-shaped sapphire. Later the Emperor informed me through the Grand Duke Serge Mikhailovitch that he and the Empress had chosen it together, and that the serpent was the symbol of wisdom.

I had chosen for my benefit performance the two ballets which I had just danced at the Hermitage Theatre, Drigo's *Arlequinade* and Glazounov's *Les Quatre Saisons*. At the end of the show I danced in the *divertissement*. In *Les Quatre Saisons* I danced the Ear of Corn, partnered by Oboukhov (the Faun), Chiraiev and Gorsky (the two Satyrs). This ballet received the greatest success.

I received a vast number of gifts and ninety-three bouquets or baskets of flowers, several of them from the Grand Dukes and the St. Petersburg Prefect of Police. The Grand Duke Serge Mikhailovitch gave me a magnificent present. Among many different gifts was an illustrated album, specially published for my tenth anniversary under the title *Biographical and Critical Outline*, by two admirers who modestly concealed their names under the initials A.K. and V.O.

One page in this album, describing the theatre after the performance, gives a good impression of the atmosphere of that memorable evening:

"The ballet was just over. People flocked from the theatre into the street, but seemed to have no intention of leaving. The balletomanes remained in front of the theatre, jostling, pushing round the narrow stage door where the dancers who had performed that night would emerge. The crowd consisted mostly of gallery regulars ('the hencoop' spectators) and especially of students. By the stage door one could make out the uniforms of all the scholastic establishments: the high school student's grey overcoat jostled the undergraduate's elegant cloak.

"There was the high school student in his best clothes, twirling a non-existent moustache; there was the pimply undergraduate casting a disdainful eye on his junior's grey overcoat; there was the new made intellectual, the son of some tradesman ceaselessly fuming, 'Those ladies are taking a long time to get their make-up off!' Finally, there was the inevitable moustachioed figure in his beaver fur collar, puffing at cigarette after cigarette; not to mention, last in this picturesque assembly, the fifteen-year-old who kept on looking nervously at his watch! They had all come to pay a worthy farewell to their idols, especially those of the fair sex.

"The stage door kept on opening and closing, more and more often, letting out the dancers in their everyday clothes. But these first 'swallows' passed almost unnoticed: they only meant that the removal of make-up was nearing its end.

"The public was not waiting for them, but for the 'real' dancers, the famous names, the stars!

"Two or three minutes more, and Mlle. Kschessinska in person appeared in the passage. The ballerina was not yet in the street when a chair emerged as if by magic. The balletomanes installed their idol in it, and with ceaseless cries of 'Bravo!' and 'Hurrah!' they bore her in triumph to the doors of her carriage. The farewells were enthusiastic."

This performance was to alter my whole life. A few days afterwards I gave a dinner party to which the Grand Dukes Cyril and Boris Wladimirovitch came, bringing their youngest brother (he was not quite twenty-one), the Grand Duke André Wladimirovitch, whom I had not yet met.

That evening—which was also our first meeting—the Grand Duke André Wladimirovitch made a great impression on me. He was exceptionally good-looking and also very shy, which did not spoil things at all—quite the reverse! During dinner he accidentally knocked over a glass of red wine whose contents spilled on my dress. Far from being angry, I saw in this a happy omen, an incident which was to bring me much happiness and joy. For from that moment my heart was filled with an emotion which I had not felt for a very long time, and was not just another flirtation.

After our first meeting, I saw the Grand Duke André Wladimirovitch more and more often, and our feeling for each other soon turned into mutual attachment.

I started once more to write my journal, which I had completely abandoned since my separation from the Tsarevitch. I can no longer remember what I wrote, except that I admitted experiencing the same feelings as before. But now I was no longer a naïve girl but a woman who had known the sufferings and joys of life.

During the summer the Grand Duke André Wladimirovitch began to be a frequent spectator at rehearsals at the Krasnoïe Selo Theatre, and M. A. Pototzka, our fine dramatic actress and my great friend, never stopped teasing me and saying, "Since when are you interested in kids?" The Grand Duke was indeed nearly seven years younger than I!

Then he often came to see me at Strelna, where we spent the time most agreeably. Unforgettable evenings spent walking in the park by moonlight and waiting for him, or if he was still later, after the manœuvres, at about one in the morning, with the heady odour of cut hay about me when the first rays of the sun appeared on the horizon. . . . On July 22nd, the Grand Duchess Marie Pavlovna's birthday, a picnic was arranged every year at Ropcha, with the assistance of gipsy musicians. That year the Grand Duke, who had been unable to come in the morning, had promised to come and see me at Strelna, even just for a few minutes, if the garden party did not end too late. I was alone that evening and I waited for him impatiently; my happiness was all the greater when he finally appeared. We remained for long hours on the terrace in the beautiful night, now talking of everything and nothing, now keeping silent to listen to the calls of distant birds in the dawn, and the light rustle of the wind in the leaves. It was like the discovery of the earthly Paradise for us, over which broke an unforgettable dawn, like a great song of gladness. Our memory of that night was so intense that later, every year, we celebrated the date as an anniversary.

During the same summer, on July 7th, a new gala performance was arranged, this time at Peterhof, in honour of the Shah of Persia. For my share in the gala, which consisted of the third acts of *Bluebeard* and *Paquita*, I received from the Shah a medal adorned with turquoises.

In autumn, when the manœuvres were over, André got two months' leave, and we decided to meet in Biarritz in order to spend a few weeks together in complete freedom. But André had first to go to Sebastopol and then to Ai Todor, the estate of the Grand Duke Alexander and the Grand Duchess Xenia Alexandrovna, who had invited him, before going to Biarritz via Constantinople and Paris.

The day before he left André came to see me in St. Petersburg, where we spent a last unforgettable evening. The next day I drove to the Nevsky Prospect to wait for him to pass. . . . I drove very slowly so that he could overtake me and say goodbye once more, even from afar.

Our time at Biarritz left me with both a happy and a sad memory. Friends often invited André to functions which he could hardly refuse, and we could not appear together before all eyes. Besides, he was still very young and could not behave as he liked. On our way back we stopped in Paris for a few days. But I had to hurry back to St. Petersburg, where the season was about to begin.

I was very jealous, and found it particularly painful to leave André in Paris. He came to see me off on the Nord-Express at the Gare du Nord, and I actually persuaded him at the very last minute to come with me to the first station, Saint-Quentin. Thus we put off the moment of parting by two hours! . . . After that I had to resign myself to the inevitable, and my sadness increased as time and space separated us from each other. My heart was heavy when I arrived in St. Petersburg, and I was counting the days till we met again.

During that season I took part on February 27th 1900 in the benefit performance for Delorme, the actor in the French company, at the Michel Theatre. It was the first performance of the two-act pantomime, *De la Lune au Japon* (libretto by M. Lopoukin, music by Kislinsky), with choreography by Cecchetti, who directed the production. But it was a work of little interest. And, besides, I had other things to think about!

CHAPTER XI

ITALY WITH ANDRÉ

ON DECEMBER 3RD 1900 I made my first appearance in *La Bayadère*, a ballet in four acts and seven tableaux with an apotheosis, with choreography by M. I. Petipa, book by Houdékov and music by Minkus. The first performance, with entirely new costumes and décors, was given at P. A. Guerdt's benefit.

I was very fond of *La Bayadère*, both because of its interesting choreography and the number of mimed scenes in which I could shine. I was not disappointed in its success.

On January 28th 1901 came Pierina Legnani's farewell benefit performance. She was finally retiring from the Russian stage and was to be the last Italian dancer invited to join the Imperial Theatre Company.

After she left I was given two more ballets, *Le Petit Cheval Bossu* and *La Camargo*.

The former, a ballet in four acts and eight tableaux, with choreography by Saint-Léon and music by Léo Delibes, is based on a story by Erchov. It was a beautiful work, with a great many delightful and effective dances, and I believe it would still be a great success today if somebody revived it. The male roles were taken by Chiriaiev and Stoukolkin, and the Press gave us the warmest notices.

On April 15th I appeared in the other ballet I had inherited from Legnani, *La Camargo*, a work in three acts and five tableaux in Louis XV style, by Saint-Georges and Petipa. It was responsible for another clash between Prince Volkhonsky, Director of the Imperial Theatres, and myself. Legnani had performed the Russian dance in a Louis XV style costume, whose billowing skirts, supported by hoop petticoats, hindered her movements and robbed the dance of all its charm.[1] Legnani was certainly an excellent dancer, but she paid far less attention to costume than I did. I knew perfectly well that in these clothes I would look ugly, on account of my small size, and that I would also find it quite impossible to execute the Russian dance in the way I wished to do it. It consists of imperceptibly subtle touches, which

---

[1] It was a copy of the costume which the Empress Catherine II had worn at a fancy dress ball in honour of the Emperor Joseph II.

contribute its value. I had therefore given my reasons to the wardrobe-keeper, adding that I would naturally put on the prescribed costume, but without the tiresome hoops, whose absence would anyway not be noticed under the billowing skirts. My remarks, wholly justified as they were, were doubtless misrepresented to the Director to appear a mere whim. In any case, my observations were disregarded and I was again told that I must put on the hoops without fail. I then received the impression that someone was trying to pick a quarrel with me on a trifling excuse.

Just before the performance began Baron Koussov, Theatre Manager in the Imperial Theatres, entered my dressing-room and insisted once more in the Director's name that I should put on the hoops. The disagreement had now gone on for some time, and the public, who knew all about it, was impatiently waiting the outcome of "the affair". The outcome was that I categorically refused to put on the hoops and danced without them! If it had not been for the publicity given to the quarrel, nobody could ever have known if I was wearing the hoops or not.

The next day when I arrived at the theatre for rehearsal I read on the Administration's notice board: "The Director of the Imperial Theatres fines the ballerina Kschessinska [so many roubles] for an unauthorised change in the costume prescribed by regulation for the ballet *La Camargo*". Bearing in mind my salary and position, the fine was so small that it was clearly meant to provoke and not to punish me. I could not submit to such an insult without taking steps to put it right. I had no other resource but to apply once more to the Tsar, begging him to have the fine remitted through the same channel. And now a notice went up on the board: "The Director of the Imperial Theatres hereby orders a remission of the fine imposed on the ballerina Kschessinska for an unauthorised change in the costume prescribed by regulation in the ballet *La Camargo*." Following this incident, Prince Volkhonsky felt that he should not remain at his post and handed in his resignation. However, his prestige and independence did not suffer as a result. He left in July 1901 and was succeded by V. A. Teliakovsky.

I was very sorry for this incident then and am sorry for it today after so many years. Prince Volkhonsky was not personally responsible; but he had allowed himself to be influenced by the false picture which my too numerous enemies had given him. I respected and thought highly of him then, and the emigration was later to turn us into fast friends.

In the autumn André and I decided to make a journey to Italy, which he did not yet know and of which I was never weary. We agreed to meet in Venice.

So I left with my brother's first wife, Sima Astafieva, who was also a dancer in St. Petersburg. Sima, who was as lively and charming as one could wish, was the ideal travelling companion: she was delighted and attracted by everything. We stopped first in Paris, where the Exposition Universelle was in full swing. There was also a play adapted from the famous novel of Sienkiewicz, *Quo Vadis?*, which we had all read excitedly. We went to see this play. The principal part of Petronius was taken by the famous actor De Max, a most handsome and elegant man. Sima fell in love with Petronius at first sight!

However, we got to Venice, arriving in the middle of the night. Venice renewed its hold over me every time I went there. As for Sima, she at last forgot to sigh over her Petronius and was thrilled by the Grand Canal, where black gondolas silently glided against a background of distant cathedrals bathed in moonlight. Our windows opened on to the canal, and we fell asleep to the soothing strains of some romantic melody, no doubt the craze of the moment, sung by all the gondoliers.

As we had agreed, André joined us in Venice, with his aide-de-campe, A. A. Beliaiev. We all four got on very well. Between visits to the various monuments and festivities, we often went to a well-known little restaurant called *Il Vapore*, where we sampled the local specialities and drank Chianti.

We went on to Padua, where we bowed over St. Anthony's tomb: there were holy images being sold there which could be blessed by rubbing them against the sarcophagus. Then we went to Rome, where we spent almost a fortnight, generally devoting our mornings to visiting museums, while in the afternoon we toured Rome or the surrounding district to see the monuments and historic spots.

Thus we visited the chapel on the Appian Way, built, so legend has it, on the very spot where Jesus Christ appeared to Saint Peter, who was fleeing the city and asked Him, *"Quo Vadis, Domine?"* (Where are you going, Lord?) This was the theme of Sienkiewicz' novel, and we were shown in the chapel a deep footmark left on the flagstones by Jesus Christ when He stopped to answer the Apostle's question. But Sima, madly in love with Petronius, insisted on being shown the latter's statue, convinced that it was an authentic representation of Sienkiewicz' character. The guide's attempts to set her right were useless; she would not give up and remained certain that among the statues of Nero's period could be found one whose hair-style or toga might evoke her hero's appearance. I can still see her going through museums and suddenly pointing, at every turn, to the inevitable Petronius!

In the evenings at the hotel so affected were we by the atmosphere of ancient Rome that we played at dressing up as Romans, and Nero would appear—or Sima's idol! These extempore masquerades brought tears of laughter to our eyes.

One day, in a museum, we tried without success, for all Sima's pointed mime, to ask some house-painters perched on their scaffolding the title of the melody which one of them was singing at the top of his voice. The tune had pursued us from Venice. But we did not know a single word of Italian. It was only at Genoa, almost at the end of our journey, that we were able, by strumming the tune on a piano in a music shop, to find out that it was *O, Sole mio!* and to carry off the music in triumph.

From Rome we went on to Assisi, Perugia, Florence, Pisa and Genoa.

Assisi and Perugia are very close to each other. The way to visit them was to go straight to Perugia, where there were good hotels, and to visit Assisi from there. But by a misunderstanding we got out at Assisi, where a carriage was waiting for us and we had rooms booked.

We left Rome by the evening train, and it was pitch dark when we reached Assisi, sure that it was merely a halt and not the station we wanted. Our coach was in the rear of the train and we could only make out a few lights twinkling in the distance. Two carriages, one for us, another for the luggage and our servant, were waiting for us at the station. We expected to emerge right into the town, to cross well-lit streets—but thick darkness reigned about us, and our carriage took a completely deserted road. There was not a trace of a town, not a sign of a building along the road. We could not even see where we were going, and were all four seized with fear, especially as Sima kept on picturing bandits and hold-ups. Was this a presentiment? At any rate some horsemen in long capes, with rifles slung over their shoulders, suddenly emerged from the shadows and stopped our carriages. We were going to be robbed! But as soon as we got a closer view of the bandits, we sighed with relief: they were mounted carabineers sent to meet us in order to protect us and escort us into town. What had happened was that in Rome André had all the time been followed, most discreetly, by a policeman who had only identified himself at the station, just before the train left, when he wished us a pleasant journey. He knew where we were going and had warned the carabineers in

13a. My sister, later Baroness Julie Zeddeler.

13b. In the ballet *La Fille du Pharaon*.

14a. The Grand Duke André when I first met him.

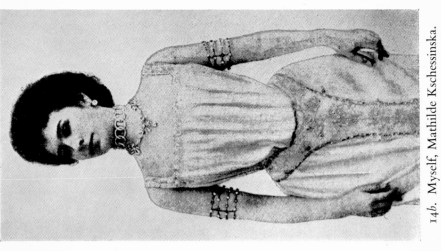

14b. Myself, Mathilde Kschessinska.

14c. In the ballet *Esmeralda*.

Assisi of our arrival. So all was for the best and at last we saw the lights of the town. But there was a bitter disillusionment in store for us. Our hotel was terrible and so bug-ridden that, exhausted, disappointed and furious, we spread our own blankets on the floor and slept as well as we could on them, fully dressed. However, when we woke and glanced out of the window we were rewarded with an astonishing sight: fifty mounted carabineers, with a Major at their head, were drawn up in front of the hotel! Shortly afterwards André was told that the worthy Major wanted to present his respects. He explained that his task was among other things to facilitate the visit of the town, the basilica and tomb of St. Francis, as well as the Convent founded by St. Clair, and to escort us to Perugia, where we were at last able to find a comfortable hotel. Next we visited Florence, Pisa, with its leaning tower, and finally Genoa, where we made quite an extended stay.

I became sick when I arrived in Paris and consulted a doctor, who informed me that I was in the first month of pregnancy. I was filled with happiness at the news, but thought immediately of what was waiting for me in St. Petersburg.

If the immediate future had much happiness in store for me, I was going to have to go through some very painful moments.

CHAPTER XII

OUR SON IS BORN

THE 1901-1902 SEASON promised to be a very interesting one. Several of my favourite ballets came in my repertoire, and new creations were foreseen.

I danced *Esmeralda*, *La Fille du Pharaon*, *The Sleeping Beauty*, *Le Petit Cheval Bossu* and *Paquita*.

On January 20th 1902 I appeared in *Don Quixote*. This ballet, composed in Moscow by the Moscovite maître-de-ballet, Gorsky, was given at the farewell benefit performance for Christian Petrovitch Johanson, my beloved teacher, who had adorned the Imperial scene for over sixty years. Considerably improved with new choreography by Gorsky, this sensational ballet included a large number of stylised Spanish dances. I danced the classical variation *sur les pointes*, using castanets merely to stress the beat lightly. My dance was performed to an extraordinarily rapid rhythm. I executed pirouette after pirouette, and the public was delighted.

As I expected, I had to stop dancing in February. Neither my dancing nor my appearance allowed my condition to be suspected. My last public appearance was on February 10th, still in *Don Quixote*. I was in great form and enjoyed the usual success.

However, I had to dance once more, this time at a performance at the Hermitage, on the 15th of the same month. These performances always took place during the winter season, between the Feast of Epiphany (January 6th) and the first day of Lent, sometimes twice a week, before an audience exclusively composed of members of the Imperial Family and Court guests. The repertoire consisted of small ballets and short pieces; décors and costumes were always specially made. For a certain period Serge de Diaghilev had an active part in arranging these performances, which were always of a very high artistic level.

Just before the beginning of Lent an adorable ballet, *Les Elèves de Monsieur Dupret*, in two tableaux, was performed, with choreography by Petipa and music by Léo Delibes.

In the first act I took the role of La Camargo, in a delightful *soubrette's* costume, while in the second act I appeared in a *tutu*. The stage projected almost as far as the first row of the stalls, where sat the Emperor, Empress and members of the Imperial Family. I had carefully to calculate each of my attitudes so as not to let them see the change in my silhouette, a change which was only visible from the side.

So I finished the season. Now that I could no longer dance, I decided to hand on my ballet, La Bayadère, to Anna Pavlova. We were on excellent terms and Anna often came to my house. She greatly enjoyed having fun and especially liked the company of the Grand Duke Boris Wladimorovitch, who called her "my angel". She had been noticed and praised by public and critics ever since graduating from the Ballet School in 1899. For my part, who saw in her the beginnings of great talent, I predicted for her a brilliant future. But Petipa at first refused to give her this ballet, which he had created for me, and I had to insist for a long time before he would give in. To help Pavlova, I rehearsed La Bayadère with her, from beginning to end, despite my state of health. She also worked on the ballet with E. P. Sokolova, who had danced it long before me.

When interviewed by a journalist after the performance, Pavlova only mentioned E. P. Sokolova, and forgot me completely. I knew Anna Pavlova too well not to be certain that this "lapse of memory" could be attributed to people who were trying to damage our relations, in particular a journalist who was most influential at the time, apparently pleasant and polite, but capable of the worst meanness. I was greatly hurt by this injustice from Pavlova, especially as I had helped her, from her first steps on the stage, by all the means in my power. These things, however, sometimes happen, and despite a few shocks of this nature my relations with dancers remained on the whole excellent.

In the spring of 1902 the delightful Tamara Karsavina graduated from the Ballet School, a beautiful girl, gifted, simple and full of infinite kindness. Unlike what happened in 1890—the year of my own graduation—the Emperor and Empress did not attend the performance, at which the Grand Duke Wladimir Alexandrovitch was the only representative of the Imperial Family. As soon as the performance was over the Grand Duke came and asked me to take Karsavina under my wing. He was very fond of her. My affection for the Grand Duke was such that his wish amounted to an order. But Karsavina proved so gifted and so finished an artist that she had no need of my protection. In the autumn of the same year, when she was to appear in a very difficult pas-de-deux, I gave her one of my own costumes, so that she might appear under the best conditions. For I had my own costumes of the best quality for interludes and *divertissement*. For ballets, however, I wore the theatre's costumes, made from artists' sketches or sometimes even from my own designs. Pale blue and deep lilac were then the fashionable colours, two shades which were present in the costume I gave Karsavina. Our company included at the time Baker-kina, a dancer transferred from Moscow to St. Petersburg after the Coronation. She very soon formed a friendship with an elderly general in a conspicuous post, an unlikeable man of disgusting cynicism. It was only recently, after the emigration, that I learnt through the *Memoirs of Tamara Karsavina* how Bakerkina, who was her friend, had explained to her the reasons for my gift.[1] She had done her best to explain to her that the theatre was a nest of intrigues, and that disinterested gestures were not to be believed in. "Why do you think Kschessinska gave you this costume?" asked Bakerkina insidiously. And as Karsavina liked the costume very much and was also moved by the value of the present and by my attention in giving it to her, she added maliciously, "You see it's in deep lilac? That's just right for grave clothes, not for a girl's costume!"

Bakerkina was also known in St. Petersburg for another reason: she was often invited to sell champagne at charity performances and never let anyone go past her table without making her drink a glass, systematically forgetting to give her back the change. Without being elegant or even well dressed, she was always very careful about her appearance and had a large number of brooches for these performances, one of which invariably adorned her head.

But this season did not leave me with bitter memories alone!

Among my friends in the theatre Vera Trefilova was outstanding. She was a delightful and conscientious dancer who had even gone to Italy to perfect her technique.

After a performance we all went to have supper: Vera Trefilova, Petrokokino, who was very much in love with her, Garfeldt and Victor Abaza, a marvellous balalaika player who was later to prove a virtuoso of international repute. Vera later invited us to her house for coffee, wonderful coffee which she would make in a marvellous new coffee machine which she had just been given! So she placed the miraculous instrument on the table and religiously accomplished the necessary preparations. She put in some ground coffee, poured in water and lit a little spirit lamp which she placed under the container. All that now had to be done was to watch the apparatus. But conversation

---

[1] *Les Souvenirs de Tamara Karsavina, Ballets Russes*, translated by Denyse Clairouin, Librairie Plon, pp. 135-136.

15.   The Grand Duke André at a Court fancy-dress ball in 1903.

16a. My son Vova, aged one year.

16b. With my son when six years old.

flowed and Abaza meanwhile had taken out his balalaika. Nobody gave further thought to the ultra-modern coffee machine. Suddenly there was an explosion, and all of us—particularly the men, whose shirt fronts were reduced to a piteous state—were splashed from head to foot in coffee grounds, while a few notes were still dying away on Abaza's drenched balalaika. . . .

The day of my confinement was drawing near and I was full of happiness at the thought of soon having a child by the man I adored. Happiness and a little anxiety, but very little, for I knew that I was strong and in perfect health. Room, cradle and clothes were all ready in my Strelna *datcha* where the baby was to be born, and we were making the final preparations.

Contrary to my expectations, the delivery was extremely painful, and at one moment the doctors despaired and wondered if they should save the mother or the child. Fortunately, they saved us both, without affecting our health.

So our son was born, on the night of the 17th/18th June, between one and two o'clock in the morning. I had to stay in bed for a long time, with a violent fever, but made a fairly quick recovery.

I was dreading the explanation I would have to have with the Grand Duke Serge, once I was recovered, for though full of my love for André and my son, in my happiness I did not stop suffering from the thought of the great pain and terrible and wholly undeserved blow I had just inflicted on him. My suffering was all the keener because the winter before, when he was courting a young and pretty Grand Duchess, I had asked him to bring this idyll to an end in order to cut short the gossip, which I found particularly unpleasant, provoked by rumours of their eventual marriage. My thoughts were only of my love for André, and I had not then reflected how guilty I was towards the Grand Duke Serge Mikhailovitch.

His attitude, however, was moving and gave me a little reassurance. Serge knew for certain that he was not the father of the child, but he loved me and had become so attached to me that he forgave me everything. Whatever happened, he told me, he would stand by me as a faithful friend, feeling that I needed his devotion and protection.

This conversation relieved me, but I still suffered over what had happened.

We decided to call our son Wladimir, in honour of the Grand Duke Wladimir, André's father.

The christening took place at Strelna, in the strictest intimacy, on July 23rd of the same year. One of our greatest friends, Colonel Markof, of the Lancers of the Tsarina's Guard, and my sister Julie were godfather and godmother. According to tradition, I did not attend the christening, at which the Grand Duke Wladimir gave Vova a magnificent platinum cross and chain which, unfortunately, were lost in our Petrograd house during the revolution.

The Grand Duke Wladimir, who had always shown me such kindness, gave me new and moving proofs of his feeling during these happy painful days. He gave his glad and immediate consent to our son's bearing his Christian name, and often came to see me during my convalescence. I remember one of his visits particularly clearly, since it once more showed me his goodness and magnanimity.

I was still very weak and received him lying on a divan, with my baby in my arms. . . . He sat down next to me and began to comfort me, stroking my head and pouring out words of consolation to me, with a paternal tenderness that deeply moved me. He knew, he understood my torment, and these marks of affection were an immense source of consolation to me.

Two months later, when I was finally well, I was able to dance on August 19th at Peterhof, in the gala organised for the marriage of the Grand Duchess Ellen Wladimirovna to Prince Nicholas of Greece, the marriage being celebrated on August 16th 1902 at Tsarskoïe Selo.

I did not travel abroad that year. André had to prepare for his entrance to the military Law Academy in the autumn, and he devoted the whole summer to it.

In the same year my sister Julie completed her twenty years' service on the Imperial stage, and, following tradition, she retired. A few months later, on December 11th 1902, she married Baron Alexander Logguinovitch Zeddeler, who left the Preobrajensky Regiment after his marriage to enter the Ministry of Communications.

My sister had lived with me, by my father's wishes, since I had left my parents. Now that she was gone I converted her room, which adjoined mine, into a nursery.

I have a precious memory dating from the same period. During the winter the famous Moscow tenor Sobinov came to see me in St. Petersburg and I invited him to dinner. Before sitting down he begged me to show him the baby, who was then six months old. The nurse was just about to put him in his cradle and he looked at us half asleep. Then Sobinov began to sing *sotto voce* Lermontov's famous lullaby.

He sang softly and beautifully, in such a rich voice that the tears came to my eyes. Vova slept now. "When Vova is grown up," whispered Sobinov across the cradle, "tell him I sang for him. . . ."

CHAPTER XIII

VIENNESE WALTZ

ON FEBRUARY 16TH 1903 I danced *La Fée des Poupées*, a ballet in two tableaux, based on the story of Assreuter and Gaul, with choreography by Nicholas and Serge Legat and music by Bayer. The décor represented the interior of a toyshop on the Gostinny Dvor in 1830. Through the window could be seen the Nevsky Prospect, with the people of St. Petersburg walking by in costumes of the period.

At the beginning of the year I had received a very flattering invitation to appear at the Theatre Royal in Vienna in the six weeks of Lent, during which our theatres were always closed. I was to dance *Coppélia* and *Excelsior*, a ballet new to me, with very complicated choreography by the Viennese maître de ballet.

So I left for Vienna in mid-February with my maid and dresser. My usual partner, Nicholas Legat, my friend, Olga Borkenhagen, and Liouba Egorova the dancer came too. Egorova continued to work with Legat even during the journey. At this time I was also taking lessons with Legat; I thought that Cecchetti's Italian school robbed ballet of its grace and lightness, which I wanted to preserve.

We all of us stayed at the Imperial Hotel, a former palace whose vast, high rooms, with their old-fashioned furniture, were unattractive. My suite consisted of an enormous sitting-room and a bedroom which led into the bedroom shared by Olga Borkenhagen and Liouba Egorova. The maid and dresser slept on the same floor. I have not forgotten our terror, one of the first evenings after our arrival, when we were convinced that there was someone watching us from behind the silk curtains hiding a sliding door which separated the sitting-room from my bedroom, in which were all my jewels.

On the day of the first rehearsal the company gave me the warmest welcome when I arrived at the theatre. We established excellent relations from the very beginning, which greatly contributed to my success in Vienna.

At my first appearance, in *Coppélia*, the public greeted me as warmly as the artists. I introduced the *Valse Capriccio*, by Rubinstein, in which I was partnered by N. Legat, into the second ballet, *Excelsior*.

However, everybody was sorry that the Emperor Francis Joseph, now very old, did not attend the performance. For nearly fifteen years, ever since the tragic death of his son, Rudolph—followed by the equally tragic death of the Empress Elisabeth[1]—the Emperor had not been to the theatre.

The artists' surprise and joy may be imagined when the rumour went round before the performance at which I was to appear in *Excelsior* that the Emperor was contemplating attending! And ten minutes before the curtain went up the Emperor entered his box. All Vienna spoke of the event!

The Emperor was lavish in his applause, and the audience was not behindhand. The dancers, whose enthusiasm was almost delirious, thanked me and gave me a triumphal reception after the performance, thinking that I alone was responsible for the presence of the Emperor, whom several of them had never seen! Before I left the company gave me a medal to commemorate my appearance at the Theatre Royal in Vienna.

Among the countless flowers and plants I received was one that I prized particularly, a four-leaf clover plant given me by a young student who had bought it out of his modest funds. I was very moved, and brought the plant back to my *datcha*, where it spent the summer on my drawing-room table. In winter it was put in a hot-house. The following summer, as soon as I came back to Strelna, I asked the gardener for news of my plant from Vienna. In reply he showed me a small path from the *datcha* to the sea, fringed here and there, to my great surprise, with four-leaf clovers!

While I was in Vienna I received a telegram from the Grand Duke Wladimir Alexandrovitch announcing his coming arrival and inviting me to breakfast. When he arrived he stayed in the same hotel as I and we talked without reserve. I was happy to see him again and particularly touched by his attention. He was only spending one day in Vienna, and was very sorry to be unable to come and applaud me at the theatre.

Viennese life of the period was a delightful whirl of balls, celebrations and galas. I gave a reception in the hotel salons in honour of the Press, whose tributes had been so warm, and also invited some of the artists of the Viennese ballet.

Needless to say, invitations poured in and I received countless attentions. I also had the pleasure of a reunion with one of my great

[1] The Archduke Rudolph, heir to the throne, died aged thirty on January 30th 1889. The Empress Elisabeth was murdered by an anarchist in Geneva on September 10th 1898.

friends, Youry Beliaiev, a gay and witty man, a journalist on the St. Petersburg *New Times*, and an eminent theatre critic and pamphleteer. We went out a lot together.

In Vienna I first saw Isadora Duncan dance. I was wholly conquered. Isadora, who danced barefoot, worked very hard and was perfectly mistress of her art. She was the utter incarnation of ancient statues in her dancing and especially in her poses. I was so carried away by her Viennese waltz, danced in a red costume, that I climbed on a chair and cheered her at the top of my voice.

There was a minor drama on the day of my departure. I had sent Sonia, my maid, to the station with my luggage. Sonia, who was sweet, very beautiful and completely devoted, adored me. She was insistent that day that she should look after my jewel case, so much was she afraid that I might forget it in the bustle of departure. And her fears were realised! In spite of her insistence, I kept the case and put it under the coachman's legs. At the station I was greeted by a crowd of admirers and friends, who gave me such an enthusiastic reception that I let the porters take care of all my luggage and forgot the jewels. When I remembered them the little case had disappeared! After panic, feverish searching, upheaval and bustle it was finally discovered in my compartment in the hands of the triumphant Sonia. She had not trusted my vigilance, had seized it as soon as I arrived and immediately entered the train. I still have the case, by the way, but today completely empty.

While I was still in Vienna I was invited to appear in America on very favourable terms, the first ballet dancer to receive such an offer. But large fees did not tempt me, and I was also unwilling to be away for a long time from my son and André. I therefore declined, but preserved the contract, which remained in Russia among my papers.

After Easter and shortly after my return to the Austrian capital, Teliakovsky, the Director of the Imperial Theatres, persuaded me to go to Moscow to replace Roslavleva, who had suddenly fallen ill, in *Don Quixote*. This project made me very anxious, as I was worried about my reception by the Moscovites, although I had already danced this ballet in Gorsky's version in St. Petersburg; the only difference was that I took the first act variation at greater speed. The artists gave me a warm welcome, but instantly warned me that the conductor was extremely obstinate and did everything he wanted. I should have a hard time persuading him to alter the rhythm. Nevertheless, I called on all my tact in my approach to him, with the result that he willingly gave in to my request.

In St. Petersburg my entrance on stage was always greeted by warm applause, so much so that I had grown accustomed to such a welcome.

When I appeared in Moscow on April 20th 1903 absolute silence reigned among the audience. This worried me. After the adagio, however, unanimous applause broke out, and when I had danced my variation at high speed the whole audience dissolved in cheers. I was wild with joy: I had conquered the Moscow audience! This performance was a great treat to me.

I was no less happy in my private life: I had a son I adored, and I loved and was loved by André. I lived for them and through them alone. The Grand Duke Serge, with true nobility, was so kind to me, he continued to spoil me as he had always done, and was always ready to come to my defence, which he could do better than anyone else. He adored Vova and treated him as his own son.

The Grand Duke Wladimir Alexandrovitch was now a constant visitor. In the evenings he passionately devoted himself to a card game called "Aunt", which was then all the rage. He gave me wonderful presents: a pair of vases from Prince Vorontzov's collection, for instance, and at Easter he always gave me an enormous egg-shaped bouquet of lilies of the valley, with a precious stone, also in the shape of an egg, from Fabergé. He also once gave me a bracelet with a very fine sapphire. He also liked sending me many new pieces of dance music and one day brought me a chaconne, which he wanted to have performed, and which later, in a simpler version, became a ballroom dance.

On April 10th he came to celebrate his anniversary with his sons, Boris and André. He had evidently grown fond of me, and he told me one day that he prized my feeling towards him and my frankness very highly. "Am I really loved for myself," he used often to say, "or is all the respect I receive due solely to my rank?"

During the summer of 1903 he used sometimes to walk over from Peterhof with his aide-de-camp, Baron V. R. Knorring. Our son was then a year old, but could not walk yet; I did my best to tie his scanty hair into one curl surrounded by a pale blue ribbon. He was brought to be shown to the Grand Duke, who caressed Vova and exclaimed, "His head is just like mine!"

I have one particularly precious memory from the same year, 1903, which always moves me when I think of it. At my request, the Tsar sent me his photograph. He had not signed it "Nicholas", but "Niki", a discreet and delicate touch, giving proof of his loyalty to our memories; many years later I was to have additional proofs of it in his *Journal*.

At the theatre I continued to enjoy unfailing success. But there were isolated manifestations which almost cast a gloom over my stage appearances. From time to time there were boos and even occasional hisses among the public's enthusiastic applause. I needed an iron will to keep on smiling and bring the performance to a successful end. I found these demonstrations all the more painful because I knew perfectly well who was at their root.

I was exhausted by all this spite, and my desire to retire, to escape these horrible intrigues, kept on increasing.

My father, who loved his art with his whole heart, was very much grieved by my decision to retire. He tried hard to dissuade me, but finally gave in to my reasons. I asked for a farewell performance, which was granted me, and I fixed the date for February 4th 1904. It remained now only to finish the season.

In the autumn I was invited by the cadet officers of the Michel Artillery School to their traditional ball. I had warned them that I would only be able to arrive after *The Sleeping Beauty*, which I was dancing that evening. They first showed me over the School, and then asked me to join the ball. The dances were new ones, and I did not know these ballroom steps, so on the pretext of resting I carefully watched the dancing couples before venturing myself. It was a delightful evening and I left amid enthusiastic farewells.

On December 7th I danced *La Fille Mal Gardée* in Moscow, with N. Legat, at Grimaldi's benefit performance, and took advantage of my visit to invite Gueltzer to dance in my own farewell performance and to take the part of Marceline, Lise's mother, in the same ballet. He at once agreed, and gave a marvellous rendering of this female role.

The *Journal of the Tsar* for January 21st 1904 reads:

Wednesday: Dined alone together.[1] Went to the theatre, where *The Sleeping Beauty* was being performed. Marvellous: I had not seen her for a long time. Returned at a quarter to twelve.

But to whom did the remarks "Marvellous" and "I had not seen her for a long time" refer? This was what I wondered as soon as I read the *Journal*. Now, the *Imperial Theatres Annual*, which gives a list of each season's repertoire, reveals that on January 21st 1904 I danced *The*

[1] With the Empress.

Sleeping Beauty. It was my one performance of the ballet in the whole of the 1903-1904 season.

Could I have dreamed that that evening, on his return from the Maryinsky Theatre, the Tsar would have sat in his enormous study in the Winter Palace and noting, as was his custom before going to bed, his impressions of the day, would have mentioned me?

And can he have imagined that those lines, which I treasure so highly, would be read by me fifty years later, long after his death?

I cannot hide one very painful circumstance which calls for a correction from me.

Others have claimed and spread the story, both on the eve of the Revolution and after it, that I received bribes, particularly for orders from the Artillery. Such insinuations, needless to say, were not worth considering. Moreover, had they had the least foundation the Provisional Government would have carefully dealt with my case, as it did with so many others.

But when I started to write these memoirs and consulted a great many documents and impression of this period, I came across the letters written by the Tsarina to the Emperor during the Great War, and was deeply pained to read two of these in which the Tsarina repeats certain slanders which had fallen on me. She says in so many words that I behaved like Mme. Soukhomlinov,[1] taking part, according to different stories, in shady affairs of bribes and Artillery orders.[2]

I suffered acutely when I read these lines. How could the Empress have believed such calumnies? Why had she passed them on to the Tsar without even trying to verify them?

I know that the Emperor had told her of our meeting, but over a long period of years and through tiny details I had always felt the Tsarina's goodwill towards me.

What happened later? Somebody no doubt tried to blacken me in their eyes.

I have never in my life tarnished the honour of my name nor taken

[1] The wife of the War Minister.

[2] The authentic text of these letters may be found, in English, in *The Correspondence of the Tsarina Alexandra Feodorovna and Tsar Nicholas II*, published by the Berlin "Slovo" firm. The two extracts referring to me are as follows:

Letter No. 97, June 25th 1915: "Kschessinska is mixed up again—she behaved like Mme. Sukhomlinov it seems with bribes and the Artillery orders—one hears it from many sides."

Letter No. 192, January 9th 1916: ". . . There are very unclear, unclean stories about her and bribes, etc., which all speak about, and the artillery is mixed up into it."

advantage, to material and dishonest ends, of the protection which the
Tsar constantly granted me. And I am sure that he never believed a
single word of these accusations, which he showed by the tone in
which he spoke of them to the Grand Duke Serge. How greatly I
regret having known nothing of this in Russia, so that I might have
told the Tsar it was pure scandal and he might have done me the
favour of making sure.

At the end of January, just before my farewell performance, the
Russo-Japanese War broke out. In the first days of the conflict, however, the situation was still confused, and people were not yet de-
moralised.

My performance took place as arranged, on February 4th. The
audience greeted me extremely warmly, and my enemies kept quiet:
their boos would in any case have been smothered by applause. These
unanimous cheers were sincere and moving evidence of the public's
goodwill towards me.

I had chosen the first two acts of *La Fille Mal Gardée* for the programme, and I introduced a *pas-de-deux*, the same with which I had
started my stage career in 1890. Thus I was able to execute and give an
encore of my thirty-two *fouettés*, which critics said I was the first, after
Legnani, to execute faultlessly. Gueltzer, who had come specially on
my behalf from Moscow, filled the role of Marceline to perfection.

I next danced the second tableau from the first act of *Swan Lake*,
when the Swan Queen slowly moves back on points, as if to say
farewell to the spectators.

Thus I took my leave of the public. An unwilling leave—but,
however sad I found it, I could not do otherwise.

I received an enormous number of flowers and a great many valuable
gifts, including a gold laurel wreath, made to measure, each leaf
engraved with the name of the ballets I had danced: a real floral tribute.

Carried away by enthusiasm, the young people gathered at the stage
door, unharnessed the horses from my carriage and brought me home
themselves, some distance from the theatre, an experience which had
once befallen Fanny Elssler!

After this farewell performance I immediately left for Moscow, to
take part in Katia Gueltzer's benefit performance on February 6th.
I danced an adagio with Nicolas Legat and the variation from *La
Bayadère*. The Moscovites acclaimed me wholeheartedly, and for my
return to St. Petersburg I was provided with a whole sleeping car,
which was fixed on to the night express. It proved very useful to the

balletomanes who had come to Moscow for the performance. I had ordered supper, which was served in the coach: the party lasted the whole night and we did not notice time passing. The next day, in the capital once more, I had to attend the balletomanes' dinner given in my honour at Cubat, when I was crowned with the gold wreath and had to make a speech. It was a wonderful evening and another sleepless night.

I now spent most of my quiet and peaceful life in my Strelna *datcha*, and it was there, on July 30th, that I heard the announcement of the birth of the long-awaited heir to the throne, the Tsarevitch Alexis Nicolaïevitch. The birth was greeted by the Imperial Family and the whole of Russia with the greatest joy, in which I joined whole-heartedly. Later I was able to read in the Tsar's *Journal* for August 24th 1904: "Went for a long ride with Micha. Passed by Strelna."

They must have passed in front of the *datcha*, and possibly the Tsar expected to see me in my garden. I might by chance have come out at that very moment, seen him, and been able to show him my joy in learning that he had a son, an heir for Russia.

When the Emperor returned from Krasnoïe Selo to Peterhof, André used to telephone me and I climbed up the hill leading towards the bridge where the assemblage passed. Police watched the road and stopped all access to the bridge; but they knew me and even used to ask me if the Emperor had set out, for I was always fully informed by André. When they saw me near the bridge, that meant that the Tsar had left Krasnoïe Selo. How can I forget these fleeting moments, which are still fresh in my mind? The Emperor approaching while I stood motionless, hoping to catch his glance, and his hand slowly came up to his eyes. . . .

CHAPTER XIV

RETURN TO THE STAGE

I HAD BEEN ABSENT from the stage for several months when, at the beginning of the 1904-1905 season, the Director of the Imperial Theatres, Teliakovsky, urgently begged me to reconsider my decision. So far from ceasing after my departure, the intrigues for which I had been blamed had become still worse.

I had grown used to the idea that my theatrical life was over; I only finally gave in when Chiriaiev begged me to dance the ballet *Brahma*, to be revived for his farewell performance. This took place on December 12th 1904, and my rendering was inspired by the memory of Virginia Zucchi.

Most of the corps de ballet were glad of my return, with the exception, of course, of a small group of diehards. But the public's welcome made me forget everything. Nevertheless, I refused to sign a contract, as the Director would have liked, and only agreed to appear in certain performances, like a guest artist. In fact, I wanted to remain perfectly free, and told the Administration that no contract could bind me and no attack frighten me; but that I would always be ready to be of service. So I returned to the stage on these terms, and was never to retire.

I was invited more and more often to Moscow after my first appearance in 1903. I danced there at benefit performances for Katis Gueltzer, for Grimaldi, for the corps de ballet, and, finally, for the old artists. Once even, so as not to disappoint my friends, I left for Moscow with a sore throat, shaking with fever, and still danced, out of sheer will power. I saw double when I came on the stage, but nobody noticed, and by the end I had almost recovered.

I had also been to Warsaw, with my father, to dance *Esmeralda*. My father as usual danced the Receiver, Claude Frol. Other parts were taken by local dancers. I received as great a success as ever.

That summer, on July 3rd 1905, my father died on his estate at Krassnitsy, aged eighty-three. In spite of his age, he would have lived much longer had it not been for an accident the previous year. During a rehearsal of *The Sleeping Beauty* a trap-door suddenly opened under him. Luckily, he was able to hold on to the stage with his elbows, but the shock was so violent that the doctors forced him to go to bed. This change in his way of life had an effect on his general health. Accustomed to a life of overflowing activity, he was suddenly condemned to complete quiet, which he found unbearable. It is true that he recovered quickly, but he categorically refused to follow the way of life which the doctors advised. By next season he felt so much better that he was able to appear on the stage once more: in the spring of 1905, a few months before his death, he gave a swaggering performance of the mazurka with me in the theatre. He was eighty-three! He must be a unique example in the annals of ballet!

With the confused situation in Russia I was not immediately able to fulfil his last wishes and inter his remains, together with those of his deceased mother, in our family vault in Warsaw, where my grandfather already rested and on which I had a little chapel built. So his body was embalmed, transported to St. Petersburg and provisionally placed in the Catholic Church of St. Stanislas. As soon as things settled down, the bodies were transferred to the Powonsky Cemetery in the Polish capital. Warsaw had not forgotten my father and gave him a magnificent funeral. The road from the station to the cemetery passed through the outskirts of the town, but nothing troubled the calm majesty of the funeral procession.

My father's death was a hard blow. His disappearance somehow broke the chain linking me to my happy childhood, when, thanks to his burning passion for the stage, I began to love my art. Now, with his departure for a better world, the theatre itself was beginning to move a little further away.

In the autumn of 1905, when I had fulfilled my father's last wishes, I went with my son to Cannes, where I stayed at the Hotel du Parc, outside the town. Only my maid and a nurse came with me. André had arrived before us and had been spending the time in Nice. Later Micha Alexandrov, one of the company's dancers and a most exhilarating companion, joined us. Micha was the son of the dancer Alexandrova and Prince Dolgoroukov, Princess Yourievska's brother.

The hotel, which was in a vast park, was completely empty when we arrived, which was none the less very agreeable; but at night sepulchral silence reigned all round. It was now late autumn, and darkness fell quickly. Vova, who was only three, was put to bed very early, after which the maid and nurse went down to dine in the staff dining-room, so that I remained alone on our floor with its long, deserted corridor. The walls of my narrow dining-room were covered almost to the ceiling in oak panelling. The night of my arrival, at dinner, I noticed that the veins of the panelling formed a pattern which reminded me of

my father's features. I was afraid and thought at first that it was a mere
trick of the imagination. But the panelling again drew my eye irresistibly, and I made out the same resemblance, particularly clear this
time. . . . It was a horrible night. Although the room was brightly lit,
I felt every moment that my father's ghost was about to appear in the
doorway. Micha Alexandrov arrived next day. I placed him on my left
at dinner, where he could see the panelling which worried me and
asked him if he could see anything strange in it. Without hesitation, he
replied that he could clearly see my father's face, and André, when he
joined me, expressed the same opinion. Next day we asked for another
suite. But I still felt that this was a bad omen and that family worries
awaited me. Sure enough, I soon received a letter from St. Petersburg
with the news that my brother had just had serious trouble in the
theatre, and that the Administration had dismissed him on the instiga-
tion of the all-powerful Kroupensky, Manager of the Imperial Theatres,
who had formed a hatred for him. Later, at my request, he was
restored to his position. At the same time I learned to my infinite
sadness that Serge Legat had put an end to his life. Legat was a wonderful artist, extoradinarily handsome and full of talent.[1] We had danced
together in many ballets and he had been an excellent partner.

We soon decided to rent a little lodge in the hotel grounds, and I
sent for Basil, my valet, and Denis, my French chef, from St. Petersburg. We continued to eat in the hotel until they arrived, but sometimes, for fun, we cooked our own dinner, each doing what he could!
And the kitchen was constantly full of loud laughter, for our dishes
brought us a variety of surprises. Thus André boasted one day that he
was going to give us a succulent *bœuf Stroganov*. So we all went off to
the butcher together, acting like perfect connoisseurs. We finally
decided on what seemed to us the best and least red piece, after which
we settled down to our task, André tackling the "beef" with the
assurance of a true chef. But instead of becoming darker the meat
became whiter and whiter! It was veal! But we still christened it
"Stroganov", since the dish proved excellent.

At Christmas I prepared a beautiful Christmas tree for Vova and
invited Rockefeller's little niece, who also lived in the Hotel du Parc
and often played on the beach with our son. She came and gave Vova
a lovely pair of woollen slippers. Unfortunately, we never saw her
again.

Since I was in mourning, we did not go out much. At most I

[1] He was also the author, with his brother Nicolas, of a delightful album of
caricatures.

occasionally went to Monte Carlo. But Micha Alexandrov, who moved around enough for four, went everywhere and kept us informed of news and minor gossip!

In the spring of 1906 André was unexpectedly recalled to St. Petersburg before his leave expired. Shortly afterwards I too left Cannes and returned to Russia.

On my return home the first stone of my new house was laid. After our son was born I had decided to build a larger and more comfortable house so that he might have several rooms and feel at home there when he was older. My old house was so old-fashioned that it was almost out of the question to transform it. In the architect's opinion, it was simpler to pull it down and build a new one in its place. However, I preferred a smarter district far from the factory chimneys which had begun during these last few years to spring up on the English Prospect.

I was naturally sad to leave a house to which I was tied by the most precious memories. But would it not be sadder still to stay in a place where the smallest detail brought back the past?

Out of all the proposed sites, I finally chose one on the corner of the Kronversky Prospect and Great Dvorianskaïa Street, where there was a whole cluster of little wooden houses. I liked the position, which was in the best part of town, far from the factories, and its width allowed room for a large bright house surrounded by a beautiful garden. Alexander Ivanovitch von Gogen, a very well-known architect in St. Petersburg, was commissioned to do the work. I designed the interior decoration myself. The main drawing-room was to be in Russian Empire style, the small corner drawing-room in Louis XVI style, and the architect gave me the choice of various plans for the other rooms. Thus my bedroom and the dressing-room were to be in English style with white furniture and cretonne hangings. A few rooms, notably the dining-room and the sitting-room adjacent to it, were to be modern. All the period pieces as well as the furniture for my rooms and my son's were ordered at Meltzer's, St. Petersburg's most famous dealer. The rest—for the servants' rooms, the offices and so on—was put in the hands of the large Platonov firm.

In addition I ordered from Paris all the bronze pieces for the Empire room and the Louis XVI drawing-room (chandeliers, brackets, candelabra, door and window handles, locks, window fastenings) as well as the carpets and furniture fabrics. The drawing-room walls were hung in yellow silk. I must also add that the house possessed a charming winter garden.

We moved in just before Christmas 1907. My new house was a real success. Von Gogen had done a wonderful job and satisfied my every desire.[1]

But if the reception rooms and my private rooms deserved to be admired, I was especially proud of the staff's quarters; in fact I thought that one could not ask for impeccable service if one's servants did not receive good lodging. The kitchen, the kingdom of my French chef Denis, was indeed luxurious and always stirred my guests to envy.

I naturally had a cellar of excellent wines, which André had selected with particular care. It was so arranged that I could have supper for my guests there after the theatre.

Another object of pride were my two wardrobes, one for my everyday clothes, which were arranged in large oak cupboards, another for my theatrical costumes and accessories. Each cupboard had an inventory of the contents, and I had a copy. Since the clothes were numbered, I could have anything I wanted sent to me.

But one never thinks of everything, and I can remember a funny thing that happened. When I left for my *datcha*, the care of the house was entrusted to my chief doorman, Denissov, a Chevalier of the Order of Saint George, and a man of exemplary honesty and devotion. I left him all the keys. In spite of his great virtues, Denissov had a weakness for drink. Being aware of this failing, he had joined an anti-alcoholic league whose members had to promise only to drink wine once a year. One day I needed one of my costumes in a hurry and so I asked a friend, Olga Borkenhagen, who lived with me and whom the doorman knew very well, to bring it to me. When she arrived Denissov was in his lodge, but he firmly refused to open the door. It was his intemperance day, and he was only going to open to the mistress of the house! "One never knows what may happen," he told me later, by way of explanation.[2]

The second courtyard, behind the house, contained sheds and garages for carriages and cars. There was also a stable for the cow brought from the country so that my son should always have fresh milk. But the cow was not the only animal we had: there was also a little fat pig, a great pet of Vova's, and, in the house, a little goat which appeared on stage with me in the ballet *Esmeralda*. I had had to train

---

[1] I sold my old house to His Imperial Highness Prince Alexander Gueorguievitch Romanovsky, Duke of Leuchtenberg.

[2] Good Denissov remained loyal to me during the worst moments of the Revolution, and when he died, twenty years later, he sent a message through my brother that his last thoughts were of me.

17. The family of the Grand Duke André at the time of his parents' Silver Wedding: the Grand Duke and Grand Duchess Wladimir with their children: the Grand Dukes Cyril, Boris and André, and the Grand Duchess Ellen, Princess Nicholas of Greece.

18.   The Grand Duke André in the uniform of the 6th
Cossack Horse Artillery Battery of the Imperial Guard.

her: I fed her myself and took her to the theatre to get her used to music and the stage. She became so tame that she could be photographed, on my knees, in the drawing-room! Finally, there was Djibi, my favourite fox terrier.

They made a charming menagerie; and if one went past the garden one could see goat, fox terrier and pig going for walks and romping together.

The appearance of Isadora Duncan in St. Petersburg made an enormous impression on the young dancer and future maître de ballet, M. M. Fokine, who at once began to cut out new paths for classical ballet. Fokine rebelled against fixed poses, against the arms raised like a crown around the head. Without rejecting the framework of classical technique, he wanted a free expression of emotion. For his ballet, *Eunice*, whose theme was drawn from Sienkiewicz' *Quo Vadis?*, he went to the Hermitage Museum in order to study classical dances in vase paintings, and made a close inspection of everything which could reveal Greek and Roman art to him. The music was written by A. V. Scherbatchev. *Eunice* caused a great stir and provoked heated arguments and repercussions. There was a violent clash between the upholders of tradition and the supporters of what was new. Fokine had to wage a real war, both in the theatre and out, against certain critics and balletomanes; but the conflict merely gave him more energy and strengthened his convictions. The old balletomanes reproached him with the taint of "Duncanism". Young people, on the other hand, gave an enthusiastic welcome to this breath of fresh air which had come to give new life to the unalterable canons of classical ballet, which Fokine had certainly never intended to demolish. I am proud of having been from the beginning a supporter of Fokine, whose ideas I thought were those of genius. And I remained faithful to him to the very end. The first night of *Eunice* was on December 10th 1906. I danced the main role. All the dancers were first class: P. A. Guerdt brought his admirable mime and style to the role of Petronius. Anna Pavlova gave a marvellous performance as Antoia. The part of Claudius the sculptor had been given to the excellent dramatic dancer, Boulgakov, who was so much at home in dramatic roles that he had once considered joining the Alexandre Theatre company. Chiriaiev, a brilliant artist who gave birth to a real school of character dancing, had the part of Petronius' Greek slave, while the black slave was danced by Leontiev.

I put all my soul into *Eunice* and had a resounding success. But most important of all were Fokine's new ideas, embodied in this memorable production, which took the public by storm. There was a second performance on February 10th 1907, with equally outstanding success. Violent arguments were to continue for a long time still, both in the theatre and in the artistic group led by Baron N. V. Driesen, Editor of *The Imperial Theatres Annual*, and at other gatherings where Fokine warmly developed and defended his theories. Marius Petipa,[1] whose authority had been unchallenged since the middle of the nineteenth century, and who had managed to subdue as remarkable a maître de ballet as Leon Ivanovitch Ivanov, felt his power shaken and took a violent stand against Fokine. He succeeded in assembling round him the old dancers and a few talented young ones. But Fokine was able to carry the public and the company, and the first performance of *Eunice* remained a date of major importance.

I always supported Fokine, although I felt it a pity that, in order not to break the rhythm of his ballets, he did not allow dancers who had just danced a variation and been applauded to take a bow, thus drawing from the audience's enthusiasm the strength which comes from communion in the same art.

Fokine liked me and thought highly of me. During the same season we danced together in Moscow, on January 21st 1907, at Katia Gueltzer's benefit performance in *La Fille Mal Gardée*. We were bound by strong ties of friendship, both in Russia and, later, abroad.

[1] Marius Petipa died in 1910, maintaining the title Principal Maître de Ballet until the end of his days.

CHAPTER XV

PARIS, 1908-1909

IT WAS DURING the 1907-1908 season that I first appeared with Vaslav Nijinsky, who had newly graduated, in the spring of 1907, from our Ballet School. We danced Chopin's *Nocturne* at the Maryinsky Theatre, and later in Moscow, at the corps de ballet's benefit performance. Nijinsky had impressed me greatly at the School's graduation performance, and I had then formed the plan of taking him as partner in the near future.

Meanwhile, in the middle of the winter season, M. Broussan, Director of the Paris Opéra, arrived in St. Petersburg. On Sunday, the day when I was appearing in *Esmeralda*, Teliakovsky invited him into his Director's box. I did not like receiving visitors in my dressing-room when I was dancing this ballet, fearing that my inspiration might be disturbed, but I made an exception that night for M. Broussan. With the eloquence of which the French are perfect masters, he paid me a thousand compliments and showered praises on me for my performance of *Esmeralda*, ending by begging me, in the name of the Directors of the Paris Opéra, to appear on the Paris stage, during the coming spring season, in *Coppélia* and *La Korrigane*, in which Rosita Mauri had given a brilliant performance. Of course, I accepted this extremely flattering invitation, and André gave a big dinner party in his palace in honour of M. Broussan, who greatly appreciated this attention.

I could choose my own partner, and I thought at once of Vaslav Nijinsky, impressed more by his prodigious talent than his amazing leaps. I longed to dance with him in Paris, but unfortunately he fell ill, and I invited my usual partner, Nicolas Legat, promising myself that I would dance with Nijinsky in the summer at Krasnoïe Selo. Had it not been for this mischance, Paris would have applauded Nijinsky two years before his appearance in Diaghilev's company, when he was still free from all engagements; and many things might perhaps have happened differently!

I left for Paris at the end of April, on Monday 21st if I remember rightly, by the Nord-Express. With me came Vova, his governess, my friend from the ballet, Claudie Koulitchevska, my maid, my valet, and, as always on these occasions, my dressmaker-dresser, whose job was to dress me in the theatre and, if need arose, to repair my costumes.

The Grand Duke Paul Alexandrovitch travelled in the same coach, with his daughter, the Grand Duchess Marie Pavlovna, and his son-in-law, Prince William of Sweden. The Grand Duchess and the Prince had been married the day before.

The Grand Duke came to pay his respects and to chat in my compartment. He told me about his daughter's marriage and decided there and then to introduce her to me. I protested, maintaining that it was more for me to move, but the Grand Duke would not hear of it and soon came back with the Grand Duchess and her husband. We took to each other immediately, and the friendly relations which sprang up there and then between us were later to turn into a warm, sincere friendship.

In spite of having been married the day before, the Grand Duchess looked sad and rather preoccupied. Her husband did not appear any happier. I knew nothing of the circumstances, but I felt sorry for the Grand Duchess setting off so sadly on her honeymoon. The young married couple left the train on the following day, in Berlin, to continue to Sweden. But the Grand Duke Paul Alexandrovitch remained with us until the end of our journey.

On the journey, while we were still in Russia, Vova fell ill, as often happened when we were travelling. Understanding my anxiety, the Grand Duke immediately wired Verjbolovo and asked for a doctor to meet our train at the station. Fortunately, all went well and we reached Paris without further complications.

As I was to stay almost two months in Paris, I settled in an intimate comfortable flat in the *17 ème arrondissement*, rue Villaret-de-Joyeuse. André stayed at the Astoria Hotel.

Ballet in the Paris Opéra at the time had been relegated to a minor position; it only came at the end of the performance. The works performed were in any case only of minor interest. I did not like *Coppélia*, even though A. A. Plestscheev, in his book, *Our Ballet*, says that I always danced it well. As for *La Korrigane*, this was to be the first time I danced it, and I studied it under the tutelage of Rosita Mauri. But there were no effective solos in which I might have shone, either in this ballet or in *Coppélia*, with the result that, though successful, I was not so successful as I might have hoped if I had been allowed to choose my own ballets. In addition, the Administration of the Opéra made no publicity about my arrival, and this had an obvious effect on the performances. Nevertheless, I was invited for the following year, and the French Government decided to mark my first appearance at the Opéra by awarding me the academic palms in silver. At the end of the

19*a*. My house on the Kronversky Prospect, St. Petersburg.

19*b*. The entrance hall.

19*c*. The winter garden

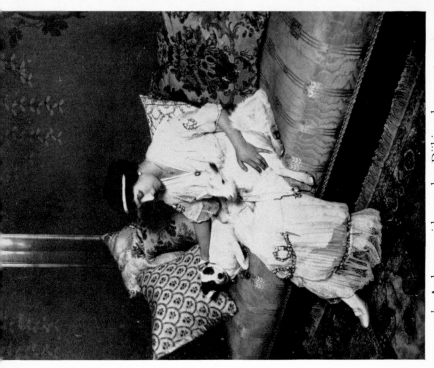

20b. At home with my dog Djibi and my pet goat from *Esmeralda*.

20a. The Grand Duke André in Bulgarian uniform.

season the dancers gave me a commemorative medal, as in Vienna, showing the Opéra on one side and bearing the following inscription on the other: "From the ballet dancers of the Paris Opéra to Mlle. Kschessinska in memory and affection, June 13th 1908."

During this Paris season Nicolas Dmitrievitch Benardaki, a Greek from Russia and husband of the beautiful Marie Pavlovna, *née* Leibrück, arranged a wonderful performance in his private house which contained a little theatre. Legat and I danced Chopin's *Nocturne*. Chaliapin and Smirnov also took part, and the spectators included the Grand Duke Paul Alexandrovitch and his wife, Princess Paley, who was then called Countess Hohenfelsen. The performance was followed by a sumptuous dinner, during which our host made a very witty speech.

S. P. Diaghilev was giving his first lyrical season at the Opéra and I had the fortune to see the first performance of *Boris Godounov*, with F. I. Chaliapin as Boris. I shall never forget that performance. The scenes in the theatre were indescribable. The public was completely carried away by Chaliapin's singing and acting. In the night scene, where Godounov thinks he sees the ghost of the Tsarevitch Dimitri, our neighbours were nudging each other and murmuring, "Look! There he is in the corner!" as if a ghost really had appeared. Chaliapin's acting was so powerful that he hypnotised the whole audience. We Russians were especially struck by the fact that the Opéra public, which was then so cold and difficult to move, gave the singers such an ovation that those who saw it still remember it today as a great event.

Diaghilev, whom I saw almost every day, was delighted at the reception given to his first opera season, and also that Russian music should be so successful.

Finally, Princess Lobanov-Rostovsky, an eminent figure in Paris society, invited André and myself to lunch at the Café de Paris, where Chaliapin was also invited.

After staying in Ostend to allow Vova to enjoy himself by the sea— he still remembers the magnificent cake which the hotel gave him on his birthday—I returned to Russia at the beginning of June. Vaslav Nijinsky was completely recovered. So I was able to rehearse with him the works for the summer season at Krasnoïe Selo and to achieve my wish of helping young talent and giving him an immediate position on the stage. I felt that a brilliant future awaited him; and in fact his truly exceptional career dates from then.

During the performances at Krasnoïe Selo I was able to see for certain that Nijinsky was not only an excellent dancer, but also an ideal partner. So I decided to invite him as my partner whenever the occasion arose. I was his first stage partner, as people have often commented since. Nijinsky was a charming boy, friendly and very modest; he became very close to me, and we often danced together, both in St. Petersburg and Moscow.

It gives me great happiness and deep moral satisfaction to stress that Vaslav Nijinsky appreciated all I had done for him from the beginning of his career and was grateful to me until the end of his life. As a sign of his gratitude he gave me a magnificent icon in mother-of-pearl, with a silvered halo, a present which truly reflects his great nobility of soul. I put the icon in the cupboard for holy images in my room, where daylight lighting showed up the subtlety of the work. Of the many precious objects I lost during the Revolution, I regret this icon almost the most, for it was not only a memory of some of the finest times of my career, but also, above all, the offering of a chosen spirit, an incomparable artist, who had to abandon the stage prematurely, when he had still so much to give his art.

As Anna Pavlova was still in St. Petersburg I had the idea of inviting all the ballerinas, as well as the best soloists, to dance in the *grand pas* from *Paquita*. Thus I brought together A. Pavlova, T. Karsavina, O. Preobrajenska, V. Trefilova and others of our outstanding dancers.

It was a wholly exceptional performance. Each artist as she appeared was greeted with thunderous applause. At ordinary performances only the ballerina dances a solo, but I asked each of them to dance a solo of her own choice for this occasion. This made the evening more brilliant still, since each artist had an effective variation with which she could conquer the audience.

After the show was over I arranged supper at Cubat for the *premières danseuses* who had participated in the performance and agreed to dance with me. Only the ladies were invited to supper, served at a round table, which made the distribution of seats easier. The table was in the middle of the room and drew everybody's attention. When coffee had been served the men were allowed to come and sit at our table and I offered them champagne. One of the balletomanes present seized a plate and began to collect copper and silver coins, without revealing why he was doing it. Shortly afterwards I received from him a silver plate from Fabergé to which had been soldered all the coins collected that night, with a commemorative inscription.

We suffered a grievous loss early in the year. On February 17th 1909 the Grand Duke Wladimir Alexandrovitch died suddenly. He was less than sixty-two years old. His sudden death grieved me all the more because, as I learnt from André, the Grand Duke and he had been together two days before to the patronal window of the little church in the Winter Palace, and nothing then led one to suspect this premature end. I lost in him a great and beloved friend, one who had shown me the sincerest kindness in difficult times, and unreservedly given me his moral support in my most painful moments. Was it some dark foreboding which had led him, shortly before his death, to send me Sibelius' *Valse Triste* that I might adapt it for ballet? His cruel death left me stunned.

Meanwhile S. P. Diaghilev, who had just brought his season of Russian opera to a triumphant conclusion at the Grand Opéra in Paris, formed the idea of organising an opera and ballet season for the following year. He asked for my help and advice, inviting me to take part in the projected season. He wanted above all to gain the patronage of the Grand Duke Wladimir Alexandrovitch: knowing that I was on good terms with the Grand Duke, he hoped that I would not refuse to help him in his attempt. Moreover he needed my support to obtain a State subsidy of 25,000 roubles.

The Grand Duke's death robbed Diaghilev of the powerful patronage he had hoped to win. He tried to obtain another important person's patronage, but his attempts failed. The question of the subsidy remained in suspense; in spite of my efforts, Diaghilev had received no reply even during the Grand Duke's lifetime.

During my further discussions with Diaghilev about the projected season and the repertoire I noticed that his attitude towards me was beginning to change completely, in spite of our former friendship. Tackling the question of the distribution of ballets, Diaghilev proposed giving Pavlova *Giselle*, in which she was incomparable and had always won brilliant and deserved success. As for me, he offered me an unimportant role in *Le Pavillon d'Armide*, which would not have allowed me to prove my worth and to be certain of success with the Paris public. In spite of violent arguments on this point, Diaghilev would not give in. I could not accept his invitation to appear in Paris on these terms. I therefore declined to take part in his season.

I could not intercede on behalf of a project in which I was no longer taking part. I therefore asked that my requests for a subsidy should not be followed up. All Diaghilev's efforts to obtain that subsidy by other means failed. Serge Lifar, describing this period of Diaghilev's artistic activity, in one of his works,[1] sides entirely with me and considers that

[1] Serge Lifar, *Diaghilev*.

Diaghilev had done me an injury as well as showing flagrant ingratitude towards me.

I now decided to take advantage of the invitation which I had received the previous year, to make another appearance at the Opéra in Paris, an invitation to which I had as yet given no final reply.

My second Paris season took place under entirely different conditions: this time Paris knew me; publicity had been better organised, I was no longer a stranger to the Company and Administration of the Grand Opéra. In short I found a free and easy atmosphere and felt at home. I therefore decided at whatever cost to introduce my own variation into *La Korrigane* which I was to dance again. This would allow me to win the success I banked on, and also confirm, beyond dispute, my reputation on the Opéra stage. The rules did not allow the music of another composer to be introduced into a ballet. I intended to insert my variation from *La Fille du Pharaon*, with music by Cesar Pugni. To gain my ends I had to wait for the right moment which was not long in coming.

I cannot remember who then arranged the garden parties in the suburbs of Paris for the artists of the Opéra. In any case, I was invited to one of these parties as a member of the company. The Opéra's two directors, Messager and Broussan, were also there. I was on excellent terms with all the corps de ballet, but on terms of particular friendship with Aïda Boni. We arrived together at the garden party in Messager's car. Boni, who knew that I wanted to dance my variation, advised me to approach Messager directly on the way back, when, she said, he would be in the most favourable mood. She assured me, moreover, that exceptions to the rule had already been allowed by the Director. On the way back Messager was certainly in an excellent mood. He sat between myself and Boni, who never stopped pinching my arm behind his back, thus showing me that the moment to act had come. I began by telling the composer how unenthusiastic I was at having to rehearse the same old thing tomorrow, in which there was no chance for me to shine or prove myself. Messager asked me why I did not insert some variation into the ballet, to which I replied that I could not do so without his permission. But, I added after a short pause, if he was willing to let me, I would begin rehearsing my variation the very next day. Messager at once agreed and gave me his permission. I thus danced my own variation in *La Korrigane*, and scored an enormous success. I even had to give an encore, which scarcely ever happened at the Opéra.

After the last performance I gave sweets and little vases from Gallet to all the dancers.

I had hired a car for my stay, driven by a young and very nice chauffeur who showed me a charming attention. Wishing to thank him for his services, I had given him a ticket for one of my performances. And that evening, when I returned to the car after the show, I had the happy surprise of finding it all decorated with flowers.

During the same season the Paris Press Syndicate had organised a charity evening at the Opéra in aid of the earthquake victims from the *départements* in the South. The performance opened with Bizet's *L'Arlésienne*, in which I appeared with Aïda Boni, Lobstein and the Opéra company. The orchestra was conducted by André Messager.

One section of the programme was devoted to Russian ballet and included three numbers: a *pas-de-deux* danced by Pavlova and Mordkin, a mazurka danced by Vassilieva and M. Alexandrov, and a *pas-de-deux* in which I appeared with N. Legat. As a member of the Opéra company, I had the right to appear last. Just before the ballet programme began someone said that Pavlova was not ready, and I was asked to take her place, in order, so it was claimed, not to hold up the performance. All the evidence showed that this suggestion did not come from the Administration of the Opéra, nor from Pavlova herself. But Pavlova was at that time always in the company of Dandré, whom she later married, and Beobrasov. These two men had been behind a great deal of trouble I suffered in St. Petersburg, and were clearly responsible for the suggested change. I had too much experience of backstage tricks to be taken in, and I refused. It then turned out that Pavlova was quite ready! This little incident proved once more that even far from St. Petersburg intrigues continued to flourish against me.

Serge de Diaghilev had finally succeeded in organising his season of ballets and operas, but this time at the Théâtre du Châtelet, where Vaslav Nijinsky won a dazzling success. Before his time, the male classical dancer, considered far inferior to the ballerina, was limited to supporting her and to dancing a few steps to give his partner a rest. Thanks to Nijinsky, he was raised to the highest level and became the ballerina's equal. Nijinsky, who danced very important parts, succeeded in giving male dancing a new direction and style, which proved a veritable revolution in the art of ballet.

Tamara Karsavina charmed the whole of Paris with her beauty, grace and talent. She was truly marvellous that season and her success exceeded that of the genius, Pavlova.

I left Paris sorrowfully, taking with me a magical memory of the hours spent with Mme. Juliette Adam, of her garden at l'Abbaye de Gif, of her luncheons, where the social, artistic and literary celebrities of Paris rubbed shoulders, and I am really happy to have been able, during this stay in Paris, to meet such artists as Sarah Bernhardt, Réjane and Duse.

CHAPTER XVI

LE TALISMAN

BACK AT STRELNA, I plunged again into building. There was no electric light in Strelna at the time, not even in the palace. I therefore decided to have a small private power plant built near the *datcha*, with a house for the electrician and his family. My visitors were very envious of this sensational innovation, which added greatly to the villa's charm and comfort. Two years later, in 1911, I also had a small lodge built in the garden for my son, who was just nine. He had often complained of my many absences, due to rehearsals, and I had promised him, to make up, to spend one season's salary on building this lodge, which comprised two bedrooms, a drawing-room and a dining-room as well as china, silver and linen. Vova leaped with joy on making his owner's round, but I suddenly noticed that he looked put out: the lavatory had been forgotten! And I had to promise him to put this right at the end of another season.

I made my first appearance of the 1909-1910 season rather late, on December 13th, as the Sugar Plum Fairy in *Casse-Noisette* at a performance in aid of the corps de ballet.

Shortly before this, on November 24th, there had been a new production by Nicolas Legat of a ballet by Drigo, *Le Talisman*, for O. O. Preobrajenska's benefit performance. The general opinion was that this new choreography was most successful, and helped the ballet greatly. However, after the first performance of *Le Talisman*, N. Legat came to see me and begged me to take it over. In spite of a favourable reception from the public and the critics, he told me that he was disappointed in the ballet's success. He thought that Preobrajenska should have made more of her role. But he was convinced I could save the ballet, turn it into a great success and thus keep it in the repertoire. In short, he intimated that the fate of *Le Talisman* and his reputation as a choreographer depended on my acceptance.

At first I had refused to accept a role given to another dancer, but Legat's pleading was so persuasive that I agreed.

The second performance of *Le Talisman*, destined for December 20th with Preobrajenska, was cancelled. This four-act ballet, with additional prologue and epilogue, was particularly difficult, and I had to rehearse hard.

A month later, on January 3rd 1910, I appeared in *Le Talisman* with triumphant success. Nicolas Legat had been right: the ballet came through brilliantly and remained in the repertoire. Legat was overjoyed and did not know how to thank me!

Prince Chervachidze had designed new costumes from my plans. *Tutus* generally began at the waist, and I asked him to lengthen the bodice. This innovation became very popular, and the old fashion was only kept for long *tutus*—in *Les Sylphides*, for instance.

I always seemed taller on the stage than I really was; and this illusion was strengthened by the new cut of the bodice. We did not then wear today's scanty *tutus*, which are more concerned with exhibitionism than aesthetic beauty and make it impossible to design beautiful costumes. Even in his last years, the great Fokine refused to allow these *tutus* in his ballets.

My costume in the second act of *Le Talisman* so delighted Anna Pavlova that she asked me if she could have a similar one made for her foreign tour, to which I agreed with the greatest pleasure.

The success of the costumes in *Le Talisman* led me to ask Prince Chervachidze to design me new ones, in a more definite Egyptian style, for *La Fille du Pharaon*. He fulfilled this task to perfection and also designed for the second act a very pretty gilt diadem, which made André buy me a real one, with diamonds and sapphires, from Fabergé.

I loved dancing *Le Talisman*, even though there was no strongly dramatic scene in it; but Nicolas Legat had composed some beautiful dances, which were always greeted with loud ovations. At every performance I had to repeat the coda from the last act four times—even five times, at my twenty-fifth anniversary performance.

Dancers were allowed to give two or even more encores; there were no restrictions. But when the Tsar and Tsarina were present, if the audience demanded a third encore, we had to turn to the Imperial Box and wait for a signal from the Emperor and Empress. The Dowager Empress Marie Feodorovna liked *Le Talisman* and came to almost every performance. When she nodded her consent I curtsied low and re-embarked on my coda to a veritable storm of applause. The Grand Duke Serge Mikhailovitch told me that the Empress consulted him every time, asking him if I was strong enough to give another encore of the coda; to which he used to reply that the very fact that I was waiting for her consent proved that I had sufficient strength.

R. Drigo's music for the ballet was as delightful to dance to as it was to listen to. He appreciated my keen ear, and said that dancers without an ear were a real penance for the conductor.

On February 6th 1910 the French Embassy, with the Emperor's special approval, organised a charity performance at the Maryinsky Theatre in aid of the victims from the floods which had ravaged France. It was a mixed programme, and I danced the third act of *Raymonde*. The French Government wanted to give me two Sèvres vases as a sign of gratitude, but I asked for academic palms in gold. I had received silver palms the year before, and, by law, I could only receive gold palms four years later. I was granted them, nevertheless, and the decree was signed on March 7th 1910 by Gaston Doumergue, Minister of Education, and a future President of the Republic.

Soon after I moved into my new house, Lina Cavalieri came to pay me a visit. A woman of outstanding beauty and charm, she completely conquered Vova, who was just six years old, and who asked her for a photograph which showed her lovely eyes! Furthermore, since he was mad about stuffed dolls, and especially plush monkeys, he at once named her commander of his battalion of monkeys, the highest award he could confer on her!

At about the same time Prince Troubetzkoy, a highly talented sculptor who made the monument of the Emperor Alexander III in Znanensky Square in St. Petersburg, said he wanted to make a statuette of me. But I was so bursting with energy that I felt unable to keep up a pose before a sculptor or painter. Already in 1901 Constantin Makovsky had attempted to paint my portrait and I had only been able to bear a few sittings. So I gave a guarded consent to Prince Troubetzkoy. It was in summer, at Strelna, and the Prince set to work in the greenhouse, where he had an abundance of light and could spread his clay in the fire of creation as much as he liked. Although several cases of cholera had been reported in St. Petersburg, the Prince, who was a convinced vegetarian, continued to eat an enormous quantity of raw fruit. Sometimes, in the middle of a sitting, he felt ill and would run out, assuring me that he had caught the terrible disease! All this was both entertaining and unbearable. At first the statuette—which was half life-size—looked very much like me, but the resemblance later diminished.[1] Anyway, after I returned to town, the work

[1] Many years later, after the war, I spotted the statuette in Prince Troubetzkoy's studio in Paris, together with one of André, far more successful to my mind, which the Prince had made in Russia in 1910.

continued for a time in my winter garden, until the opening of the ballet season soon took up all my spare time. The work was thus relegated to a shed.

Next year, at Easter, I had several guests at home, including Prince Paolo Troubetzkoy and my half-brother, Philippe Ledé, my mother's son by her first husband. A lively and enthusiastic man, I liked him very much. At a certain point in the conversation Philippe asked Prince Troubetzkoy's leave to see the statuette. The Prince was delighted, and we set out together for the shed.

With his customary expansiveness, Philippe was soon full of praises, admiring the likeness, the movement, the workmanship. All this was very much to the point, and the Prince was smiling with contentment. But my brother, wishing no doubt to add weight to his compliments, suddenly declared, "Now, that's a piece of sculpture! That's a really talented work! Not like that ghastly statue of Alexander III which some useless man has put up!" And he continued for quite a time in this vein. In horror, I realised that my brother had no idea that the statue of the Tsar was the work of Prince Troubetzkoy! I hastily left the shed and ran as far as possible, helpless with laughter at my brother's blunder, but most embarrassed at the very idea of seeing the Prince again. . . .

I think of my brother Philippe with particular tenderness. He was very fond of me, both as sister and dancer, and came to all my performances. When applause and cheers rang out, Philippe applauded and cheered louder than anybody else. And when I told him that such enthusiasm was out of place towards a sister, he replied that he was so delighted when I danced that he could show his enthusiasm in no other way. In the end he disarmed me, and I stopped scolding him; not that anybody would have been able to make him change his mind!

That spring Nina Nesterovska, a member of the Company, came often to the house, and I grew to love her for her vitality, gaiety and cleverness. She was of modest background and had never known the splendid and delicate things of life; but she was very observant, carefully noted my way of living and entertaining, remembered what she had seen and soon adapted herself to her new milieu.

Diaghilev, forming plans for a new Paris season, made new attempts to obtain a State subsidy.

After our last year's quarrel, he had obviously refrained from asking my aid; so that I remained, I am glad to say, a complete stranger to the often unattractive processes of the whole business, on which I need not dwell.

That year André spent the summer at Louga, with the Artillery Officers' School. He lived in a charming house deep in a pine forest, by a river, where he invited us to spend a week-end. I was accompanied by my sister, her husband and a few friends. It was an enchanted time, alas too brief.

On July 22nd André and I celebrated the tenth anniversary of our meeting. André gave me a beautiful piece of jewellery: two large cabochon sapphires in a diamond setting. These sapphires, I was told by Fabergé, came from the famous piece belonging to the Duchess Zenaïde de Leuchtenberg, the wife of the Duke Eugene Maximiliano-vitch de Leuchtenberg.

I must here mention the great artists of the Drama Company at the Alexandre Theatre, Varvara Vassilievna Strelska and Kostia Varlamov, whom everybody loved. They were wonderful company and the source of ceaseless gaiety to guests by their scintillating wit.

Kostia Varlamov was famous for his hospitality and especially for his gigantic *kapoustnik* (artists' suppers), and everybody knew the dwarf who served at table. I shall never forget the day when we set out together by bicycle from Strelna and dined with him at Pavlovsk: our epic return journey of sixteen miles may be imagined.

The same summer, which was so full of happiness, also brought a very sad piece of news: Marius Ivanovitch Petipa had breathed his last on June 2nd 1910 at Gourzouf, aged eighty-eight. He was born at Marseilles on March 11th 1822.

My whole artistic career, until Fokine's appearance, had been linked with Petipa. The success of his ballet, *La Fille du Pharaon*, which was, as I have said, to become my favourite role, had at once assured him fame in Russia, where he came on May 24th 1847, invited by the Imperial Theatres Administration, after working several years in Spain. I can still see his check plaid; I can still hear him whistle. . . . I remember too that at rehearsals he always gave us instructions which he had prepared beforehand, unlike Fokine, whose works were often improvised. I did not often see Petipa off stage, but during our whole collaboration in the theatre we never had the slightest quarrel, nor, as far as I can remember, did he ever make an unkind remark or utter an ungracious word about me. He liked me very much as a dancer and I worked smoothly with him. With his death one of the most renowned figures in nineteenth-century ballet took his place in history. His name remains closely linked to the life of Russian ballet, and his works have kept their charm till the present day. Petipa's death caused me great sorrow: he took away with him the memories of my youth!

CHAPTER XVII

TWENTY YEARS ON THE STAGE

THE WINTER SEASON was a whirl of dinners, suppers and masked balls. I adored masked balls and enjoyed myself with all my heart, forming numerous intrigues under my mask and domino.

Vladimir Lazarev was then my young and fervent admirer. His beautiful sister, Irene, who was later to marry Count Vorontzov-Dachkov, won every man's heart.

I met Vladimir Lazarev under very odd circumstances. Our first meeting was at a masked ball at the Little Theatre, where I had been invited to preside over the refreshments. I was wearing a very pretty dress made by a famous Paris dressmaker: the skirt was a very close-fitting one of black satin, and the bodice, very low cut, was in fine white silk with a large bright green bow at the back. Shoulders and top were covered by a shawl. The headdress was a Venetian net covered with a white bunch of bird of Paradise feathers. I wore an emerald necklace and on my breast an enormous brooch set with diamonds and emeralds.

In order not to be recognised, I entered the ballroom in a black domino with a lace mask which only showed my teeth and . . . my smile.

Struck by Volodia's gaiety and almost childlike appearance, I determined to make him my first victim! After arousing his curiosity —"What teeth!" he said. "What teeth!"—I vanished in the crowd and furtively left the room in order to shed my mask and put on my evening dress. Then I made for my table as if I had just arrived. Volodia drew near. He could not but recognise my teeth, so I tried to remain silent and to look solemn. But he talked so much that finally I could not help smiling. . . . Volodia at once recognised me. "What teeth!" he burst out, and we went into a peal of laughter. In this way we became warm friends. We had many good times together; together we endured the hardships of the Revolution; we fled Russia together and remained lifelong friends.

Among my many friends a high place goes to Michel Alexandro-vitch Stakhovitch, whom I liked very much for his wit, intelligence and charm. Michel was no longer young then, but he was full of life and high spirits. He swore that he had fallen for me as a young man and thought it his duty to come and applaud me every Sunday at the ballet. When asked where he was going he invariably replied, "To Vespers," adding that the ballet was for him on Sunday what Vespers were for others on Saturday! One day he sent me flowers on the stage with a card on which he had written the first notes of Siebel's aria from *Faust*, "*Contez-lui, mes fleurs* . . .". From being almost blind to ballet before we met, Michel Alexandrovitch Stakhovitch thus became a fervent balletomane.

I often had guests in the evening, and these parties, which were always very lively and gay, often brought together M. A. Stakhovitch, Basil Alexeevitch Maklakov, the distinguished lawyer and politician, Alexander Alexandrovitch Mossolov, head of Chancery at the Imperial Court Ministry, and Isadora Duncan, who had become one of my great friends during her last stay in St. Petersburg. She always wore a Greek tunic, held in place by a clasp shaped like an old brooch, and so, in memory of our friendship, I gave her a fine clasp from Fabergé.

After supper, when she had drunk a little, Isadora became very amusing, and we often had passionate arguments about the merits and advantages of our respective arts. She was then at the height of her glory, and tried hard to prove to me that classical ballet was bound soon to give way to her new school, based on the study of the dance steps and movements of ancient Greece.

While granting that her ideas helped to beautify and give new life to our ballet, I maintained that neither she, her pupils nor still less her imitators would ever be able to assimilate our art; whereas our artists, who were formed in the classical school, were capable, provided they had the necessary technique, of executing any movement. If she had such a hold over her audience, I said, it was because she had put her whole soul and mind into her art, which filled her whole being, because she was thoroughly mistress of it and had devoted her remarkable talent to it. Her imitators, who lacked her gifts, and were prepared only for a narrow and very specialised form of dancing, lacking any solid foundation, were condemned to a speedy disappearance.

I cannot speak of Isadora Duncan without calling to mind the famous Spanish dancer, Argentina, who only danced Spanish dances. But in order to reach perfection in this limited sphere she took care to perform all the classical exercises every morning. Without a technical foundation, she said, one cannot reach a really artistic level in dancing. This is an example which bears out my opinion in a remarkable way: only the classical school allows artists to perform dances of all kinds.

Duncan used to bring me her little pupils to show them to me, all dressed like her in pink tunics, barefoot, which meant spreading a sheet on the floor so that they could dance.

My last meeting with Isadora Duncan was in Nice after the revolution, shortly before her tragic end (September 14th 1927). This was after her last journey to Bolshevik Russia. She was almost unrecognisable. There seemed to be nothing left of the Isadora of old except her indomitable energy.

That winter Sarah Bernhardt came to give a few performances in St. Petersburg. I heard that she had looked in vain for a greyhound, the best of which belonged to private owners, who would not sell them. However, through friends I managed to find a superb pedigree greyhound, which I was able to give her at the very last moment, at the station, before she left St. Petersburg.

On February 13th 1911 I celebrated twenty years of dancing on the Imperial stage, and a special performance was arranged. I chose February 13th, the same date as for my tenth anniversary at the Maryinsky Theatre in 1900, which also fell on a Sunday.

It was a memorable evening for me, marked by the presence of the Tsar, both Empresses and most of the Imperial Family.

How can I describe my joy, many years later in Paris, when I received the programme of that evening, with my photograph on the first page (a real innovation at the time)?

The performance opened with the first act of *Don Quixote*, which consisted almost entirely of stylised Spanish dances and took place in a Barcelona square. I was partnered by P. A. Guerdt as the rich noble Gamache and by N. Legat as Basil the barber.

This was followed by the third act of *Paquita*, in which I danced a magnificent *pas-de-deux* and a solo by N. Legat to music by A. Kadletz. Sedova, Karsavina, Will, Egorova, Vaganova and other soloists took part in the *grand pas*.

Next came the second act of *Fiammetta*, which the Tsar liked so much to see me dance. I had the role of Fiammetta, Karsavina danced Love and N. Legat the rich young nobleman, Sterngoldt; Stoukolkin danced his servant, Martini, and P. A. Guerdt his tutor.

During the first interval the Director gave me the Emperor's present: an outstretched diamond eagle in Nicholas I style, mounted in platinum and with a platinum chain, which meant that one could wear the jewel as a pendant. On the reverse there was a platinum plaque engraved with an eagle. Under the eagle hung a rose sapphire set in diamonds. The Grand Duke Serge Mikhailovitch came to see me during the first interval to tell me that the Emperor wondered if I would appear on stage with the jewel that he had just given me. Naturally, I put it on straight away, and thus adorned danced the *pas-de-deux* from *Paquita*.

During the second interval the curtain remained raised, and a delegation of artists from all the Imperial Theatres, representing opera, ballet, drama and the French theatre, came to pay tribute to me.

A long table, occupying the full width of the stage, was installed to show off the countless presents[1] I had received. The bouquets, arranged on the floor, formed a real garden.

The *Imperial Theatres Annual*[2] described the performance in these words:

"An event of some importance took place on February 13th 1911, when M. F. Kschessinska celebrated the twentieth anniversary of her entry to the Maryinsky Theatre. Representing pure classicism in dancing she is unrivalled in the contemporary Russian theatre, thanks to her complete control and the beautiful and pure style of her dancing and acting. Twenty years is a long time for a ballerina, but Mlle. Kschessinska's dancing has lost none of its brilliant virtuosity: this is virtuosity which makes one forget the art as one watches the artist. M. F. Kschessinska began her career at a time when the

---

[1] I cannot remember all these presents, or hope to enumerate them, except for a few particularly precious ones. André gave me the diamond diadem which I have already mentioned, made from Prince Chervachidze's design. The Grand Duke Serge Mikhailovitch gave me a mahogany chest, with gold rims, containing a collection of yellow diamonds of all sizes, to make any jewel I desired. Jivotovsky gave me a large elephant in a pink precious stone with ruby eyes, and an enamel powder-case on a gold frame. From the public I received among other things a Louis XVI table and tea service, and a diamond watch. The table, made of green malachite, was surrounded by a silver rim. Underneath the table was a fixed biscuit box. The watch, which was round, had a diamond and platinum chain. As the total subscription came to more than the high value of these gifts, at the last moment I also received some gold cups. The Moscow balletomanes gave me a table centrepiece, a Louis XV mirror in a silver setting, and a silver flower vase; in the mirror one could read the names of the donors engraved under the vase.

[2] *Imperial Theatres Annual*, 4th edition, 1911. A review of the 1910-1911 season. Ballet, E. A. Starka (Siegfried) pp. 138-139.

21. The Emperor Nicholas II.

22.   At the Paris Opera, 1908.

interest stirred by our ballet was concentrated on the outstanding virtuosity of famous foreign dancers such as Carlotta Brianza, Dell'Era, Legnani, Zambelli and many others. Venturing to appear in roles in which the most famous foreign dancers had shone, she gradually opened the way for a complete conquest of the stage by Russian ballerinas: Zambelli was the last foreign dancer invited to Russia. Borrowing the virtuosity of the Italian school and the grace of the French Mlle. Kschessinska irradiated these qualities with Slav softness and soul. To this she added her enchanting acting and achieved, down to the smallest details, an art which has delighted all ballet lovers for twenty years. And if the classical cause needs another defender, at a time when all choreographic values are on trial, no more eloquent, passionate or persuasive advocate could be found than Mlle. Kschessinska. Our gifted ballerina's benefit performance was a mixed programme: the first act of *Don Quixote*, the third act of *Paquita* and the second act of *Fiammetta*. Apart from Fokine all the leading lights of the company took part."

To crown this success, on February 18th the balletomanes invited me to a sumptuous dinner at Cubat.

My benefit performance convinced me once again that I had been quite right to leave the stage in 1904. It was now clear to all that intrigues went on and even grew worse during my absence, when I could have absolutely no part in them. Furthermore, the public's moving welcome on my return to the stage had proved beyond dispute that they had missed me.

The Easter holiday could not have been happier and André gave me a most original present. In a straw egg I found a great many little parcels, all identical in appearance, containing tiny things without value, such as pencils, ash-trays and other baubles. But others contained wonderful presents, including a pair of diamond shoe buckles.

That season André gave some brilliant dinner parties and receptions in his palace. The guests were carefully chosen, and André loved to unite the leading artists of ballet, opera and operetta, which was very fashionable just then. The scene was always one of great gaiety, and dancing often went on until dawn. It was at one of these parties that I made the acquaintance of the Grand Duke Dimitri, who was just beginning to come out into society.

While I was staying in Monte Carlo, during the spring, Mordkin came to visit me, and invited me to dance with him in London during the summer season. He had planned at first to appear with Pavlova, but had since quarrelled with her. I did not give him a definite answer, but decided later to go to London, in order to solve the question. I now learnt that the invitation came not from the theatre management, but from Mordkin himself, who had been allowed to choose his partner. Under these circumstances it would have been wrong for me to appear in Pavlova's place. I therefore declined the invitation. Meanwhile, Mordkin was invited by Baron Henri de Rothschild to dance at his home, and replied that he could appear with me. Baron Henri de Rothschild agreed and asked me to name my fee. I told him that I accepted, but that there could be no question of remuneration. He thanked me for my kindness and offered to put me up in his home. But time was short, because I had to hurry back to St. Petersburg, and in the end I was unable to take part in that performance.

The Peterhof Theatre put on a charity show at which I danced a Russian dance to the accompaniment of the balalaika orchestra of the Empress's Lancers; then, in summer, at one of the performances at Krasnoïe Selo, partnered by two male dancers, Stoukolkin and Orlov, I danced a Russian dance arranged by Claudie Koulitchevska to folk tunes. A rich and ugly merchant and a young hawker who was as handsome as he was poor were quarrelling for my heart. Then we all three performed a mimed scene in which the rich merchant offered me a ring and the poor young man his heart. The scene ended with a dance called *kamarinskaia*. My costume, made from a sketch by the painter, Solomko, who was a folklore specialist, was extraordinarily successful.

The public gave us a quite remarkable welcome, especially when one remembers that at a performance in the Tsar's presence and before an audience consisting mainly of soldiers, displays of enthusiasm were as a rule most restrained.

I was all the happier because I had been able to dance for the Tsar. When he left the theatre, after the performance, he looked up at my dressing-room window, the very one where twenty years before as a young girl I had waited for the Tsarevitch, who had since become the Emperor of the most powerful country in the world!

Ivan Orlov, one of my best and oldest friends, delighted with my success, came near the window a little later and called out, "Bravo, Maletchka! Bravo! Such a triumph in front of His Majesty! . . ."

Baron Gotsch, who had been a visitor at my parents' home when I was still a little girl, always spent the summer at Peterhof, and from time to time gave very gay dinner parties. I remember a trick that Nina Nesterovska and I, who had been invited to one of these dinner parties, played on him. We had asked him to call us when all the guests had arrived. Meanwhile, we hid in a room on the floor above and dressed up as ship-boys. And when we heard him call out, "Hey, Petia and Vania, where are you? We're waiting for you!" we ran down, creating a great impression on the guests, particularly those who liked young boys!

Among Gotsch's guests was a young Uhlan, Mitoussov, full of life and high spirits. Like all the Uhlans, Mitoussov lived in Peterhof. One day, knowing that he was at manœuvres, I entered his quarters and placed my framed photograph on a table together with a bunch of violets, asking his orderly to say nothing when he came back. And the charming Mitoussov really fell in love with me after that!

My birthday was always celebrated with festivities in my *datcha* at Strelna. The day reminded me of my childhood, the blissful holidays on the estate at Krassnitzy, and I wanted every one to share in the happiness as before. But that year, on August 19th 1911, my birthday was a real planned performance, and particularly brilliant.

I put up large posters in the garden announcing that the artists of the Imperial Theatres, Pavlova, Kschessinska, Preobrajenska, would take part in the performance, which would be followed by supper at Félicien (a famous St. Petersburg restaurant, standing on a large raft on the Neva), with a firework display organised by the Serebriakov firm as a finishing touch. N. Bakerkina, it was announced, had kindly consented to sell the champagne. Finally, there would be a special train to bring guests back to St. Petersburg.

In fact, only the part about the train and the fireworks was true. For the performance, the balcony was transformed into a stage, with scenery at the back, footlights and curtain, not to mention the stage door, for which we used my bedroom window, on the ground floor. Never-ending preparations and rehearsals took place, needless to say, in an atmosphere of feverish nerves.

This fine programme, however, very nearly fell through owing to a completely unexpected dinner party arranged for that very day at Peterhof, in honour of King Peter I of Serbia, who had just arrived in St. Petersburg to attend the marriage of Prince Jean Constantino-vitch to Princess Hélène of Serbia. All the Grand Dukes, as well as Prince Gabriel Constantinovitch, were bound to attend this dinner, which, fortunately, did not last long. Thus my guests were able to come as arranged and the small delay did not harm the evening in any way.

After receiving my guests, I ran to my room, on the pretext of making sure that everything was ready, hurriedly put on an evening dress and covered myself, like Bakerkina, in brooches, including one on a headband on my forehead. With gloves drawn to my elbow and a highly dramatic expression, I then settled at the champagne buffet, and the guests were invited to move into "the theatre". Boris Wladimirovitch was the first to come in, and I gave him a programme, imitating Bakerkina's voice and movements. He burst into such a peal of laughter that the right atmosphere was at once created. When the audience had sat down, Boris began to tap with his feet, like the Paris audience when it becomes impatient, and to call, "Curtain! Curtain!" a cry which the rest of the guests at once took up.

The "renowned" artists were greeted with a terrific ovation. It was an absurd spectacle: Kschessinska was impersonated by Baron Gotsch, who danced my Russian dance dressed as a Boyar. (I had rehearsed this number with him with meticulous care, and he imitated me to perfection; but he had assimilated his "model" so much that he had spent the whole day lying on a sofa in a woman's dressing-gown, eating, still like me, nothing but caviar sandwiches!) He also acted Preobrajenska in one of her classical variations. Pavlova, in *Giselle*, was imitated by Micha Alexandrov, in a *tutu*, as was right. Nina Nesterovska imitated Katia Gueltzer in *Don Quixote*.

After this everybody went to Félicien, which meant by the sea, on the jetty, where supper was served in the open. The alley about a kilometre long leading to the jetty was lit with lamps and each table with a lantern. A wonderful view extended before the diners: on both sides, the lights of St. Petersburg and of Cronstadt; immediately opposite those of Lachta. As a final touch of beauty there was a wonderful firework display at the end.

At dawn a special train (which only cost me 55 roubles) carried back the inhabitants of St. Petersburg towards the capital.

At this party Nina Nesterovska met Prince Gabriel Constantino-vitch, whom she later married.

On August 27th André left for Kiev in order to attend the man-œuvres, in which the regiment of which he was honorary colonel was taking part.

P. A. Stolypin, the Prime Minister, and Count Kokovtsev, Finance Minister, also went to Kiev, as well as many members of the Court.

The first days were devoted to manœuvres and the visit to historic sites; on September 3rd there was to be a gala performance in the city theatre in the presence of the Tsar. During the morning of that day the police received some alarming news: terrorists had been reported; an attempt at assassination was feared. But investigations led to nothing, and anxiety increased among the members of the Security Service. The police thought the most dangerous moment was likely to be when the Tsar went from the Palace to the theatre: the route which the retinue was to take was known to all. But all went smoothly. In the absence of the Tsarina, who had stayed away, only the senior Grand Duchesses accompanied the Emperor. But during the second interval, while they were drinking tea in the annexe to the box, suddenly a terrible commotion was heard from the auditorium. The Tsar, who did not know of the threat that hung over him, thought that the box had given way. Everybody rushed forward: in the first row of the stalls, near the Imperial box, stood Stolypin, quite upright, in a white tunic, with his hand to his chest; the blood was gushing out between his fingers. . . . Perceiving the Emperor, Stolypin raised his arm and motioned to him to leave his box; then he began to make the sign of the cross over him many times from afar. He was immediately supported by the people standing round, became completely pale, soon lost consciousness and collapsed into a seat. This had lasted no longer than a flash of lightning, and according to André it was difficult to say what happened next. Everybody was shouting, some were running, while officers with drawn swords ran after a man whom they caught up and wanted to stab in the corridor, near the exit of the theatre.

Stolypin's assassin, seriously knocked about, was in fact arrested in this corridor. He was called Bagrov. Employed as an informer, then dismissed before being re-engaged just before the Kiev festivities, he had himself warned the police of the terrorists' presence, with the result that searches had continued the whole day for the man who had been the whole time under the police's eye. On the pretext that he knew the terrorists by sight, Bagrov had been allowed to enter the theatre as an assistant to the secret police without being subjected to the least supervision. He openly approached Stolypin and fired at him point-blank; he then tried to reach the exit, where he was stopped.

Stolypin was immediately transported to a private clinic, where doctors declared that they were afraid he could not be saved: the bullet had perforated his liver. He died on September 8th 1911, after five days' death-struggle.

The news of the attack on Stolypin reached St. Petersburg the next morning. I could not help noticing how implacable Fate was towards the Tsar, how it was dealing him blow after blow: his father's premature death; a marriage celebrated amid sadness and mourning; a coronation darkened by the Chodynka catastrophe; the ill-fated war against Japan; the loss of his best Foreign Minister, Count Lobanov-Rostovsky, who died shortly after being nominated, and now the death of his Prime Minister, who had smothered the revolutionary rising of 1905! And we had no idea then, not even a glimspe, of what the future had in store for him!

There were many in 1917 who thought that Stolypin might have stopped the Revolution.

CHAPTER XVIII

LONDON, VIENNA, MONTE CARLO

Two years having elapsed since our quarrel, Serge de Diaghilev appeared to come to the conclusion that it was time for a reconciliation. He therefore decided to re-establish our friendly relations of old. In 1911 he invited me to dance for him in London at Covent Garden during the autumn season, then in 1912 in Vienna and Budapest, and finally in Monte Carlo for the spring season.

Arnold Haskell, the ballet historian, has since given an exhaustive account of my relations with Diaghilev:[1]

"At last Kchessinska and Diaghileff were united. Two of the strongest personalities in Russia, they had met in many a stormy encounter, both as allies and as enemies, and each of them had great respect for the other, and the rare gift of never bearing rancour. In 1925, when Diaghileff introduced me to her in Monte Carlo, he said, 'Voilà un adversaire bien digne de moi', and that was their attitude throughout. Kchessinska was all-powerful in Russia, able to have everything her own way at the Maryinsky Theatre, with the result that more absurdities have been written about her by imaginative writers than about anyone else, identifying her with nearly every sensational happening of her time—absurdities and identifications which she has never troubled to contradict. What emerges is a woman of infinite charm, wit, and intelligence, generous in instinct, a fighter, because one must be a fighter on the stage, whose greatest fault was never to lose her fights. If she and Diaghileff had been at daggers drawn the year before, there were no signs of it now."

Diaghilev and I agreed that in London I should dance Le Carnaval, two acts of Swan Lake and the pas-de-deux from The Sleeping Beauty. Vaslav Nijinsky was to be my partner.

I took Vova to London, with Miss Mitchell, his English governess, and Dr. Milk, for Vova often fell ill on journeys. My old friend Baron Gotsch also came, together with my faithful maid and my dresser. André left St. Petersburg with us.

It was an eventful journey, from the moment I forgot the keys of

[1] In Diaghileff, by Arnold Haskell, Gollancz, 1935 (pp. 239-240).

my suitcases and only noticed their absence at the very last minute at the station. My chauffeur at once left in the car to fetch the precious keys, and the station-master very kindly agreed to hold up the train for a short time. But when the chauffeur had not returned after ten minutes, the signal to leave had to be given. We were to travel to London by Calais and Dover, but when we reached Berlin we found that a derailed train had damaged the track and were directed to Ostend, from where we could reach Dover by sea. We arrived at Ostend at dinner-time. As the boat was due to leave at midnight, we set out in search of a hotel. With the end of autumn, the town was deserted and the best hotels closed. The weather was terrible, a real storm, with rain pouring down; we walked in Indian file in the poorly lit streets, staggering under the violence of the squalls which swept across the sea, making a bee-line from lamp-post to lamp-post so as not to fall down. Poor Gotsch, who had a dread of the sea, kept on asking if the boat would dare leave harbour in spite of the storm. I too was seized with anxiety when we went on board; but our departure could not be postponed: I was due to rehearse in London next day. The boat reached the open sea somehow, and we have not forgotten the sight of Baron Gotsch, in his pyjamas, sunk in a deckchair on the upper deck, while a compassionate sailor poured a bucket of water over his head.

When we finally reached the station at London we had to explain to the Customs officials that we could not open our luggage. Of course, I was to receive the keys immediately by post, but meanwhile there were only two alternatives, each as unpleasant as the other: we could either leave the cases in bond or break open the locks. However, when they found out who I was the Customs officers very politely, and as a special favour, believed me about the contents of the luggage and allowed us to take them away.

We all stayed at the Savoy, where Diaghilev and Nijinsky were also staying. Vova slept in a large room next to mine and we had a drawing-room. André had the adjacent suite, which also had a large drawing-room.

Dr. Milk left us two or three days later to return to Russia, and next day, of course, Vova developed a high fever. The Grand Duke Michel Mikhailovitch most obligingly telephoned his doctor, a child specialist, who proved very competent and sent us a nurse to look after the young patient, a task which she performed admirably, although she frightened me the first day by leaving the window wide open and assuring me that it was the best way to avoid catching cold at all times of the year!

23. Paris, 1908–1909.

Mlle KSCHESINSKA
Première Danseuse Etoile du Ballet Impérial
(Ph. Boissonnas et Egler).

M. Nicolas LEGAT
Maître de Ballet des Théâtres Impériaux

24.   The opera programme, Paris, 1908–1909.

However, it proved a most effective method and Vova had no other health troubles during his whole stay.

London life at once captivated me by its elegance: at dinner men were always in tails and women in evening dress. Even Vova became impressed with this social necessity. Lacking an evening suit, he fixed a table napkin to his back to represent imaginary tails and thus arrayed he sat at table with great dignity. So I had a child's evening suit made, which he proudly wore each night at dinner.

For my first performance Diaghilev advised me to appear in the *pas-de-deux* from *The Sleeping Beauty*, partnered by Nijinsky. I was very fond of this *pas-de-deux*, but in a new town and before a strange audience I should have preferred a more effective number. However, since I was sure that Diaghilev knew London better than I did, I followed his advice. He himself chose me a very beautiful blue costume, and together we discussed the question of the jewels I was to wear.

My diamonds and other precious stones were so valuable that they raised delicate problems. On the advice of Agathon Fabergé, the famous jeweller's son, who was also one of my great friends, I had entrusted the dispatch of my jewels to his firm, the London branch looking after them until my arrival. Two catalogues were made, and each piece of jewellery was numbered: I had only to know the numbers of the jewels I needed every evening, without giving further details. At the appointed hour an official of the firm, who was also a detective, brought them to me in my dressing-room and prevented any un-authorised person from entering; when the performance was over he took the jewels away again. I also had a number of pieces which I wore every day, and these the hotel management had asked me to place in their safe at night. One night there was a big dinner-party at the hotel, and I asked Fabergé to send me my diadem, which was very valuable. The official brought it, but must have told the management of the Savoy, who informed me that as an added security measure plain-clothes police would dine at a neighbouring table; so I was not to be surprised at their presence. Two young Englishmen in tails did in fact follow me like my shadow the whole evening, but so skilfully and discreetly that nobody except the initiated could tell them from the Savoy's elegant clientéle.

I had an undeniable success at the first performance, but in spite of Diaghilev's claims it was not as great as I had hoped. It was more a *succès d'estime*, due to a famous artist, the prima ballerina of the Imperial Ballet.

I firmly decided now to insert my classical solo to music by Kadletz into the ballroom scene from *Swan Lake*, counting thus on scoring a true success. Diaghilev agreed with me. He was only presenting two scenes from *Swan Lake*, the swans' scene and the ballroom scene. In the swans' scene the adagio is played on the solo violin, as was my solo to Kadletz's music. At the Maryinsky Theatre in Russia this adagio was always played by the famous violinist Auer, who taught at the Conservatoire. I wanted the adagio and solo to be played in London by an artist of the same standing.

By a lucky chance, Mischa Elman, the Russian violinist, who was then at the height of his career and was also Auer's pupil, was giving concerts in London at the time, and I suggested to Diaghilev that he should be invited for my first appearance. Diaghilev thought this an excellent plan. Needless to say, I would pay for all the expenses.

Mischa Elman at once agreed to accompany me. We rehearsed the adagio together in the theatre, with the whole company, but the solo in my hotel. It was no light matter and Mischa Elman seemed very anxious. When André expressed his astonishment, imagining that such a piece would present him with no obstacle, Elman replied that he would find it easier to play the hardest piece in his repertoire than this solo, adding that in order not to do wrong to the artist he was accompanying he had to follow every single one of her movements and beats.

On the day of the performance he arranged to have his interval at the Albert Hall coincide with my appearance at Covent Garden. This was a very unusual case of a double appearance during the same evening.

It was a real feast! Although this was the first time he was accompanying dancing, Mischa Elman did it as a great master, and if the adagio from the swans' scene delighted the public, it was in my classical solo that I secured the resounding triumph I had dreamed of.

But my success had unforeseen consequences, and was the cause of some painful moments for Diaghilev. Nijinsky did not like anybody else but himself to receive ovations when he was dancing. His pride was hurt, and he indulged in a scene of jealousy with Diaghilev, threatening never again to dance with me; it was even said that in his fury he tore his costume. But Diaghilev was as skilled in avoiding scandal and smoothing down even the gravest incidents as he was in exciting them, and in the end everything was quickly arranged to everybody's satisfaction. However, one of the Russian dancers in the company claimed that my success was entirely due to Mischa Elman's participation; she had always been notable, even in St. Petersburg, for the number of

intrigues she started against me. In any case, the succeeding performances, at which I won the same success without Elman, proved the
reverse to her in no uncertain way.

All the works which mention my London appearance with Mischa
Elman insinuate that I had to pay a fortune for those few minutes'
collaboration. Actually, apart from a fine present, I paid nothing for
them. Elman, who had wanted to accompany me of his own accord,
only begged André to help him obtain permission to give a few concerts in Moscow and St. Petersburg, where he appeared, among other
performances, at Le Cercle de la Noblesse, in an enormously successful
recital. He played a double concerto with Auer, his former teacher, and
it was particularly moving to see them appear together on the stage.

I have some very happy memories of that trip to London. One day
Diaghilev and I decided to go and visit Windsor Castle with Nijinsky
and the leading dancers of the company. We were so numerous that
the station-master had an extra carriage fixed on to the train! When
we reached Windsor we hired enormous charabancs and in this
picturesque fashion visited the town and park. The castle was closed to
the public. But we were able from the coach to see the Grenadier
Guards in red uniforms exposing their bearskins to the rain (to freshen
them, so we were told!).

Another notable memory is the lunch to which André and I invited
Diaghilev's company in our suite at the Savoy. The hotel had a
Russian chef, and we feasted on *blinis*[1] and caviar, washed down with
vodka. Later we gave a supper party for Diaghilev, Nijinsky, Leon
Bakst, A. P. Benois, to which we also invited Reynaldo Hahn, the
composer, and the members of the company. Dinner at the Savoy was
particularly fashionable at the time, when London society frequented
the restaurant. The women wore superb dresses and brilliant jewels.
Since English restaurants had to close at midnight, the head waiter
offered to move supper into a private room, where we could go on
until dawn. We did; and it was a very gay and successful party.
Finally, we gave a last luncheon for all the dancers before leaving
London.

My success with the London public, the happy settling of my
relations with Diaghilev, the charm of English society, all helped to
make our stay the happiest—though, alas, the briefest—of experiences.

I went straight back to St. Petersburg, where I wanted to spend

[1] Savoury pancakes traditionally eaten at Carnival time, in the week preceding Lent.

Christmas and the New Year and also prepare for the coming performances.

During this season I was asked to form part of the delegation sent by
the ballet to present a crown and illuminated address to an actress at
the Alexandre Theatre. I had chosen my clothes with the greatest care,
for the ceremony was to take place with the curtain raised before the
Tsar and the Imperial Family. And I had the great joy of hearing that
the Tsar went up to the Grand Duke Serge Mikhailovitch after the
performance and said to him, "Malia is extraordinarily beautiful
tonight!"

Before leaving for Vienna in February, I appeared on January 20th
1912 in *Carmen*, at Médée Figner's farewell performance. It was she
who had begged me, in the name of our old friendship, to dance the
Spanish dances from the opera. There was some risk in this, for the
only Spanish dances we had been taught were stylised ones (it was
Fokine who introduced the more authentic kind). However, I was
prepared for the performance by Boris Romanov, an expert in Spanish
dancing. Meanwhile, the Administration ordered me a new costume
from Golovin—a magnificent affair, but quite unsuitable for me!
My despair reached its depth when I heard that the Tsar was coming
to the theatre. By a miracle, at the last moment I spotted Nina
Nesloukhovska, one of our dancers who was also appearing, wearing an enchanting Spanish costume, which was far simpler and more
practical than mine. I suggested to her that we change, which
delighted her, and I easily got permission from Golovin. Thus I was
able to dance unimpeded and scored the greatest success. Boris
Romanov was delighted. He later created a dance for me performed
entirely on points, with my hands in a muff, to be inserted in the
skating scene from the opera, *Le Prophète*. The work was produced
at a benefit performance for the chorus, and Romanov's dance was a
triumph.

At the same time, with two of my best friends, Anna Nikolaievna
Ostrogradska and Louise Alexandrovna Likhatcheva (stage name,
Borhardt), I decided to throw a rather original supper party at Cubat.
Each of us was to invite three men from among our best friends, so
that we should be twelve at table. In fact, we were fourteen; the Grand
Duke Dimitri Pavlovitch expressed a last minute wish to attend, and
so we had to invite someone else, so as not to be thirteen. It was a
wonderfully gay supper, particularly owing to the original idea,
whereby the ladies were paying! The same evening I played the mute
Fenella in the opera of the same name at the Conservatoire Theatre.

This was a private production, in which I appeared by leave of the Administration.

During my whole career I only very rarely consented—three times, if I remember rightly—to dance in private houses as a favour to friends. If one accepts these invitations blindly, they multiply so quickly that one is bound to refuse them, such refusals leading inevitably to misunderstandings and grudges.

One day I danced the "apache dance" with my brother and Orlov. Another time I performed my "Russian dance" at the house of Anna Nikolaievna Ostrogradska, whose husband, Basil Alexandrovitch, was a member of the Douma. They gave brilliant and gay parties, bringing together a select assembly of guests. Everybody loved Anna Nikolaievna for her gaiety, charm and intelligence.

My third private appearance was at the house of Nicolas Platonovitch Karabtchevsky, a famous lawyer at the St. Petersburg Court of Assizes. An amateur musician and poet, he had written a short musical comedy for ballerina and singers which he begged me to perform. I liked the idea and agreed. Karabtchevsky had invited three singers from the Imperial Opera to take the singing parts, Tcherkasska, Nikolaieva and Zbroueva. The three singers stood on stage (which was decorated with flowers) behind a screen, and I danced in a pink semitransparent costume, to a sung melody, transposing the words of the poem into movements and mime.

N. P. Karabtchevsky was so enthusiastic at the end of the performance that he ran into my dressing-room, kissed my hands and cried out ecstatically: "Mathilde Felixovna! I beg of you to kill somebody so that I can defend you, and you'll be acquitted!" I thanked him warmly for this devotion, but assured him that I had no intention yet of killing anybody. Could he then foresee that his offer to "defend" me was to acquire a deeper and more serious meaning, in very unexpected circumstances?

I left in February for Vienna with Nina Nesterovska to rejoin Diaghilev and his company. I was glad to meet several old friends there whom I had known since 1903. Next we went on to Budapest, where, for the first time, I danced Le Spectre de la Rose, with Nijinsky. There were several very jolly suppers, with the added entertainment of Hungarian rhapsodies, and one evening I invited all the dancers to the theatre, where we occupied several boxes. Such a large number of young, pretty faces caused a sensation.

I was very eager to be back for my anniversary on March 2nd,

St. Mathilda's day, which I was accustomed to spend at home. My son would also have been hurt by my absence. But that meant missing the last performance. I begged Diaghilev, at the risk of annoying him, to let me go a day earlier. Although he was sorry, he understood my wish completely. Nina, whose name-day was on the day before mine, left with me. We expected to reach St. Petersburg on the eve of my name-day, but just before Warsaw, in pitch darkness, the train stopped. As on my London journey in 1911, the train ahead of us had jumped the rails! The lines were overloaded, and I could not get a special train. We had to spend the night in Warsaw, and arrived in St. Petersburg on St. Mathilda's day.

After spending some time in St. Petersburg I had to leave Russia again on March 18th, this time for Monte Carlo, where Diaghilev's season at the Casino Theatre was about to begin. I was accompanied by my son, Vissotzky, his tutor, and Nina Nesterovska. On my intervention, Nina was able to dance for Diaghilev, but without pay, because the company was full.

The Grand Duke Serge, who was also going to Monte Carlo, came on the same train, with his elder brother, the Grand Duke Nicholas.

As Vova was growing up, the question of his surname had come up. We had therefore decided to ask the Emperor to grant him the name of Krassinsky, my family's real name. The Tsar consented and accorded it to him, together with the hereditary precedence.

Thus Vova left for the first time with his own passport.

We went to Cannes, where we intended to spend the end of Holy Week and Easter before rejoining Diaghilev in Monte Carlo. But my son fell seriously ill on the journey.

As soon as we arrived in Cannes, we consulted the best local practitioners, but they were unable to give a diagnosis, and showed considerable anxiety. While waiting for Vova's doctor, Dr. Von Hasse (whom I had asked by telegram to come at once) to arrive from St. Petersburg, I appealed to a famous child specialist who was on holiday in Nice. The consultation was more or less secret, for he could not practise abroad. His clear and definite diagnosis, confirmed by Dr. Von Hasse, the moment he arrived, reassured us. Vova was suffering from acute colitis, caused by food poisoning. Fortunately he made a fairly rapid recovery, and the Grand Duchess Anastasia often came to see him in bed and made a great fuss over him. We had to wait for a complete recovery before thinking of moving to Monte Carlo, where we stayed at the Hotel de Paris.

Meanwhile, in order not to inconvenience Diaghilev, I used to travel by train to Monte Carlo, and after dancing return in pitch darkness to Cannes by car. Whenever there was a performance, Diaghilev, in a fever of anxiety, wondering whether I was going to come or not, would telephone me a hundred times a day for news of Vova. But in spite of all difficulties, I did not miss a single performance, and was constantly successful, especially in the second scene of *Swan Lake*, in which I always had to repeat my solo. When I entered the Sporting Club after the performance everyone present applauded. After the last performance of *Swan Lake*, at the public's urgent request, we even had to repeat the ballet. Diaghilev was delighted. He was having a triumph. Our reconciliation had borne fruit.

On my return to Russia I spent the summer at Strelna, making frequent visits to the theatre at Krasnoïe Selo, not only to dance there, but also to watch performances and meet friends. André had a pretty *datcha* just inside the town, where he gave charming supper parties after the performances. The Grand Dukes Boris Wladimirovitch and Dimitri Pavlovitch came, and I invited my friends among the young dancers.

On my father's death, his estate at Krassnitzy, near Siverskaïa, had been sold to His Serene Highness Prince Henry of Wittgenstein, and my mother used to spend the summer at Strelna, where she had rented a villa, in order to be closer to me. In August she suffered a third stroke, which left her almost completely paralysed. This was a terrible blow for all of us, for our mother, so affectionate, had also been our close friend, our adviser and our comforter in times of stress. Vova, who was still young, loved her deeply, and she was good at spoiling him!

The autumn of 1912 brought me other causes of distress. André now fell seriously ill: afflicted with acute bronchitis, he had to stay in bed for the whole of August, and the doctors, fearing tuberculosis, sent him at once to the Crimea. Thus he had to miss the centenary celebrations of the Battle of Borodino.

I had to choose between two people I loved: I must either stay with my mother and leave André to go alone to the Crimea, or go with André and leave my mother. The doctors assured me that no immediate danger threatened my mother and she might still live a long time; they said that I could easily go to the Crimea and return to St. Petersburg without difficulty if necessity arose, since the journey lasted only two days.

André left on September 4th with his aide-de-camp, F. F. von Kube, and all his staff. On the invitation of the Grand Duke Nicholas Nico-laievitch, he settled at Tchaïr, the Grand Duke's property, in the aides-de-camp's house, and rented a *datcha* for me at Novy Mishkor, near where he was staying. He warned me, however, that neither cook nor servants could be found in the Crimea.

This meant that I had to reserve a whole sleeping-car, because I was taking a large party: my maid, the valet and Vova's two tutors (Scherdlin, his French tutor, and Pfluger, the Russian), my butler and two cooks.

I was enchanted with my first visit to the Crimea. I went constantly to see André, who was beginning to recover, but was still tired by the slightest effort. He could not receive guests, and in any case did not want to. He sometimes visited us on his drives, but never went out in the evening.

Not far from our villa, near the Baidar Gate, was one of the biggest and finest estates in the Crimea, Foros, belonging to Ouchkov, whom I knew very well. The beautiful Miloucha, his wife, was later to be-come Countess Vorontzov-Dachkov. Ouchkov always sent me not only beautiful bouquets, but vast ones; once he sent me a huge bundle containing a small almond-tree surrounded by flowers! Although he was in St. Petersburg at the time, he heard that I was in the Crimea, and told his steward to invite me to visit the estate and ask me to lunch. I went with Micha Alexandrov. The estate was certainly worth visiting, and we enjoyed an excellent meal, washed down with Crimean wines.

Although our *datcha* at Novy Mishkor was lit by oil, it was none the less comfortable for that. There was a tennis court where Vova could play. We led a quiet, simple life, going for lovely walks in the district. I took advantage of my stay to visit the old castle at Livadia where Alexander III had breathed his last. I was able to see the room where the Emperor had died, the Empress Marie Feodorovna's rooms and those where the Tsarevitch had lived until, aged only twenty-six, he had ascended the throne.

At the beginning of November, alarming news about my mother's state of health made me return in haste to St. Petersburg. Soon after-wards André entered a sanatorium which had just been opened at Reichenhall, near Munich, since his doctor thought that the mountains would be better than sea air.

My mother was in a very bad way. I shall never forget her reproach-ful words when I returned: "Mala, you've quite forgotten me!" Deeply anguished, I realised that she had been fully aware of my absence. From then on my sister and I remained by her bed day and night. She died peacefully, without pain, on November 22nd 1912. After a solemn service at the Catholic Church, where I met many of her old friends, who suddenly brought back my childhood to me, her body, embalmed, was transported to the monastery of Saint-Serge, at Serguievo, near Strelna.[1] By permission of the Archimandrite Serge, who was replacing the aged and ill Superior, the coffin was placed in a mortuary chapel until the chapel which I had built in the monastery cemetery was ready. The interior of this chapel, whose bronze door was the work of the sculptor Khlebnikov, was decorated with marble and mosaic.

In memory of my mother and to show my gratitude to the Archimandrite, I gave some priest's vestments to the monastery for Solemn Masses.

This cruel loss left me without the energy or the wish to dance, and I decided to rest for a time.[2]

---

[1] The same monastery where Vova went to Communion.

[2] In an article entitled "Ballet" (*The Imperial Theatres Annual* 1913, a review of the 1912-1913 season) A. Levinson wrote: "We sincerely hope that Mlle. Kschessinska is only leaving the Imperial stage for a short time; her retirement would be a very severe loss for our company" (3rd edition, p. 142).

CHAPTER XIX

THE END OF AN EPOCH

IN SPITE OF BEING in mourning and having decided not to dance that season, I could not, in all conscience, refuse the members of the corps de ballet to make an exceptional appearance at their benefit performance. I was asked to dance *Le Petit Cheval Bossu*, slightly modified and completed by Gorsky. My refusal might have had serious repercussions on the box office takings and thus hurt the artists. The performance was on December 10th 1912, and during the last act I danced Tchaikovsky's Russian dance on points. This is a very sad dance and I performed it with tears in my eyes, communicating my own feelings to the audience.

In January 1913 I paid a few days' flying visit to St. Moritz, where André had settled in accordance with the wishes of his mother, the Grand Duchess Marie Pavlovna, who was not convinced by the remedial properties of the Reichenhall sanatorium.

André met me at St. Moritz Station. We went up in a sledge drawn by two horses wearing bells, in which we drove to the Kulm Hotel. St. Moritz, muffled in snow, immediately won my heart. A summer sun was shining and the town was like the window of a toy-shop with its passers-by dressed in multi-coloured pullovers and mufflers, their skis over their shoulders, drawing their toboggans.

Our rooms were a kind of independent flat overlooking the ice-rink and the valley far off. The first thing we did, of course, was to go the round of the shops in order to fit me up. At about eleven in the morning I accompanied André to the ice-rink, content at first to watch him perform. Then I took lessons, but I did not have enough time to learn skating properly. In the afternoon, riding in a sledge drawn by two horses with bells, and well wrapped in warm blankets, we went for long expeditions in the beautiful and majestic country around. Then back before sunset, and dinner, eaten with great appetite, at the hotel restaurant or in our rooms.

André had with him his aide-de-camp, F. F. von Kube, and his doctor, G. Maak, who had arrived just before me from Russia to look after his health. We at once became friends with him. He proved not only an excellent doctor, but also a charming man, whose destiny was to be linked with ours for many years.

I was unfortunately unable to enjoy St. Moritz with its ice-rink and pine forests for long. My son was waiting for me in Russia, where I also had to perform in the gala for the tercentenary of the Romanoff Dynasty.

In St. Petersburg I met Anna Pavlova, who had come to give a few performances. We were always on the friendliest terms, in spite of the sowers of discord. When she came to see me, the conversation happened to turn on jewellery, and she begged me to show her mine, which she found superb. I gave her a platinum propelling pencil, decorated with rubies and diamonds, in memory of me.

Owing to my decision not to dance that season, all my ballets had been withdrawn from the repertoire. Pavlova, however, was invited to appear in *La Fille du Pharaon*. Knowing, as an intelligent artist, that it was not a ballet for her, she was rather apprehensive and begged me to come and see her when she danced it. Since I was in mourning, I said I would only watch from the wings (where, with touching thoughtfulness, she provided me with a chair on which was a box of sweets). Although she gave an admirable performance, her fears were justified and she only scored a moderate success.

The gala for the tercentenary of the Romanoffs took place in February in the presence of the Tsar, both Empresses, the Imperial Family and the high dignitaries. I had been asked to dance the famous mazurka from the second act of the opera *La Vie pour le Tsar*, and I could not refuse to take part in this particularly solemn performance. The public was not admitted, and the only spectators were people invited by the Court. In the last act a quite unprecedented event took place when the Tsar Mikhail Feodorovitch, the first Tsar of the dynasty, appeared on the stage. This part was taken by Sobinov, replacing Chaliapin, who had fallen ill at the last minute.

In March I left with Vova for Cap d'Ail, where the year before I had rented the Comtesse de Morlat's villa. André arrived just before me from St. Moritz. So when I arrived I found a cook, Margot, and a young Swiss butler, Arnold, admirably skilful and endowed with multiple talents. He arranged the table like a real artist, and that first evening I was full of admiration for large dark blue ribbons, with bouquets of red roses in their knots, decorating the table-cloth.

The Grand Duke Serge Mikhailovitch joined us later for Easter.

André and I received many invitations, particularly to Monte Carlo, where we had a great number of connections and friends, whom we entertained in return.

At the beginning of our Holy Week we all went to Cannes, where

André was preparing to go to Communion. We stayed at the Carlton, which had just been opened, and at midnight, in the large salon, we had our Easter supper, with the traditional *koulitch* and *paskhas*.

We went back to Russia at the beginning of June. After his winter in St. Moritz, André had so far recovered his strength that he decided to resume his normal life, and as a start to join in the ceremonies which were to take place at Kostroma and later in Moscow for the tercentenary of the Romanovs.

I was to pass through moments of anguish and despair that summer. Vova, his tutor and my electrician, who had fixed the electric motor of our canoe, had taken advantage of the magnificent weather to put out to sea. They were surprised far from shore by one of those terrible, unexpected hurricanes which are one of the great dangers of the Gulf of Finland. When the storm was over they were able to return to shore, not far from the Imperial Palace, from where Vova and his tutor telephoned me to reassure me. But meanwhile I had endured two hours, two centuries, of terrible uncertainty, during which I ran out to the jetty, telephoned the lifeboat station at Strelna Harbour, but in vain, for no boat had been signalled at sea. Alone and appalled by my helplessness, I had fallen on my knees and weeping I prayed God to save my son.

Since I was in mourning, I did not dance or appear at the Krasnoïe Selo Theatre, and the Grand Duke Dimitri Pavlovitch, disappointed by my absence, told me through the Administrator of the theatre that he would expect me without fail at the next performance. I agreed to come, but did not enter the auditorium, and we spent the evening chatting in my dressing-room.

Equally I did not arrange large parties, and only entertained friends, including the Grand Duke Dimitri Pavlovitch and officers from the Uhlan Regiment stationed at Peterhof. Once the party went on until dawn, and the Grand Duke Dimitri, who, as the Tsar's aide-de-camp in attendance, had that day to attend a parade of two cavalry regiments, of which the Grand Duchesses Olga and Tatiana Nikolaïevna had just been named honorary colonels, barely had time to dash to St. Petersburg to change, reach Peterhof and take his place in the Imperial suite. We watched the parade, and I sighed with relief when I saw him appear. This was the Grand Duchesses' first review, and how proud they looked on horseback in their well-fitting uniforms!

In the autumn, when almost all social life stopped for us until the winter season, I left again for Cap d'Ail, this time to live in a house which belonged to me. For home life had appeared pleasanter and

1891   1911.

Diner du 18 Février.

———

Hors d'oeuvres

Potage Bisque de Homards

Rastigaïs au foie de lotte.

Poularde Archiduc

au maïs

Jambonneau d'Jork garni de

filets mignon financière

Punch Danois

Perdreaux et cailles sur crouton

Salade romaines

Haricots vert nouveau de Kline

à l'Anglaise

Parfait aux violettes de parme

Gateaux fruit

Café. Liqueurs.

———

25.   The menu for my Jubilee supper, 1911.

26.   At the Jubilee reception, surrounded by dancers and balletomanes.

altogether easier than hotel life. André and I had therefore decided in June, before leaving the Morlat villa, whose lease we could not renew, to find another house for the autumn. Our agent told us that there was a magnificent estate for sale at an attractive price. The idea appealed to me, especially as the site, on the edge of a mountain and over-looking the sea, was really wonderful. We settled the deal during the summer and called the villa Alam, which was just the diminutive of my name, Mala, spelt backwards.

We had a charming guest staying with us on the Riviera. During the spring, when we were living in the Morlat villa, my butler had given me a tame white pigeon. He was afraid of nothing, would share my breakfast and walk quietly about the table. In the daytime he flew into the garden, but came back before nightfall. I became so attached to him that I at once took him with me to Strelna and St. Petersburg; he lived in the winter garden, where there was a window which allowed him to fly out freely. He grew so tame that he formed the habit of perching on my head and sleeping on my bed with Djibi my dog, who was his best friend. When the Revolution broke out and I had to leave my house in great haste, the pigeon stayed in the winter garden. My servants later told me that when the house was occupied by the Bolsheviks, my tame white pigeon, prompted apparently by some mysterious instinct, flew out through the window . . . and never came back!

While waiting for the repairs to be finished and to move into the villa, we spent a week at the Eden Hotel. We still had a great deal of shopping to do, and I was as happy as a child at the prospect of living with André in such a delightful setting. Thus we moved in amid joyful celebrations.

As often happens, although the villa was big, we did not have enough rooms for André's aide-de-camp and his doctor. Nor was there a garage. So we decided to build another villa for our guests and servants. Work started at once, and from our window we could watch the workmen dynamiting the cliff: they ran off when the siren sounded, clapped when the explosions were successful and did not conceal their disappointment when a charge failed to explode.

The end of that year, 1913, became coloured with golden light as it fades into the distance. After two happy months at Cap d'Ail, I left St. Petersburg, while André, whose health still caused a little alarm, returned to St. Moritz for the winter. It was a sad parting, but I rejoined him at St. Moritz for the Catholic Christmas. As Vova could not interrupt his studies, I left with Micha Alexandrov. We spent two wonderful weeks. I resumed my skating lessons and we went again for long sleigh rides, towing Micha on his toboggan: one day we fell asleep and lost poor Micha, who had overturned, unknown to us, when crossing a pit! How happy we were to return, soaked and frozen, to our cosy room with its magnificent Christmas tree!

But once again we had to part. I had to return to St. Petersburg to prepare the Russian Christmas for my son. It was my habit to invite Vova's little friends and to give them presents distributed round the Christmas tree. But sometimes I also arranged little performances for them. That year I had Dourov, the famous clown, with his performing animals, including a large elephant, which arrived wrapped up in check blankets. In order to get him into the house, we had to draw apart the side wings of the front door. He was hidden in the cloak-room before the performance. Dourov showed us his trained animals and did conjuring tricks, but the climax was undoubtedly the entry of the elephant, and the children's happiness reached its peak when he lay on an enormous bed and took a chamber pot, both of which had been brought in during the interval.

Meanwhile I was working uninterruptedly, preparing for my return to the stage.

I made my reappearance in *Le Talisman* on February 2nd 1914, at the corps de ballet's benefit performance. On the 9th there was a benefit performance for N. Legat, to celebrate the twenty-fifth anniversary of his entry to the Imperial Theatres in 1888. Legat had chosen *Esmeralda*, in which he gave an admirable interpretation of the role of Gringoire.

I had no idea that the Tsar would be at the theatre that evening. He lived regularly at Tsarkoïe Selo, and did not often come to St. Petersburg, especially in the evening. We learnt that he would be there just before the performance. I was in the wings, from where one could see the Imperial box. When the Tsar appeared, I could not believe that my age old dream would at last be realised, that he would see me dance *Esmeralda*!

When I danced this ballet I used to spend the late afternoon lying down in the half-darkness of my room, in order to concentrate and really enter into the heroine's role.

I had always danced *Esmeralda* with passion; but that evening I lived the part with all my heart and soul! The tears were in my eyes as I danced the jealousy scene at the ball, where Esmeralda and Gringoire dance before Phoebus and his fiancée, putting such life and fire into it that it might have been my own destiny at stake. And there must have been spectators who understood me and lived the drama with me, for I was given a real ovation.

But alas, I was never to know what effect I had on the Tsar. The Grand Duke Serge Mikhailovitch, to whom he always confided his impressions about me, was away from St. Petersburg that day.

Knowing that I was preparing to leave for the Riviera, the Director tried to persuade me to stay, and to appear the following Sunday in the new version of *The Sleeping Beauty*, but I refused. In spite of my desire to dance again in the presence of the Tsar, who liked me so much in the old version of *The Sleeping Beauty*, I wanted to leave him with the impression of *Esmeralda*.

André rejoined me at Cap d'Ail, returning from Florence, where a new statue of Tsar Alexander III had been erected.

The new villa, situated lower down with a roof that was the continuation of the old villa's terrace, was at last finished. On the first floor there were four guest-rooms, overlooking the sea, and two servants' rooms. The ground floor comprised a huge garage and the chauffeur's room. When everything was ready, the Arch-priest Gregory Ostroounov came to bless the house. Then there was a house-warming party, and everybody signed the guest-book.

The first to settle in the new villa were André's aide-de-camp and doctor.

My half-brother, Philippe Lédé, and the Grand Duke Serge Mikhailovitch soon joined us. As usual, we spent Holy Week in Cannes, and on Easter Saturday we went once again to the church in Cannes for the Easter night service, with a number of friends in four cars. After the service we returned to Cap d'Ail, where the traditional Easter supper of *razgoveni* was awaiting us. It was a charming happy journey, and I can still see the procession in the garden round the church, a few seconds before midnight when the chorus *Christ is Risen* is sung. Sadly I recall that my son and I are the only survivors of that Holy Week in the South of France. The season ended with André's birthday and we returned to Russia.

André's birthday, dinner-parties in Monte Carlo, Nice or Cannes—the days passed, filled with untroubled, carefree gaiety; and so many friendly faces remain linked to that happy spring of 1914, among others Nicholas Johnson, who was to die at Perm with the Grand Duke Michel Alexandrovitch.

Shortly before leaving, we bought part of the park adjoining our estate, in order to build a tennis court and a miniature fort for Vova.

In May we sadly left villa Alam—with so much luggage that the train had to be held up for at least five minutes to load it in the guard's van—promising to return in the autumn. We did return, but not all of us, six years later. We returned after passing through the horrors of war, the Revolution, Bolshevism and flight from Russia, to live out our days in exile.

After returning to St. Petersburg, I soon went to Strelna, where on June 18th we celebrated Vova's birthday, a day whose ceremonial he had carefully arranged once and for all, allowing no lapses from the programme. Early in the morning he put on his military tunic, with countless decorations, a lanyard and a sword. Tradition required that breakfast should be served in his little house; but although this house was right next-door to the villa, the same tradition required that he should ride there in his child's motor car. He then reviewed his many presents, and we had a group photograph taken.

His name-day, on July 15th, was marked by a big party, the last birthday party he was to have. The guests poured in, and the children organised a grandiose *corrida*, with a box, Spanish sovereigns, procession, toreador and a fierce bull, whose corpse, after the killing, revealed two young friends who had been the front and rear.

This birthday was the end of our peaceful life and our gaiety. Painful days were ahead of us. Could I have guessed that I was entertaining these young officers for the last time, that they would go off to the war, and that some of them I should never see again?

I shall make no attempt in these memoirs to deal with the political side of the terrible years we had to live through and the events we witnessed. Nothing at the time seemed to point to war. It is enough to recall that at the beginning of June the King of Saxony came to St. Petersburg, and that there was a succession of dinners and military parades. On the 15th an English squadron under Admiral Beatty, on an official visit, anchored off Cronstadt. On the 28th, it is true, the Austrian Archduke Franz Ferdinand and his wife were assassinated at Sarajevo, but on July 7th M. Poincaré, the French President, was solemnly received by the Tsar at Cronstadt. A gala dinner was given in honour of the President, who also attended the military parade at Krasnoïe Selo before returning to France, almost on the eve of the declaration of war.

The day after President Poincaré left, life at Krasnoïe Selo resumed its normal course. There was horse-racing in the Emperor's presence;

then came a regimental dinner with the Horse Guards, followed by the last gala performance.

As usual, everybody came to see me in my dressing-room. Everybody hoped that the clouds gathering on the political horizon would clear, and that we should be spared war.

At that last performance of the Krasnoïe Selo season I appeared in my best Russian dance. Could I then imagine that this was the last time I was to dance before the Tsar?

When he left the theatre I stood at my dressing-room window, as I had stood twenty-two years before, that distant time when, still young and madly in love, I had waited with beating heart to see him appear on horseback in front of the theatre . . . where, a few hours later, I had gazed after him with tears of joy at the hope of seeing him again soon!

But this time he was troubled. Alarming news had been received that very evening: Austria was sending an offensive ultimatum to Serbia. A terrible rumour passed among the audience. War, they said, was imminent. I returned home tormented, with a heavy heart, thinking of all those I loved.

My son has kept a deep and lasting memory of that evening. Until then he had been almost a child, and life and its political problems had been for him the dim and far-off world of the grown-ups. But this was for him the tangible revelation of patriotism. When the Tsar entered the auditorium to sit in the front row, the audience spontaneously paid him an indescribable ovation; never was a national anthem sung and listened to with such religious fervour. One felt that the Tsar and his people were one, and the Emperor's grave face showed how aware he was of his responsibilities. We artists were separated from the audience by the curtain; we heard the anthem, but could only guess the symbolical spirit of that spontaneous display.

The next day we learned that preparations for mobilisation had begun. Then came general mobilisation, followed, a week later, by the declaration of war.[1]

I had a lot of friends and acquaintances in the Army, particularly the officers of the Uhlans of the Guard, stationed at Peterhof, not far from Strelna, with the Empress Alexandra Feodorovna as their honorary colonel. In the summer these officers used to come to see me almost every Sunday. All the officers I knew came to say goodbye,

[1] This was the last time, July 20th, that I saw the Tsar. It was at Peterhof, when, amid the people's cheers, he entered the capital to read the manifesto announcing to Russia the declaration of war.

and each of us wondered, without daring to say it, whether destiny would allow us to meet again in Peterhof.

I blessed them all with a small miraculous icon representing Our Lady of Czenstokov, a legacy from my father, who had never been separated from it in his lifetime. This same icon protected us all later during the whole Revolution.

As I say, I blessed all the Uhlan officers with the exception of Goursky, who had no time to come and see me, and said goodbye by telephone. He was killed during the first days of the war, on August 6th, near Kauschen. When I heard that his body had been brought to Petrograd,[1] I went to Warsaw Station and was able, not without difficulty, to find a goods waggon on a minor line in which were several coffins containing the remains of soldiers who had fallen during this first encounter. And in front of Goursky's coffin I remembered the young Uhlan brimming with life and joy whom I had known at Strelna. I was alone, and I wept bitterly before that poor victim of the terrible war. Nobody could see me. Nobody could prevent me from weeping. . . .

The Grand Duke Dimitri Pavlovitch had also to leave for the front among the first, with his regiment. Unable to come and say goodbye to me at Strelna, he begged me to come to the capital and bless him. I went at once, and we met in my house in Petrograd. It was a heart-rending moment when he knelt before me to be blessed. . . . Thus day after day I saw those I loved go towards a death which could strike them at any moment.

At the end of September André, who had been attached to the staff on the north-west front,[2] left in turn and my sadness increased. We still cherished the hope, at the time, that the war would be short, for nobody seemed able to bear a long-drawn conflict.

A few days before the war the Grand Duke Serge Mikhailovitch was attacked by arthritis and fell seriously ill; he had to stay in bed at Mikhailovka, where I went constantly to see him. When his health improved a little, he was moved to his palace in St. Petersburg, but his life was to remain in danger for a long time. He was Inspector-General of the Artillery, to which he had always passionately devoted himself and which he knew better than anyone; and he felt keenly his inability to serve his country at such a time.

When it was clear that there was no threat to Petrograd and that

[1] The name given to St. Petersburg in 1914; changed to Leningrad in 1924.
[2] Later, when his health allowed it, he took over the command of the Horse Artillery Brigade of the Guard.

the fighting would take place far from the capital, life slowly resumed its normal course, but without excitement.

The war was becoming more and more bloody, and far from thinking of festivities, many civilians started hospitals. I myself found, not far from home, a large apartment overlooking the Kamennostrovsky Prospect. The conversion took some time, and the hospital was not ready until December 1914. It consisted of two operating theatres and three rooms for the wounded on the ground floor, a total of twenty beds, with one room reserved for the seriously wounded. I made sure of the collaboration of the best doctors in Petrograd, who came to the hospital in the morning. The permanent staff, who lived in the basement, consisted of a sister, two male and two female nurses, and a cook, who had been in my employment first as a scullery boy and later as assistant cook.

On the day the little hospital was blessed, Prince Obolensky, the Prefect of St. Petersburg, A. A. Polovstov, the Red Cross representative, and all the administrators of the Public Health Service, as well as medical inspectors and several of my friends, attended the ceremony, which was followed by a collation.

The hospital remained empty for several days. Then, one evening, I was warned that a number of wounded were about to arrive. Staff and doctors were all ready. I felt very anxious, conscious of the moral responsibility which would henceforth be mine. One of the first to come, very seriously wounded, died that same night, which affected me deeply. I wanted to send for the doctor at the end, but I was advised against it: he had just examined the dying man and prescribed the necessary treatment. Sending for him now would only have meant depriving of his aid those whom he could still relieve. This was true enough; nevertheless in my desolation I continued to think that the doctor might perhaps have saved the dying man.

I never attended operations or the dressing of wounds, since I could have been of no assistance there. But I did my best to be useful, trying to spoil the wounded by all the means in my power and to bring some light, however small, into their lives far from their families; looking for ways to comfort and encourage them. I sent presents to their families; I questioned them to find out whom I could help and what their families needed. One day, to entertain them, I organised a party and danced before them, with Orlov and Stoukolkin, in our costumes, the Russian dance which we had once performed at Krasnoïe Selo. We had never had such a grateful audience!

CHAPTER XX

WARTIME

During those war years I sometimes left Petrograd to dance in provincial towns.

My first tour was arranged by Sokolovsky, who took a whole company to Reval for a single performance. He succeeded in obtaining for me a splendid saloon carriage, decorated entirely in Karelian birchwood and furnished in Empire style, known as the "Vialtzeva carriage" because that artist had used it for her tours across Russia. Baron Gotsch accompanied us. At Reval I danced my famous *pas-de-deux* with Vladimirov, a very talented dancer who had graduated from the Theatre School in 1911. The performance was extremely successful and we went straight back to Petrograd. For the return journey a restaurant car was attached to the train and supper was served to the whole company, who were in high spirits for the whole journey.

Shortly afterwards the famous impresario Reznikov invited me to dance with Vladimirov in Helsingfors. Vitting, the tenor, and Latchinov, the conductor, came too. This was a remarkably successful performance. It was winter time, and the naval officers who had attended the show invited me to come to see their ships trapped by ice not far from the town. We reached the squadrons by sledge, and then on foot. It was a strange sight, and I was photographed on the ice by the ships, in the company of the officers.

Our success at Helsingfors encouraged Reznikov to invite me at once to Kiev for a single performance. I got a very cold reception from the Kiev public, while Vladimirov, my partner, was far more successful than I. The inhabitants of Kiev were very jealous of their city, which they considered the second in Russia, after the capital. Also there was a magnificent theatre in Kiev, where all the greatest artists felt more or less obliged to appear, though I had never done so until now. Next Reznikov arranged a two week tour across Russia. This time we were to appear in Moscow, Kiev, Kharkov, Rostov-on-Don, Baku and Tiflis. Vitting was to sing in the intervals so that I could change costume and get a breathing space between my dances. To make my travelling easier the Grand Duke Serge Mikhailovitch lent me his saloon-carriage, which was very large and specially arranged for long journeys; Vladimirov, Vitting and Latchinov, as well as my staff, all benefited from it. It comprised a drawing-room, bedroom, lavatory, luggage compartment, kitchen-buffet, two sleeping compartments and a further two for the staff. Arnold cooked breakfast for us. Our meals came from the station buffet and the carriage was attached to the train when it was about to leave. It was our ambulating palace, and we travelled all across Russia in it in the greatest comfort.

We left at the beginning of April, and gave our first performances at a private theatre in Moscow, the Zimin Theatre. I had already won over the Moscovites, who gave me a warm welcome. The public in Kiev, our next stopping-place, seemed determined to redeem itself by the most ardent enthusiasm.

We went on to Kharkov, where Vladimirov developed a sore throat, and the performance at Rostov-on-Don had to be cancelled. Rostov Station, where we arrived late in the evening, was crowded with admirers who had come to welcome us, and we replied to their greetings through the window.

Leaving Rostov, we suddenly found ourselves in a dream landscape: the Don had overflowed and the train seemed to be floating in the middle of a huge moonlit lake.

Our penultimate stop was Baku, a millionaires' town and head of the oil industry. The public was exceedingly smart, and the women, covered in jewels, wore lovely evening dresses. I was invited after the performance to the best restaurant in town, and given a true ovation when I entered. My wonderful reception in Baku surpassed my expectation, but at Tiflis, for which I had chosen appropriate dances, including that of the Indian butterfly, which I danced with Vladimirov, my reception was beyond all bounds.

I had no time to visit the town properly, but was enchanted by its picturesque appearance. I was taken by officers to a nearby restaurant, by the River Koura, where I was able to hear the *zourna*[1] and see the national dances.

Tiflis gave me a moving send-off. The corridor of the carriage was invaded by an enthusiastic throng, and the officers who had been my hosts the night before had great difficulty in bringing me an enormous round basket full of fresh fruit and vegetables. These baskets, called *tabakhi* in Tiflis, have the same significance as bread and salt offered as a token of welcome in Russia. Since there was no room for all the flowers in the carriage, they were tied to the rear platfrom.

We went straight back to Petrograd, where I presented my fees for these performances to the Committee of the Grand Duchess Olga

[1] A form of Caucasian trumpet.

Nikolaievna, the Tsar's eldest daughter. She was anxious to thank me, and presented me with a medal and a testimonial.

I was really sorry that our tour was over: I had been enchanted with this journey across Russia. But the war and its attendant horrors continued. I fought with all my might against the war's depressing atmosphere, trying to raise my own morale and that of others, and this earned me the nickname, *"radouchka"*.[1] Vladimir Lazarev called me "the miracle girl".

During the summer of 1915, in order to provide some distraction for the wounded and allow them to breathe better air than in the hospital, I invited them in turn to my *datcha* at Strelna; they came in Army lorries specially lent for the purpose.

Vova was delighted at spending a day with soldiers. He followed the progress of military operations with care; he knew every battle by heart, asked the wounded hundreds of questions and often came to play draughts with them.

At the same time, in the summer of 1915, Vova had decided to organise a small body of fire-fighters. We bought him a pump and the training of the members began. For Vova it may have been nothing more than a game, but it was none the less a very useful game, since our house was of wood. A proof of this was given us one night when I was awoken by the smell of smoke. I hastily rose, and made a tour of the whole *datcha*, at the end of which I noticed that the chimney of a room directly under André's room was on fire. I quickly roused everybody in the house, and Vova's fire-fighters extinguished the beginnings of the fire before the arrival of the Strelna fire brigade, who were too far away to intervene in time. Without my son's quick action, we should all have been burnt alive on the first floor of the house, since the fire had broken out just next to the staircase. Vova's favourite partner was "the Bulgarian", so called because of his country of birth. On the Bulgarian's regimental day, the Grand Duke Serge kindly brought him a present and sweets for the other wounded.

In 1915, looking for a piece of music which would suit dancing perfectly without having been composed for it, Fokine chose two of Tchaikovsky's works: *Francesca da Rimini*, an orchestral *fantaisie* inspired by the famous episode from Dante's *Divina Commedia*, and *Eros*, a string serenade, op. 48, composed in 1880 and inspired by *L'Ange Fiosolé*, a short story by Valerian Iakovlevitch Svetlov. (It was about this work that P. I. Jurgenson wrote, on May 31st 1882, to

[1] Literally, bringer of joy.

Tchaikovsky: "Your serenade has been a great success . . . you must have borrowed something from *Swan Lake*; or is it just a family resemblance?")

Rehearsals were very lively. Fokine, a consummate artist, knew exactly what he wanted; he pressed his ideas relentlessly, picked holes in every pose and allowed no personal initiative which reflected the dancer's individuality.

I may here be allowed to quote from an article by George Bakhrouchin[1] dealing with these ballets:

"The first performance was on November 20th 1915, at the Maryinsky Theatre, in aid of the reception centre for refugee children. The leading female roles were taken by Egorova in *Francesca*, and by Kschessinska in *Eros*, in which the part of Paolo was danced by Vladimirov. 'The fact that the performance was in aid of the charity,' wrote N. Chebouiev, 'meant that the organisers had to reduce the expenses generally incurred in a ballet production. Décors and costumes had to be chosen from stock.' Only *Eros* had special scenery, designed by Bobychev, who thus made his name as a designer.

"*Francesca* did not arouse particular enthusiasm, and was removed from the repertoire after the first performance. This may have been chiefly due to Egorova, who danced the role of Francesca. The reviewers did not devote one word to her. Nobody ventured to criticise the distinguished ballerina, but there were no grounds on which to compliment her.

"*Eros*, on the other hand, received unanimous praise. Stark wrote: '*Eros* is indeed better on the purely dancing scale. Tschaikovsky's music might perhaps have been differently interpreted. But what does it matter? The fact remains that, choreographically speaking, everything was beautiful, bright and endued with a clearly expressed elegiac note. The ballet was excellently performed by Kschessinska and Vladimorov.' The critic F. M. wrote: 'Mlle. Kschessinska and M. Vladimirov created this magnificent stylised piece like artists of true class. The dancing was particularly noble, endowed by Mlle. Kschessinska with incomparable poetry and grace. The décors were ideal.'

" '*Eros*,' writes Bobychev, 'owes its success largely to M. F. Kschessinska, who was wonderful. In spite of her years, she proved full of spontaneity, youth and true lyricism. There is no need to mention how excellent was the dancing. Kschessinska surprised us by her discipline;

---

[1] "Tchaikovsky's Ballets and their Stage History," by George Bakhrouchin, in *Tchaikovsky and the Theatre*, published by the Soviet Government, Moscow 1940 (pp. 124-126). Bakhrouchin reproduces the entire programme.

always the first to arrive at rehearsals, she listened to Fokine's remarks with the greatest attention. To her, his instructions were law.' "

Eros was acquired by the Administration and brought into the repertoire. Its first performance as a work of the Imperial Theatre Company was at the Maryinsky Theatre on December 20th 1915.

Every year, before the beginning of the season, I subjected myself to a kind of examination. After a period of intense work I asked my sister and several faithful friends to attend a rehearsal and to tell me frankly if they thought I could still appear on the stage. From the technical point of view I was gaining in strength and experience every year, but it sometimes happens that, at the end of her career, an artist does not realise that it is time to leave the stage and retire while still fresh. It is an error frequently made to retire only when strength is beginning to fail, and thus to leave a poor impression.

Before a performance I often blamed myself for continuing to appear when I had won fame. Was this not the moment to step aside? But the dance had an irresistible attraction for me, and I had too much of the sacred flame and still too many things to express, to give up my *raison d'être*.

It was in these last years, when Vladimirov became my partner, that I think I began to dance particularly well. Vladimirov, who danced with passion, inspired me more than anyone else. We appeared together in *Swan Lake*, and our movements harmonised and blended ideally. He supported me admirably in the adagio in the second scene of the first act, throwing me and catching me like a feather, in a way that brought forth enthusiastic cries from the audience. At the time all this was a real innovation. *Le Talisman*, which had always been one of my great successes, gained still more brilliance when Vladimirov partnered me, particularly in the second act, when, as the Spirit of the Wind, he appeared like an arrow on the stage, bearing me on his shoulder. This had an enormous effect on the public. Youry Beliaiev, the famous critic, wrote that Vladimirov burst on to the stage as if he were carrying a glass of champagne to offer to the audience.

If I was always anxious before the show, I was still more so while waiting to appear in the wings, afraid that I might spoil the renown I had won during my career. But with the first notes of music all fear vanished, and I leaped forward confidently and joyfully to renew my challenge to the public.

I had now been dancing on the Imperial stage for a quarter of a century; and I asked for a benefit performance, the takings to go to the

27. In costume for the Russian Dance.

28. Myself, 1911.

Imperial Theatre Society,[1] which helped the families of artists who
had been called up.

I chose *Le Talisman* for this performance and considerably put up
the price of seats. But all the tickets were sold, and often I was sent
more than the price of the tickets. Thus I received a total of 37,000
roubles, an enormous box office taking for the period. The performance took place on February 21st 1916 and I had to give five encores
of the coda from the last act, which was a record. Although I had asked
the public through the Press not to send me flowers in view of the
war, I received a vast number of bouquets. One lady who was sitting
in the stalls, under my son's box, had voiced her indignation at such
quantities, and Vova (who was then thirteen) replied sharply, "She
deserves them!" an answer which delighted those who heard it. I still
have the solid silver ladle which the public gave me that evening,
together with a large crystal and silver vase intended for wine-cup. I
found the ladle by chance, with a few other things stolen from my
house, at a second-hand dealer's in Kislovodsk after the Revolution,
and it was restored to me.

On April 17th I decided to dance *Giselle* for the first time. I knew
that this was not really my part, but I was still slim and light, and I
risked it. It was at a performance in aid of the sanitary services directed
by the Grand Duchess Marie Pavlovna, mother of the Grand Duke
André, and I expected to increase interest by my appearance in *Giselle*.
My expectations were right: the takings were high, and the Grand
Duchess, delighted with this success, sent me her inscribed photograph.
I was certainly not like Anna Pavlova, who was absolutely peerless as
Giselle, but I nevertheless had a pleasing success, and the public appreciated the motives of my action. Pavlova's admirers, however, together with a number of my private enemies, did not fail to run me
down; but their attacks left me quite indifferent, accustomed as I was
to these mean pin-pricks.

In the spring of 1916 I decided to visit the front in order to distribute
presents to the soldiers. As a member of the Red Cross, Alexander
Dmitrievitch Viktorov, one of my great friends, arranged for me to
visit a sector in the Minsk district, held by an army corps whose
commander was an acquaintance of his. I invited Vladimirov to escort
me, and we all three set out. The front was fairly calm at the time. We

---

[1] This society was under the high patronage of the Tsar. The Grand Duke
Serge Mikhailovitch and Moltschanov were respectively President and Vice-
President.

reached Minsk by train and spent the night in a shabby little hotel.

The following morning an officer from headquarters came to fetch us by car. It was a lovely day. We crossed fields and forests laid waste by recent fighting: trees torn to pieces, shell-holes, and wooden crosses planted on still fresh graves. . . . A bright sun added to the desolation of the scene. When we arrived at headquarters we were courteously greeted by the commander, who put his own house at our disposal, a kind of hut containing two comfortable rooms. Before the meal we went to a forest hut, where I distributed presents to the soldiers. After which, to my great surprise, we were given an excellent supper.

The hut, open on one side, had a projecting wooden floor, covered by a roof. An orchestra sat there, and one of the guests, an engineer by profession, danced a spirited cakewalk. I was very sorry not to have brought my costume or music with me to perform my Russian dance.

Early in the morning we left to visit the various positions held by the army corps. On the way I was shown barbed-wire defences, a camouflaged battery and a long-range gun, set apart and cleverly concealed. We finally halted before a church damaged by enemy artillery and surrounded by a great many funnels. The officers explained to me that the Germans did not fire at lunch-time: so for the moment we were safe. Seeing how interested I was, some young officers wanted to bring me even further towards the advanced posts, to show me the enemy trenches, but the commander absolutely refused, adding that he was responsible for my safety. To make up, I was allowed to venture behind the church, from where I was able to see a German soldier, calmly walking up and down along the other river bank. I can remember all that today, as if it were a dream.

We returned to headquarters before dark, thanked our hosts for their warm welcome, and left them. Forty-eight hours later, returning via Minsk and Moscow, we were back in St. Petersburg.

During the 1916-1917 season the Administration asked me to appear on stage on the same conditions as before: I agreed, but I was unhappy. Dancing gave me no pleasure. We were all, dancers and public, in the grips of dark foreboding of imminent sorrow.

I spent the summer as usual in my *datcha*, paying frequent visits to town to call on my wounded and help them. But the policy was now to assemble the wounded in the distant provinces, which were more accessible, so it was said, than the capital, and the hospitals were almost empty. As it now proved too difficult to maintain them, I decided in December to close mine.

My decision saddened both the wounded and the staff. But I was
sadder still. The moment of closing the hospital was unbearable. After
the *Te Deum* I went the round of the rooms for the last time, saying
goodbye to the wounded who were leaving that very day for various
hospitals. All the staff came with me, and in each room Chabanov, the
head nurse, exhorted the wounded in these words: "Follow my
example, my friends! Do as I do!" and he knelt before me, bowing
down several times. In spite of my protests, the wounded followed him
as well as they could. I was overwhelmed. I was never going to see all
these young people again; but we did not altogether lose touch, and
several of them later sent me touching letters of gratitude.

Serge, the musician, joined the staff of the Grand Duke Serge
Mikhailovitch, at Headquarters. Dr. Maak, who had looked after
André in St. Moritz, was also working under him.

On the night of 16th/17th December 1916, Gregory Rasputin was
invited to the Youssoupov Palace in Petrograd on a false pretext, and
assassinated by Prince Felix Youssoupov.

I had never seen Rasputin, either close to or at a distance, nor had
I ever had the slightest connection with his followers. I cannot therefore
give a personal impression of him. But he was talked of a great deal,
and with many details, at the time.

A great many people, myself included, thought that the over-
intimate relations between Rasputin and the Imperial Family were
harmful and undesirable. But the assassination was a fatal mistake.
Reputable witnesses confirmed that Rasputin had several times
practically saved the Tsarevitch's life by stopping a near-fatal haemor-
rhage. Once the most distinguished specialists had owned their inability to cure the Tsarevitch, the Tsarina's one hope was that her son
might be saved by Rasputin. The latter's assassination deprived the
Tsarina of this last resort. In any case, the men who committed the
murder played the game of those who had long been planning
the Revolution.

We suffered a terrible shock on learning of the Grand Duke Dimitri
Pavlovitch's banishment to the furthest end of Persia, and of his
participation in the affair. He had clearly been purposely implicated
for obvious reasons. He had had no hand in the actual murder, and the
complicity of Pourichkevitch, a politician of the extreme right wing,
appeared to justify the plot in his eyes.

Several years later, when I met Dimitri Pavlovitch in Paris during
the exile, he thought of that fatal night with unmitigated disgust. He

was trying to avoid not only those who had been involved in the affair, but all those who might have reminded him of it.

There were many who thought that all would go better once Rasputin was out of the way; the evil surrounding the throne would be removed, the bad influences at work on the Tsar would cease, and the country, able to breathe more freely at last, would enjoy a real Golden Age. This no doubt was what the conspirators in the Youssoupov Palace that night thought. It was their great mistake. For it was from that moment that Russia began her downhill passage towards her tragic fall. . . . The instigators of the crime, if, as some think, there were such, men who were able to impose themselves on the perpetrators, must surely have been expecting some such result.

CHAPTER XXI

THE STORM

THE OPERA CHORUS had chosen *Fenella* for its benefit performance, and asked me to take the leading dumb role in the opera. I practised with Fokine, who did away with the conventional mime and gave new life to the heroine. It was the first production of this work on the Imperial stage, and there was a great deal of talk about it in theatrical circles. Some said that *Fenella* brought bad luck, and quoted numerous precedents to support their claim, including one which I remember very well. *Fenella* was being performed in a private theatre, and Grimaldi had invited me to come to see her in the part. The performance was quite uneventful, and I returned to Strelna. But when I opened the newspaper next morning, I read that the theatre had been burnt down during the night.

On the night of the performance, January 17th 1917, all the artists felt uneasy, as if they were afraid of something. The scene represented a revolution with a palace being burnt down—a fiction which was to appear prophetic!

André wrote after the first night in his journal: "First performance of the opera *Fenella*. Mala was wonderful, and the public very enthusiastic." The next day André left to take a cure at Kislovodsk. He had got six weeks' leave before returning to the front, where a large offensive by the Russian armies was expected.

On January 29th, at Liouba Egorova's farewell performance, I danced my favourite Russian dance in the last act. When I had finished, Fokine, who was in the wings, told me that he never remembered the Russian dance better performed. Such praise from him made me very proud.

Finally, on February 2nd, Countess Mathilde Ivanovna Witte organised, with the Tsar's approval, a charity performance in aid of the Disabled Soldiers' Work-house, which was run by a special Commission of the Supreme Council and was under the patronage of Her Majesty the Empress Alexandra Feodorovna. Countess Witte, with whom I was on excellent terms, had asked me to help her organise the performance, and I secured the services of our leading artists.

M. N. Kousnetzova sang the second act of *Manon* and danced

Spanish dances. Lidia Lipkovska sang the lesson scene from the third act of *The Barber of Seville*. D. A. Smirnov sang Lensky's aria from the duel scene of *Eugene Onegin*. Finally, Fokine and I appeared as Harlequin and Columbine in his ballet *Le Carnaval*. Next we danced the first act of *Don Quixote*, and Tamara Karsavina performed the waltz from the same ballet.

The evening was a triumphant success. It was a very elegant and select audience, and Fokine was delighted with my interpretation of the role of Columbine, which he had wanted me to dance. It was my first performance in this ballet in St. Petersburg; it was also to be my last appearance on the Imperial stage in the Maryinsky Theatre, where I had been dancing for twenty-seven years.

After the performance Countess Witte gave a supper party to which the leading artists and various members of high society were invited. It was served at little tables, and I remember that my neighbour was Stanislas Poklevsky, Russian Minister in Roumania. I was on excellent terms with Countess Witte, who was a woman of high intelligence, and André, who had closely followed the lectures on political economy given by the Count, held them both in very high esteem.

Every day brought more and more alarming news. Nobody knew the exact reasons for this anxiety, but a menacing, stormy atmosphere hung over the capital, and uncertainty increased. It had begun with vague reports, and nobody had been able to decide whether the situation was really serious, or whether these were merely rumours spread by a troubled populace. However, in the first week of February General Halle, Chief of Police of the Fourth District of the "Peterbourg-skaia", whom I knew very well and who had already warned me in January, telephoned me to advise me urgently to leave Petrograd with my son, at least for a short time. According to him, disturbances might break out at any moment in the capital on the occasion of the reopening of the Douma on February 14th. My house, at the beginning of the Kamennostrovsky Prospect, might be in particular danger. I realised then that there was a basis to these alarming rumours and decided to leave with my son for the Rauch Sanatorium, near Imatra, in Finland, where we stayed for about a week. P. N. Vladimirov came with us. Life in Imatra was normal. Wonderful weather, snow, excursions and a pleasant atmosphere all helped to soothe one's nerves. On the 15th General Halle informed me by telephone that all was calm in Petrograd, and that we could return, which we did. The atmosphere did indeed seem more relaxed, so much so that my sister persuaded me to arrange a dinner party.

On February 22nd I therefore gave a dinner party for twenty-four friends, for which I brought out my finest Limoges service, my Danish service for the fish, and gilt cutlery copied from two sets belonging to Catherine the Great which could be seen at the Hermitage. This had been given me by André. The guests were dazzled by the dinner table decorated with forget-me-nots and real lace. It was my swan song in Petrograd, my last dinner party before the Revolution. I brought out countless precious trinkets and works of art which had been stored since the beginning of the war (among other things there was a superb collection of artificial flowers made of precious stones and a small gold fir tree, with branches shimmering with little diamonds). There were so many of these things that I complained to my sister I had not enough room to display them. The fates were to take a cruel vengeance for these words: a few days later there was nothing left to display.

Next day, while my housekeeper was checking the silver, glass and linen, as she always did after large parties, Vova burst in and told me that a huge crowd was pouring out of Great Dvorianskaïa Street. This was the beginning of what everybody had been afraid of: street demonstrations.

The first three days, despite the disturbances, there was no thought of a revolution. On February 25th I went quite normally to the Alexandre Theatre, where Youriev's twenty-fifth stage anniversary was being celebrated with Lermontov's *The Masquerade*, produced by Meierhold. The audience was tense and nervous. There was a sound of firing in some quarters. But I was able to return without trouble.

On the 26th, a Sunday, General Halle telephoned me once more to warn me that the situation in the city was very serious, and that I should save what I could from my house before it was too late. He telephoned repeatedly all through the day. Although he still considered the situation very serious, he hoped it might improve "if the abscess burst". His advice to save what could still be saved placed me in a real dilemma. Although I never kept my large diamond jewellery at home, but left it with Fabergé, I still had at home a great number of small jewels, not to mention the silver and other precious objects with which my rooms were decorated. What was I to choose? What was I to take away, and where? In the street the storm was already raging.

The next day it was clear that, contrary to General Halle's hopes, the abscess was not going to burst, and that it would be foolish to count on any lull. The situation was growing worse from hour to hour. Lorries packed with soldiers brandishing red flags kept passing in front of the house. So as not to be taken by surprise, I had put my most valuable possessions and everything which had come to hand into a small suitcase.

We were five at dinner that evening: myself, Vova, George A. Pflüger, his tutor, and two dancers, P. N. Vladimirov and Paul Gontcharov; but we were too worried to eat. All day we had heard distant firing, and now there were explosions not far from the house. One thing was certain: we must leave the house at all costs as soon as possible, before the mob invaded it. In order to be inconspicuous, I put on my plainest coat and threw a shawl over my head. Suddenly, in the fever of preparation, I thought of Djibi, my little fox-terrier. He was there, motionless, looking at me fixedly, with his enormous eyes full of fear. Poor Djibi understood instinctively that something terrible had happened, that everybody was preparing to leave and that we were going to forget him! Someone took him in his arms, someone else seized the case with my jewels, and we dashed out. But where were we to go? It was already after eight o'clock. Who in the neighbourhood could give us shelter? I suddenly remembered that Youriev, a member of our Drama Company, lived quite near. I was sure he would not refuse to take us in, even for a few days, while we waited for the situation to improve. We hurried there. He lived on the fifth and top floor of a block of flats on the corner of Kamennostrovsky Prospect. We spent three days with him, without even undressing. Armed soldiers constantly burst into the flat, to climb on to the roof. They were looking for machine-guns, and threatened to shoot us if they found any. We had to remove all large-sized objects from the windows, because the mob outside took them for machine-guns and were always on the point of opening fire on us. As a precaution against stray bullets, we all remained in the corridor.

During all this time our meals were brought from my house by my servants, who remained loyal to me to the end, with the exception of Katia, the cow-hand, and Roubtzova, my housekeeper. I was not particularly put out that the cow-hand should have taken advantage of the revolution to rob me; but Roubtzova's behaviour upset me deeply.

I had engaged Roubtzova as housekeeper after the death of her husband, Nicholas Nicolaievitch Roubtzov, a painter-decorator whom we knew well and were very fond of. He had decorated, among other places, the Grand Duchess Olga Alexandrovna's palace. He was very hospitable and lived very comfortably. After his death, however, his widow was left resourceless; I therefore took her in as housekeeper and gave her a very nice apartment in my house, where she settled

29. As Columbine in *Carnaval*, London, 1911.

30. My brother, Joseph Kschessinsky, and his daughter in the mazurka.

with her children. Since Roubtzov had often played poker with us, we began every time we played to put aside in memory of him a certain sum for his widow, and helped her out with grants from the capital so formed. At the time of the revolution this capital had reached the figure of 20,000 roubles, a considerable sum in those days. And now Roubtzova was receiving the revolutionaries with open arms and greeting them with the words, "Come in! Come in! The bird has flown!" This happened the very day after I left the house, which was already occupied by a gang headed by a Georgian student named Agabagov. This gentleman began to give a great many dinner parties, and forced my cook to serve him and his guests. My champagne flowed in torrents. My two cars were, of course, requisitioned.

We had been at Youriev's three days when my brother Iouzia joined me. It was decided that I should go and live with him. I therefore took Djibi, but left all my jewellery with Youriev: it would have been dangerous to go out with it. Since there was no other means of communication, we crossed the city on foot. It was bitterly cold, and the north wind was blowing hard, particularly on Troitzky Bridge. My light coat was not much protection, and I was chilled to the marrow when we finally reached my brother's house, No. 38 Liteiny Prospect, on the corner of Spasskaïa Street.

As soon as I was in his flat, I burst into tears—tears which seemed to relieve me of the accumulated sufferings and horrors of the last three days.

I was especially afraid for Vova, fearing that he might be taken from me. Fortunately, nobody knew where I was. The soldiers who had kept on bursting into Youriev's flat were ignorant of our identity. Otherwise Vova's fate and mine might have ended in tragedy.

I settled in with my brother on March 1st, just a day before my birthday. But even there I was not calm. I listened to the slightest noise coming from the street. The worst moments were when a lorry passed before the house. I always thought that it was stopping in front of our door, bringing inevitable searches, arrests or worse still . . .

On the second day we heard the worst news we could imagine: the Tsar had abdicated! It seemed so extraordinary that we could scarcely believe it. It was not, it could not be, true! Why should the Tsar have abdicated? What purpose had he in doing so? This was followed by a second overwhelming piece of news: the Grand Duke Michel Alexandrovitch was also resigning! A provisional Government had taken over. One by one the institutions of state were crumbling. And

Petrograd was a nightmare world of arrests, the assassination of officers in the streets, arson, pillage . . . and I thought of the dangers which all the people I loved were undergoing—André, Serge, the Emperor and his Family.

I was still in my brother's flat when my porter rang up to say that my house was being looted. I did not dare to go myself, but begged my sister and Vladimirov to go and find out what was happening. So they went and rang at my front door, which was opened by a soldier in open tunic, carrying a gun in his hand. He invited them to come into the room which they were using as a guard-room, and asked them what they wanted. My sister explained that she had been warned that the house had been ransacked. He answered that everything was as it should be, and showed them into the dining-room, where the gold cups were still on the shelves. But her conversation with this soldier revealed that some cases had been removed by the militia and taken to the headquarters of the Petrograd Prefect. Vladimirov at once telephoned the latter, who asked my sister to come and see him. The new Prefect received her courteously in his office, listened to her with attention; then, opening a drawer, he took out a gold crown (which the balletomanes had presented to me) and asked: "Do you know this object?" When she said that she did, he led her into a neighbouring room and showed her the cases from my house. My sister explained that our porter had warned us of attempts to loot the house. The Prefect promised to take the necessary steps to save what was left; but, in fact, nothing was done.

Some time later the crown and the cases of silver were given back to me by the police. I stored the crown, together with other things which my butler had managed to save, in the safes of the Friendly Society. I handed in the cases of silver-ware to the Bank of Azov and the Don, whose Director, Kamenka, was a great friend of mine. I still have the Bank's receipt, acknowledging my deposit. Later Kamenka, whom I met in France during the emigration, assured me that the cases were so well hidden that they would never be found. He even held out hopes of a speedy restoration of my property!

As I have said, my largest and most valuable jewels were deposited with Fabergé. But after the Revolution Fabergé asked me to withdraw them, since he was afraid that the premises might be searched and all the jewellery and precious stones found in the safes confiscated. So I placed the jewellery withdrawn from Fabergé and also the pieces I had taken from home in an official savings-box which I deposited in the

State Savings Bank. I made an estimate of the contents myself, naming an inferior sum on purpose so as to avoid paying excessive charges: I was in financial straits, and could not risk paying too much. "But there's several millions' worth here!" exclaimed the Director of the Savings Bank, startled by such a low estimate.

A few days after I had left home, Bers, an officer I knew who had just been appointed commander of the Peter-and-Paul Fortress, offered to let me live in the Fortress, where he could put rooms at our disposal. He did his best to convince me that I would be perfectly safe there, but I declined his offer. The idea of being shut up in a fortress hardly appealed to me; and I was also afraid that in case of another revolution another commander might be appointed, which would have put me in an impossible position.

When I was more or less recovered, I began to wonder whom I could go to for defence. During the first days I had told nobody where I was living, and my friends had lost sight of me. So I decided to return to them, and I turned first to P. N. Karabtchevsky. As a well-known lawyer, he had many strings to his bow: I had also been told that he was on good terms with Kerensky. I also remembered the performance at his house, and how he had promised: "Kill someone! I'll defend you, and you will be acquitted!" I had not killed anybody, but I was in a difficult position: the time had come for him to defend me. So I telephoned Karabtchevsky, in the certainty that he would help me and use his influence with Kerensky to spare me further trouble. The result was totally unexpected: Karabtchevsky replied that I was Kschessinska, that it was the wrong time to act on behalf of Kschessinska, and so on. I did not even go on listening, but snapped down the receiver.

Fortunately for me, one of my old friends, Vladimir Pimenovitch Krymov, editor and publisher of the famous review, *Stolitsa and Oussadba*, came soon afterwards to see me. A talented writer and journalist, Krymov was also a sincere man, with firm, unshakable opinions both before and after the Revolution. He was an intimate of our house, where he had met André, who thought highly of his clear intelligence and moderation. When I told him how I stood, he at once dictated a letter to Kerensky for me, which we immediately took to the Ministry of Justice. The moment I was back, Kerensky telephoned me. He proved extremely kind, promised to protect me against any trouble and gave me his private telephone number, with the assurance that I could telephone him at any hour of the day or night if I needed his help. I was deeply moved by his attitude: though I had never met him and we did not know each other at all, he was giving me this extremely kind reply. I felt at last that I was no longer alone.

Michel Alexandrovitch Stakhovitch, an admirer and great friend, appointed Governor-General of Finland by the Provisional Government, came to assure me that he was ready to do anything to improve my position.

A third faithful friend, Viktorov, proved his friendship not only by words but by deeds in the very first days of street disturbances. I had left the case with my jewellery at Youriev's house. I now asked Viktorov to get it back to me in any way he could. I did not give him another mission, to bring me the Tsar's last photograph, signed by him, which I had also hidden in Youriev's house. I had taken this photograph when I had fled from home, and, anticipating possible searches, had slipped it in an illustrated magazine on a table in the flat. I had left it there on purpose, for it would have been dangerous to have it on me, and I did not mention it to Viktorov, in order not to compromise him in case he was arrested in the street. But I cannot understand how I later left this treasured possession in Youriev's flat.

Viktorov soon reappeared, to my immense relief, safe and sound, and with my suitcase. He was not carrying it himself, however: it was in the hands of a soldier I had never seen! Viktorov later explained to me that as the case was very heavy he had stopped a soldier on the way and asked him to help him carry it. The soldier willingly did this for him, especially as Viktorov wore a uniform very like his own. Besides, Viktorov had quite rightly judged that nobody would take any notice of what a soldier was carrying.

After I had spent some time at my brother's, I ventured one day alone to the Palais de Tauride, to ask that the characters occupying my house should be expelled: I wanted to lend it to an embassy. I was taken in and out of the enormous rooms and halls in the Palace looking for the right official. I was conducted from department to department. every room was full of smoke and reeked of tobacco, the floor was littered with papers and cigarette stubs, everything was a mass of incredible dirt, and terrible people kept on appearing, with busy expressions on their faces. I remember that I also saw Kolontai, who is now dead; she was perched on a high stool, her legs crossed rather too daringly, a cigarette in her lips and a cup of tea in her hand. . . .

Finally, in this motley crowd, I found the person I wanted. He was a fairly decent man, whose name I have forgotten; it may have been Beliavin. Anyway, he listened to what I had to say and at once came with me to clear up the situation on the spot and try to help me.

When I entered my house I was rooted to the spot with astonishment: the magnificent marble staircase leading into the hall and covered with a red carpet was cluttered with books which women were carelessly handling. When I began to go up they assailed me furiously, claiming that I was treading on their books. I could not help indignantly retorting that I was in my own home and could go where I wanted. Then I was shown into the study on the ground floor, and my companion politely asked me to sit in an armchair, the very one in which I had so much liked resting in the past! One of the soldiers in the house was a very decent fellow. When my guide asked him why he and his companions had stayed such a long time in my house, by way of answer he showed me the corner window, which gave an excellent view of the Troitzky Bridge and the embankment. He implied that this was very important for them. I now understood that they were probably Bolsheviks, and were preparing for another uprising. They did not want to give up a convenient observation post, which allowed them to watch the bridge, and, if necessary, to hold it under fire. My guide now offered to let me telephone to my family. I was thus able to speak to Vova, and tried to reassure him by saying that I was surrounded by decent people and that everything was all right. Next I was invited to go into my bedroom, but I was greeted there by a terrible sight: a wonderful carpet had been stained with ink; most of the furniture had been taken down to the floor below; a period cupboard had had its door ripped off, hinges and all, and the remains were being used as a rifle rack. I could not bear such vandalism, and hastened from my room. The bath in my bathroom was full of cigarette stubs. Agababov, the student who had been the first occupant and had now settled here, now came up to me and insolently offered to let me come back and share the house with him, adding that I should be given my son's rooms. I did not reply. Downstairs, in the drawing-room, I was greeted by a no less sickening sight: the grand piano, a mahogany Bechstein, had been moved, for no conceivable reason, into the winter garden and wedged between two pillars, which had naturally been greatly damaged in the process. It was then that my head porter told me that on the very evening I had left the house, my tame white pigeon had flown out through the open window and never returned. I left the house which I had built with so much love in great sadness.

I went back once more, with Hessin, my lawyer, who had helped me in my endeavours, and Vladimirov and Pavloucha Gontcharov. We were received by the same soldier and shown into the little corner

Louis XVI drawing-room, where the floor was strewn with chests for silver and knick-knack cases. Pointing to them, the soldier said, "You see! It's all there, as you left it!" In fact, as I was later to learn, everything had already been pillaged: the chests and cases were empty. Two sailors kept on telling me to speak low. Vladimirov, who was walking next to them, suddenly came and whispered to me that I must leave the house immediately. I followed his order at once, realising that something serious was happening. When we were in the street Vladimirov explained that he had happened to hear the sailors' conversation, and that it was about me. I am small, and I seemed even smaller in my black coat and with a shawl on my head. One of the sailors had said, "I thought she was tall! She's tiny! Why don't we do away with her straight away?"

When all my efforts to turn the occupants out of my house had proved unavailing, I determined to approach Kerensky in person, and went to the Ministry of Justice. Kerensky received me most politely and explained that my house could not be emptied: any attempt to do so would involve bloodshed, which would merely complicate matters. Later I became convinced that he was not in a position to act.

I was overwhelmed at the idea of being homeless and of being reduced to ask for shelter, especially when I realised what an embarrassment I was to those who kept me.

I therefore decided, after spending about three weeks with my brother, to go and live with my sister in the English Prospect. I stayed there three days, then moved to the flat of Lili Likhatcheva, my great friend, before moving into Vladimirov's tiny flat in Alexeevska Street, which he lent me.

Ludmilla, my maid, and Arnold, my butler, came regularly to help me in the kitchen. Arnold was an excellent cook. As a Swiss citizen, he could go on living in my house, and took advantage of this to bring me any small things he could carry away without being noticed. Ludmilla lived with her mother, but often went to the house, and almost always succeeded in bringing me a pair of shoes from it. She took her shoes off before entering my wardrobe, which she entered on bended knees, to hide her feet under her skirt, put on my shoes and went away again looking completely unconcerned! She told me that the soldiers had broken some scent bottles and torn to shreds a magnificent lawn and cambric bedspread. Even Katia, the cow-hand, brought me back my black velvet skirt, which she had stolen and then unpicked because she was fatter than I was. When she learned that

Kerensky was protecting me, she had taken fright, and so gave me back the skirt, which was later to prove useful. She brought me at the same time a childhood photograph of Tsar Alexander III, which shows him with his brother, the Grand Duke Wladimir Alexandrovitch. The Grand Duke looked astonishingly like Vova in this photograph, and Katia had taken it for a picture of my son.

I led a fairly calm life in Vladimirov's apartment. The first wave of the Revolution was over, and was succeeded by a calm, though this was merely on the surface. For Easter, which fell on April 2nd, my dear Denis sent me a traditional meal, prepared by himself, which I shared with Babicha Romanov and his wife, Liolia Smirnova.

One day I was visited by Semion Nicolaievitch Rogov, the balleto-mane and journalist, whom I knew well. He had been called up and drafted to the reserve battalion of the Kexholm Regiment, part of the Guard; he wore the uniform and mixed constantly with the soldiers. He was therefore perfectly informed on the state of mind prevailing in the barracks and on what went on there. Rogov called on me to make me a strange and rather unexpected proposal: would I participate in a performance which the soldiers of his regiment were organising in the Conservatoire Theatre? I was naturally appalled at this idea, which seemed preposterous. I, Kschessinska, to dance before soldiers and at such a time? It was pure madness! In spite of my objections, Rogov set out to convince me that it was a serious and long-thought-out plan. He tried to prove that I would do much better to give my own free consent: these performances were becoming frequent, and artists were more or less constrained to take part. Rogov finally succeeded in gaining my support with the assurance that I should be in no danger and that my appearance would be greeted with universal enthusiasm. Afterwards I should be able to move freely about town without fear, instead of hiding as hitherto. My wardrobe was still intact, and my Russian costume and everything needed was brought.

The day of the performance arrived. I was at home, dressed and in make-up, waiting for my lawyer, Hessin, Vladimirov and Paul Gontcharov to return from a reconnaissance visit to the theatre, where they had gone to gauge the atmosphere and find out if I could also go; for in spite of Rogov's assurances, my friends preferred to find out for themselves. So they mixed with the crowd of soldiers, listening to their conversation. The soldiers' attitude to me was hostile, and so they first told me that it would be better not to go yet to the theatre. But they did so much good work vaunting my merits in the soldiers' eyes, saying that I was a wonderful dancer and that everybody would fall into an ecstasy when I appeared on stage, that the prevailing attitude gradually changed and Rogov was at last able to fetch me.

I was more dead than alive, and hardly conscious of what was going on round me. Many of the corps de ballet were in the wings, waiting as anxiously as the organisers. Even Rogov had later to admit that till the very last moment, in spite of his assertions, he was consumed with terrible anxiety. I looked very pale in spite of my make-up; but if I was afraid of the moment when I would have to appear on stage, my main preoccupation was for Vova, whom I had left alone at home in my uncertainty of what awaited me at the theatre. Nervously and with hesitation, I at last dared to leave the wings and face the audience. What happened next is difficult to describe. The whole audience rose and greeted me with a thunderous volley of applause. The ovation was such that the orchestra had to stop playing. And all this lasted some time—almost a quarter of an hour, according to Rogov! After this I was able to perform my Russian dance, which completely carried away the audience. I had to give an encore, and received such a welcome that I could have done it once more; but I no longer had the strength left. The soldiers, transported, were throwing their caps on to the stage. In the wings many people were crying, unable to bear the sudden transition from worry to enthusiasm. I returned home exhausted, but as it were relieved of a burden: I had kept my word, everything had gone off well. . . . But few knew what it had cost me!

It was to be my last appearance in Russia; and by the vagaries of fortune it took place in the Conservatoire Theatre, the scene, long ago, of my very first appearance!

A rising of the Bolsheviks, accompanied by grave disorders throughout the town, was expected on May 1st. I was afraid to remain alone with my son in Vladimirov's apartment, and joyfully accepted the invitation of our old friend, Vizan, the Siamese Minister, to spend these few days with him. We remained forty-eight hours in the Embassy, where my sister and her husband also found asylum. Baron Zeddeler had been arrested and set free at the beginning of the Revolution, and we were afraid he might be re-arrested.

At the beginning of June the Grand Duke Serge returned to Petrograd. Members of the Imperial Family were forbidden to serve in the Army, but an exception was made for him, and he was officially asked to continue his duties. He went on for three months. It was a terrible blow for him to be torn from his career and from the artillery to which he had devoted his whole life.

He had been allowed to keep a car, in which we were able to go for drives. In the course of one of these I caught sight of one of my own cars; but I distinctly felt that I had been recognised by its occupants, and we hurried back. Shortly afterwards one of my cars was given back to me, and I hastened to sell it before it was permanently requisitioned.

My faithful Djibi died after a visit to Tsarskoïe Selo. This made me very sad. He had shared in our joys and sorrows; and I still remember one night during the terrible time we had just been through when, exhausted and near to nervous prostration, I flung myself weeping on my bed. Djibi had sprung towards me, with an expression of human compassion, whimpering that he could not comfort me. Vova and I took him to the garden at Strelna, where he had so recently trotted and played. This time the soldiers who occupied my *datcha* behaved touchingly and helped us to dig and fill in the little grave.

This was not the first time I had been back to my *datcha* since the Revolution. Everything had been turned upside-down, and much of the furniture was missing. The soldiers were always very polite and correct in their behaviour towards me. They proposed of their own accord to look after my son during his walks in the park, where he sadly revisited the scenes of his happy games, now ravaged and gone to waste. The oldest soldier even offered to let Vova live in his lodge, and guaranteed to see that he would be safe. And when I wanted to have my Swedish birchwood piano with a few other things that were still safe moved to Petrograd, the soldiers gladly undertook the work; the whole load, put on a large four-wheeled cart, arrived safely home. In memory of this service, the soldiers asked me to give them some of my photographs. On the whole they had not yet been deeply affected by revolutionary propaganda, and there were some well-meaning people among them.

On June 18th, my son's birthday, Vova, Vladimirov, the Grand Duke Serge Mikhailovitch and I went to Finland, to the estate belonging to Nicolas Alexandrovitch Oblakov, a teacher in the Boys' Section of the Imperial Theatre School and P. N. Vladimirov's great friend. Oblakov's estate was not far from Bieloostrov Station. We spent three or four days there before returning to the capital, where I remained almost another month. After so many hardships, this stay was a real time of peace.

CHAPTER XXII

IN THE CAUCASUS

Almost six months had gone by since my enforced separation from André. I had but a single wish, to rejoin him in Kislovodsk. I knew from his letters that the wave of revolution had scarcely touched the district, and that life there was normal. Many families were in fact leaving Petrograd for the Caucasus and its watering towns, Piatigorsk, Essentouki and Kislovodsk. These spas were comfortable and had an excellent climate. Count Kokovtzev and his wife had already left, as had Countess Karlova with her whole family, the Cheremetievs, the Vorontzovs, and many others. Members of the world of finance had also assembled in the same region. They all thought it dangerous to remain in the capital, where rioting might start up again at any moment. There were many who also hoped that being close to the border and the Black Sea they would be able to leave Russia more easily in case of danger.

For my part, I wanted not only to rejoin André, but also to take Vova as far as possible from Petrograd, and to settle with him, if only for a time, in a safe place: I was becoming exhausted with continual fears for our safety. Furthermore, deprived of my house in Petrograd and my *datcha* in Strelna, I could not but be a nuisance to those who were sheltering me. In leaving for Kislovodsk, I expected to return to Petrograd in the autumn, to gain possession of my property once again, and to start a new life—though what kind of life, in view of the many problems I would have to face, was still uncertain. In all this two feelings filled me, happiness at seeing André again and remorse at leaving Serge alone in Petrograd, where he was in constant danger. I was also very sorry to deprive him of Vova's company, and Vova of his. He devoted his spare time to him, and kept a close watch on his education.

I was deeply troubled by all these considerations, but the thought of my son's safety and my wish to see André as soon as possible again finally decided me to settle for some time in Kislovodsk. Nobody foresaw the outcome of events, and we went on planning in the same old way.

It was dangerous at the time to travel in Russia without a safe-conduct, vouching that the bearer was not liable to prosecution for his

activities under the old régime. So I made my application to A. F.
Kerensky, as head of the Provisional Government, and soon afterwards
received the necessary permit from the Minister of Justice, Paul
Nicolaïevitch Pereverzev, a document which allowed me not only to
travel freely all over Russia, but also to live wherever I pleased.

The moment of departure and separation came. The Grand Duke
Serge Mikhailovitch accompanied us to Nicholas Station. He was
already in civilian clothes, and I can still see him standing motionless
on the platform in his long overcoat and gazing, with infinite sadness,
after the train as it moved slowly away. . . . Fate was to make this
temporary parting a final separation.

I left Petrograd on July 13th. Ludmilla, my faithful maid, and Ivan
Kournossov, my former manservant, who had just been demobilised,
left with me. Kournossov was to look after Vova, whose valet,
Koulakov, had disappeared at the beginning of the Revolution. The
first days of the journey were uneventful; but after Moscow the train
was invaded by a crowd of deserters who proclaimed the reign of
"liberty", announcing that everybody could do what he wanted.
They found their way into the sleeping compartments, entered the
coaches, and we had almost to barricade ourselves in ours.

We reached Kislovodsk at ten in the evening. André had booked
rooms for us in a furnished house. We went straight off, with André
and Kube, to dine under the arbour of a Caucasian restaurant, and
after the long, difficult journey the meal seemed exceptionally good.

We often recalled that dreamlike evening in such beautiful surroundings, the scene bathed in moonlight, while music played far off.
We were at last together again, and my joy at seeing André was so
great that for a time I forgot our trials.

We met Fokine and his wife, who were also in Kislovodsk, and who
shared our hopes and fears. There was only one subject of conversation:
Should we stay or leave? What was going to happen? What should
we do?

My sister and her husband joined us on August 29th and settled in
a wing of the villa; a month later the Grand Duke Boris Wladimirovitch and one of his best friends, Leon Mantachev, an oil magnate, also
arrived. It soon became clear that there was no point in even thinking
of returning to Petrograd. My hopes of recovering my home vanished
daily. Moreover, in view of the general situation, it was better to
spend the winter in Kislovodsk. So I started to look for a new house,
since Stcherbin's villa, which was planned as a summer residence,

had no heating. By luck I found a magnificent villa belonging to Beliaievsky, an engineer, charmingly furnished and having a little garden. My sister and Baron Zeddeler settled there with me. I immediately engaged a cook and organised my household. Although I was accustomed to greater comfort and luxury, I at last felt at peace, and happy to have a modest home after four months of wandering.

Before we moved in, Vladimirov came over to see me from Sotchi, where he was following a cure. While he was staying with me he fell off a horse; he suffered a broken nose and severe bruises, and was confined to his room for a long time.

My life was taking shape and I was surrounded by a wide circle of friends from Petrograd. But I was harrowed by the thought that the Grand Duke Serge Mikhailovitch was still exposed to the dangers of the capital. In my letters I tried to persuade him to come to Kislovodsk. He could even have stayed with Count Cheremetiev, one of his earliest friends, with whom he would have been completely at home. But it was no good. The Grand Duke kept on putting off his departure, hoping to succeed in his many attempts to recover my house. He also wanted to send and store abroad his mother's jewellery, in my name; but this project failed, because the British Ambassador, to whom he had applied, refused to help. Further, he wished to save what was left of my furniture by storing it with Meltzer. Apparently his efforts were crowned with success; but in my case this served no purpose.

When he had recovered from his accident, Vladimirov returned to Petrograd in October 1917 to resume his career in the theatre. When he left he promised me to do his utmost to help the Grand Duke Serge Mikhailovitch, and he kept his word by making attempts to obtain permission for the Grand Duke to go to Finland. But this plan came to nothing, for, like many other members of the Imperial Family, the Grand Duke did not dare leave Russia, fearing that his departure might have grievious repercussions on the fate of the Tsar. And travelling was still dangerous, still more so for a Grand Duke, even if he had a safe-conduct.

When we heard of the new Bolshevik Revolution and of the new Government's first measures—the confiscation of all bank accounts, savings and property belonging to the "bourgeois", we realised that in a single day we had become penniless.

With the loss of my house vanished any possibility there might have been of returning to St. Petersburg and recovering my most precious possessions, the Tsar's letters and his last photograph, which

31. In the ballet *Le Pavillon d'Armide*.

32. In the ballet *Le Pavillon d'Armide*.

I had left in Youriev's flat. I had put the letters in a casket which I
entrusted to a devoted friend, the widow of Inkin, the artillery officer,
whose daughter, Zoë, was Vova's childhood friend. When I gave the
casket to Inkina I believed that my friend was quite safe from prosecution and search, and was convinced that it would be quite safe with
her. As for the photograph, I hoped it could stay in Youriev's flat
until better days arrived.

As soon as we decided to remain in Kislovodsk, Vova entered the
local grammar school, an excellent establishment with first-class
teachers, where he finished his secondary education. He made many
friends there, "all as troublesome as himself!" according to Ivan, who
was indignant at seeing Vova return home, his suit and overcoat torn,
still breathless from running and playing in the park.

The Bolshevik flood, which engulfed province after province, did
not reach Kislovodsk until the beginning of 1918. Until then our life
was fairly quiet, apart from searches and looting carried out under the
most varied pretexts.

The days passed by in uncertainty and waiting. We often met with
friends for tea, dinner, or a game of cards, and especially to talk freely.

It was not until January 1918 that Bolshevism began to make itself
felt in Kislovodsk. Until then we only heard rumours of what was
going on elsewhere, nearer the large towns, and we could see that our
turn to taste the delights of the new régime would not be long in
coming.

The first of the spas to be reached by the Red wave was Piatigorsk,
the administrative centre of the district. The first moves were the
arrest of officers, the closing of banks, the post office and the telephone
exchange—everything, in fact, which had happened in Petrograd the
previous October at the time of the Bolshevik Revolution. A few days
later, without warning, the same happened in Kislovodsk.

On January 27th 1918 I had invited a few friends to dinner, and we
were sitting at table when a band of Red soldiers burst into the villa to
search it and confiscate weapons. They even wanted to remove Vova's
little dagger, and Ivan, my manservant, intervened: "Aren't you
ashamed to set on a child?" There was a threatening silence, and finally
the soldiers left him alone. Shortly after they had left one of them
secretly returned and warned us immediately to put out the lights and
to scatter, or we should be in danger. We at once followed his advice.
But I was surprised to find a decent man among them.

About six weeks went by without any other incident than a light

G

earthquake on February 14th, a natural danger scarcely designed to alleviate the anxiety in which we lived.

On April 13th a financial commission arrived in Kislovodsk, headed by Commissar Bulle, probably of Lithuanian origin, and sent by Moscow to extract from the "bourgeois" living in the spas a contribution of thirty million roubles. We were taken without ceremony to the Grand Hotel, where the commission sat. We had a great many Jewish friends among us, including Rebecca Markovna Weinstein, who then proved a true friend to me. Owing to her political opinions, she had at first refused to meet André; but she met him later, and grew to like him very much. I was severely ill that day and could scarcely stand. Seeing my condition, Rebecca Weinstein turned to Commissar Bulle and told him that Mathilde Kschessinska was in the room, that she was ill, that she had been among the first to be hit by the Revolution and that, having already lost house and money, she had nothing further to give the Commission. Bulle then drew near and enquired, with perfect correctness, about my health. He advised me to go straight home, put a car at my disposal, and ordered someone to accompany me. After that I was never again asked for a contribution.

A little later two Bolsheviks, one called Ozol and the other Martzinkevitch, if I remember rightly, came to see me in my villa. Ozol began by taking his medals and insignia out of his pocket, and told me that he had been wounded during the war and looked after in the Grand Duchess Olga Alexandrovna's nursing-home. He was boasting and obviously trying to impress me. Martzinkevitch, who was young, slim and handsome, wore a *tcherkesska* and behaved very well. The purpose of their visit was to invite me to dance at a charity performance which they intended to organise in aid of the wounded of the district. I was surprised but still more indignant at their request; and I must have shown it, because they both hastened to assure me that many of those who would benefit from the performance had kept their former convictions. They had probably realised that I would never have agreed to dance for Bolsheviks alone. When I had explained that, even if I had wanted to dance, I could not, since I had no costumes in Kislovodsk, they at once proposed to have them sent from St. Petersburg. Naturally, I refused decisively to appear at their performance, but agreed to sell tickets, programmes and even, I think, champagne. They had come to ask me to help, and I was afraid that if I refused entirely I might get into trouble, if not with them, at any rate with their friends; and I had at all costs to avoid misunderstandings with the present authorities. Ozol left, but Martzinkevitch stayed behind on some pretext; he clearly wanted to speak to me alone. He asked me to inform him at once if I had trouble of any kind. Such an offer from a Bolshevik was, to say the least, welcome and surprising.

Some time later, during a performance of a concert at the casino, Martzinkevitch saw me in the stalls, approached me and, in the sight of all, respectfully kissed my hand.

The charity performance to which Ozol and Martzinkevitch had invited me passed uneventfully and even impressed me most favourably. The organisers received me as I had always been received, vying in their attentions to me. When the performance was over, they offered to see me home, but in the end my old friend, Constantin Molostrov, a former officer in the Horse Guard, performed this task. Whenever I met Martzinkevitch after this, he always seemed very sad. Everything pointed to the fact that he was not entirely in sympathy with the new régime which he was serving. The last time I saw him, in the Grand Hotel, he told me he was being sent on a mission somewhere. I never saw him again and have never heard him mentioned.

At about the same time, in spring, 1918, before Bolshevism took its bloody appearance, Lydia Alexeevna Davydova formed the plan of organising for the Home of the Wounded a children's evening which might do something to entertain the children and take their minds off political events.

Lydia Alexeevna, _née_ Mestcherinov, had married Eugene Feodorovitch Davydov, who, like his two brothers, belonged to the world of finance. His eldest brother, Victor Feodorovitch, was Director of the Russo-Asiatic Bank, and his second brother, Leonid Feodorovitch, was head of Credit Chancery in the Ministry of Finance. Lydia Alexeevna and her husband were well off and led a comfortable life. Very beautiful, and with four charming daughters, she was fairly prominent in Kislovodsk life.

For the performance she had in mind, Lydia Alexeevna wanted my son to take the principal part in a fairy tale, _The Caliph Who Became a Stork_. I was not very pleased with the idea. I could see no acting talent in my son, and was afraid it would be a miserable failure. But by her insistence she drove away my doubts, and when I risked attending one of the last rehearsals I was more than agreeably surprised: Vova acted his part admirably. With Ludmilla's help, I made him a lovely costume, which I have kept, and two headdresses, a turban and a stork's head, for he played each part in turn. With the help of some advice from me, he and his friends had an unqualified success before a full house.

But the most original thing about the evening was that in one box

could be seen the Grand Duke Boris Wladimirovitch, the representative
of the Imperial dynasty, and in another Commissars Bulle, Lestchinsky
and Martzinkevitch, representing the new Government, the power of
Bolshevism!

Kislovodsk was not taken over all at once by the Bolsheviks, but
gradually. An armoured train would suddenly arrive with its band
of Red Guards and commissars, and then depart again, and a period
of relative calm would follow this upheaval. During these periods of
calm, life resumed its normal course, and we continued to forgather.
If we had permission to go about by night, we came back before
dawn, although this was becoming increasingly dangerous. This was
proved to me one night when I was returning home with Molostrov.
We were suddenly hailed by a threatening "Who goes there?" and the
only answer to our explanations was a rude "Hurry up, or I'll shoot
you in the back!" Another time I was coming back with Marinov, one
of our card partners: he owned a paper-mill, and passed for a rich
man. We had just passed the footbridge over the railway and were
approaching Vokzalnaïa Avenue, where my villa was, when we saw
two suspicious characters in leather jackets sitting on a bench. As soon
as we had gone by, I became certain that we were being followed. I
was carrying a box with our card counters, which rattled as we walked.
The way seemed endless. I did not dare turn round, and my heart was
beating horribly. We finally reached the gate. I said goodbye to
Marinov and went in. But I had hardly begun to undress when
there was a nervous ringing at the front door; the ringing became
insistent, in quick, impatient bursts. My maid went to the door and
saw poor Marinov, disfigured and unrecognisable, his clothes in
shreds. He told me that he had been assaulted, soon after leaving me,
by the two men we had seen on the bench. They had pulled off his
rings, seized his wallet and cigarette case, and, when he tried to resist,
had knocked him about. Thenceforth I gave up going out at night,
even when I was not alone.

My house was sometimes searched, especially at night and under
various pretexts. One day some soldiers from the Red Army burst in,
wanting to check our passports. I showed them mine, adding shortly
that it was genuine and that I was an artist of the Imperial Theatre.
One of them meanwhile seized it and proceeded to examine it—upside-down! I then snatched it from his hands and told him that an
illiterate had no need to see my passport. After which Ivan, who had
received them coldly, rapidly showed them out.

Another day, the 7th or 8th of June, some soldiers came to make a search very early in the morning. In spite of my fears, they did not touch anything; they were obviously looking for someone. I found out later that the whole of Kislovodsk had been searched that day in the hope of laying hands on the Grand Duke Michel Alexandrovitch after a rumour that he had escaped from Perm and reached the Caucasus. In fact, he was assassinated exactly at this time.

Searches generally involved the confiscation of any valuables which the soldiers found, and so we all taxed our ingenuity in hiding jewellery and silver. But the hiding-places had often to be changed, since almost everybody had recourse to the same devices, and once the soldiers had made one discovery they then went straight to the hiding-place. For instance, people would fix bank-notes under a chest in which they left only unimportant objects. One day, however, the soldiers saw this, and at once after this they started lifting cases, caskets and trunks. I hid my money on the ground floor, under the upper window frames. The few small jewels I had taken with me I secreted in a hollow leg of my bed, and fixed a string to them in order to take them out easily. Some people hid them in jars of ointment and face-cream; but the soldiers soon dipped their fingers in these. Women who could not refrain from boasting about their hiding-places ended by paying dearly for their gossiping.

I was also several times visited by a man who appeared somewhat unbalanced. He always asked where I was and insisted on seeing me. I hid as soon as he was announced and Ludmilla always told him that I was out. Hoping no doubt to accost me in the street, he then begged Ludmilla to tell him what I looked like. She realised that it would have been dangerous to give him my description, and set out cheerfully to describe our cook, who was tall, fat and red-headed. The result was that one day he spotted the aforesaid cook and thinking that it was I he cried out, "Ah! here she is at last!" But he soon had to change his tune. I met him again, when I was having tea with my son, my sister and Baron Zeddeler. He approached the last-named and engaged him in conversation. He clearly knew that he was speaking to my sister's husband, and I was afraid he might recognise me. I tried to make myself look like a little girl by making myself as small as possible, hiding my face under my hat and leaning towards Vova. Fortunately, the trick worked.

I was also visited at this time by a picturesque character wearing a coarse cloth shirt and black tie, and accompanied by a soldier, who called himself an anarchist. While the soldier searched the villa, the "anarchist" gave me long advice about where not to hide things. He seemed to like us, and became friends with my brother-in-law. Later Baron Zeddeler met him in the street, dead drunk. He admitted to my brother-in-law that it was sorrow which drove him to drink, since the cause he served had brought him nothing but disillusionment.

Thus we lived, from day to day, in this menacing atmosphere, never knowing what was going to happen to us the next day, or even from one hour to the next. Armoured trains kept on arriving from Piatigorsk, bringing more soldiers: this meant news of more arrests, new searches and fresh looting. We lived in perpetual torment, afraid for ourselves, our relatives, our friends. . . .

CHAPTER XXIII

BETWEEN LIFE AND DEATH

IN THE EARLY HOURS of the morning of June 14th, we heard distant shots, which seemed to come from near the station and which gradually drew nearer. They soon became more and more frequent, turning into a real volley. The rumour went round the town that the Cossacks were coming to Kislovodsk, pursuing the routed Bolsheviks. Mounted Cossacks did in fact ride across town, to the inhabitants' delight; but very soon the firing died away, to be followed by a sepulchral silence. We could see neither Cossacks nor Bolsheviks. Nobody knew exactly what had happened. But one thing was clear: if the Cossacks had really come, they had left straight away again, and we were still at the Bolsheviks' mercy. Our fears, alas, proved justified, and gangs of Red soldiers began to roam about town once more, arresting everybody whom they suspected of nourishing Cossack sympathies. We later learnt that it had been a partisan raid, at Chkouro's orders, with the only purpose of robbing the Bolsheviks' treasury and seizing their weapons. Chkouro had succeeded in his aim, but the town after he left suffered cruel reprisals.

On the day after this raid the Bolsheviks searched the Semenov villa where the Grand Duchess Marie Pavlovna lived with her two sons, the Grand Dukes Boris and André Wladimirovitch. After which they ordered the Grand Duke Boris and Colonel Kube, André's aide-de-camp, to follow them. The Grand Duchess Marie Pavlovna settled with André on a balcony from which one could see the little path which the two prisoners, surrounded by soldiers, were following. After the Cossack raid the Red Army might do anything, and she was afraid she would never see her son again.

Their torment lasted almost four hours. The Grand Duke and Kube came back at about midnight. They related how they owed their liberty to a young student, who had set himself up as examining magistrate, if not as attorney-general. First of all they had been made to sit down and nobody had bothered about them. Next they were shown into a room, where this young student asked them why they had been arrested. They replied that they had no idea. Whereupon the student sent for the leader of the soldiers, and inquired into the reasons for the arrest. When the soldier could not put forward the

slightest explanation, the student told the two prisoners they were free
and gave them a pass so that they could go home.

Until March we corresponded fairly regularly with the Grand Duke
Serge, who was still in Petrograd; and we learnt from him that on
March 20th he had been banished from the capital with other members
of his family. Then his letters became intermittent and rare, but they
nevertheless allowed us to follow the stages of his exile, which led him
first to Viatka and then to Ekaterinburg. Some of our letters reached
him. At the end of June we received a telegram dated June 14th for
Vova's birthday. This was one week before his tragic end, and we
learnt from it that he was at Alapaevsk. This was his last message. Then
the Bolshevik radio announced that the Grand Duke Serge and the
members of the Imperial Family who had been detained with him had
been carried off by White soldiers and escaped. The news was design-
edly false. But who would have believed such perfidy possible? The
news filled us with joy. Almost a year later, when he was no longer
alive, we received several letters and even another telegram, which
led us to believe that he was safe.

July passed in comparative calm. But towards the end of the month
the situation became more alarming.

Rumours that the Imperial Family had perished at Ekaterinburg had
spread through Kislovodsk. We had seen children selling printed sheets
and running through the streets crying, "Murder of the Imperial
Family!" This was such terrible news that we could not believe it. We
all cherished the hope that it was merely a false rumour spread by the
Bolsheviks, and that the Tsar and his family were really well. We kept
this hope for a long time in our hearts. Even today I still sometimes
seem to hear those children's cries, scattering, like echoes, in all
directions.

Then came the nightmare time. On August 7th Etten, the Grand
Duchess's chamberlain, came to tell me that the Grand Dukes Boris
and André Wladimirovitch had been arrested in the night and taken off
to Piatigorsk with a group of other prisoners. Then Lydia Alexeevna
Davydova came to see me and assured me that everything had been
done to obtain their freedom. She begged me to stay at home, and not
to try anything myself, since I was also in danger. The Grand Dukes
came back next day, August 8th, towards evening; but they remained
confined to their home and a guard was set up to stop them leaving.

I later learnt what had happened. On the night of the 6th/7th
August, the Semenov villa where the Grand Dukes lived had been
surrounded by a large detachment of Red forces. Soldiers entered the

33. With the Grand Duke on the skating rink at St. Moritz in 1914.

34b. Dancing, 1914-1916.

34a. With my partner, Vladimirov, in the garden at Strelna.

villa, and sentries were posted in front of all the doors of the Grand
Dukes' bedrooms in order to stop them going out and communicating
with one another. After a systematic search, the soldiers ordered the
Grand Dukes to dress and follow them. Kube, with his great devotion
and loyalty, had asked to be taken with André. Nobody at the villa
knew where they were being taken. At first it was thought they would
be taken to the local Soviet, as usually happened; but it was later
found out that they had been brought to the station and placed in
a carriage under surveillance. There other prisoners joined them,
including General Babitch, one time Ataman of the Kouban Cossacks,
Kracheninnikov, attorney in the Petrograd law-courts, and Prince
Chakhovskoy. The last prisoner was only brought into the coach after
eight o'clock in the morning. André was convinced that I was going
to suffer the same fate, for he had heard some Red soldiers say that
Kschessinska was at Kislovodsk and would have to be arrested. The
prisoners were then taken to Piatigorsk, first to the local Soviet, and
then, after interrogation, to the State Hotel, where they were all shut
in one room.

During the night Kube, Prince L. Chakhovskoy and Kracheninnikov
were first of all fetched to be transferred to the local prison. Then
General Babitch was removed, and lynched by the crowd at the
entrance to the hotel.

Next day, after visiting me, L. A. Davydova went to the State Hotel
in Piatigorsk, where she was able to talk to Boris and André, and tell
them they were not to worry, since all steps to secure their liberation
had been taken. She had in fact asked Commissar Lestchinsky, whom
she knew personally and used to receive in her home, to do everything
he could to obtain their freedom. She had even offered him her
jewellery as a reward for his efforts. The Commissar refused, but
promised to do all he could.

Taking advantage of his rank of member of the Directory, Lestchinsky went to Piatigorsk at about one o'clock in the afternoon and told
the Grand Dukes that he had only been able to save them at the very
last moment, and that they had almost been shot during the night.
The local Soviet had urgently pressed for their execution, but Lestchinsky, who was opposed to all bloodshed on principle, had been able
to persuade the members. He promised the Grand Dukes that he would
fetch them at about five o'clock, but added, "That is if I manage to get
you set free." They had four more tortured hours to spend, wondering
what would happen if Lestchinsky failed. Before leaving, Lestchinsky
had said that he did not trust the local soldiers, and had therefore

summoned a mountain commissar and his men from Kislovodsk, in order to protect the Grand Dukes and bring them back to Kislovodsk. At five o'clock Lestchinsky returned to the State Hotel, and managed, with considerable difficulty, to get the Grand Dukes out. The Red soldiers were not inclined to let them go without a direct order from the local Soviet, but they were impressed by the number and imposing aspect of the mountain soldiers. There were two cabs waiting in front of the hotel. Lestchinsky made Boris get into one and André into the other, each of them with a soldier on each side. He accompanied them to the station, where they caught the first train, then brought them himself to Kislovodsk, where he restored them to their villa, setting up a guard of his mountain soldiers. But he asked the Grand Dukes not to go out, or he could not guarantee their safety. He also promised to have Kube set free, and the latter did in fact return next day to Kislovodsk.

Later Lestchinsky went back to see Boris and André, and advised them to flee into the mountains; the Piatigorsk Soviet was liable to have them arrested again, and it would be very difficult for him to intervene on their behalf. To make their flight easier, he gave them special papers in false names, attesting that the bearers were on missions for the Soviet.

On August 13th, Boris, André and Kube left in a two-horse brake for the Kabarda, where they remained in hiding until the end of September. At first I did not even know their whereabouts, because they were wandering from village to village. It was only when they had settled with Kononov that they were finally able to give me news of themselves through a man they trusted. My one consolation was knowing that they were no longer in danger; but that was the main thing.

Stories were beginning to spread that the Cossacks were rising up against the Bolsheviks all round Kislovodsk. But these were only wild rumours. The longed-for day did, however, at last arrive: Chkouro again attacked Kislovodsk, this time with a larger force of Cossacks, and occupied the town. The Bolsheviks vanished and we were able to breathe freely. But the situation remained uncertain, as I soon discovered. On September 22nd a date I remember most clearly, I went out with my son for a walk in town. We went as far as the Grand Hotel, where we learned the latest news, and then returned home. Everything seemed perfectly peaceful. But we had hardly entered our villa when the proprietor ran in crying. "What are you doing here? Don't you know that the Cossacks have left and that everybody is fleeing from Kislovodsk?" He advised us to return as soon as possible to the Grand Hotel, which was the general meeting-place. Armed with a few effects, we ran to the Grand Hotel, from which we were sent to Poplar Avenue and from there taken on large waggons to Piatnitzky Market, where all the fugitives had gathered. But then we received orders from Chkouro to return home. It had been a false alarm: the Bolshevik attack had been repelled. We were happy to be home again, but remained on constant alert, with suitcases always ready for a new alarm and a new hurried departure.

The following evening the Grand Dukes Boris and André Wladimirovitch came back to Kislovodsk with Colonel Kube. They arrived on horseback, with an escort of nobles from the Kabarda. The Grand Dukes had not been able to shave while in the mountains, and with his beard André was often taken for the Emperor, to whom he bore indeed a certain resemblance.

Two days later there was another alarm. At the last moment a waggon was sent for us, and we all got in: my son and I, my sister and her husband, Zina, Boris's future wife, and her companion. Once again we made for Piatnitzky Market, where Boris and André Wladimirovitch also arrived in their own car, which they gave up to my sister and brother-in-law. André joined us on our waggon, while Zina and Boris found another empty one. Following Chkouro's instructions, the endless column set out towards the village of Tambiev. It was a heartrending spectacle. The refugees used every possible means of transport. Some were even fleeing on foot, carrying their last possessions on their shoulders. We had no idea what was going on round us or where the Bolsheviks were. Our one idea was to get as far as we could from them as fast as possible, and by whatever means!

Halfway between Kislovodsk and Tambiev the column came under fire from a Bolshevik battery. Shells whistled over our heads and burst all round. There was terrible panic. Some whipped up their horses in order to make a quicker escape; others scattered in the fields alongside the road. An Army doctor, completely lost, leaped into our waggon and laid himself out at full length, without considering that we were already too many. We could not help smiling, so funny did he seem. Towards evening we finally reached Tambiev, but the column was completely disorganised through panic, and everybody was looking for friends or relations. We all spent the night in the village. My son and I slept in the waggon, wrapped in the blankets which André had brought. The arrival of Chkouro with his staff gave fresh heart to the fugitives, several of whom were preparing to go on in spite of the dangers of an exodus in the middle of the night. We all thought that we were now protected by a large detachment of Cossacks; Chkouro kept on giving orders to his staff and showed such energy and confidence that we were more or less convinced, that he had a large number of forces. We later learned that he had no more than a handful of Cossacks, but was pretending to have more in order to mislead Bolshevik spies.

Next day we set out again towards the *stanitza*[1] of Bekechevska. But for some reason which we were not told, we only left Tambiev in the late afternoon. The delay made us very anxious and nervous; in the night it was easy to go astray and run into an ambush. However, in spite of long halts, we reached Bekechevska without incident. But there was danger in staying there, for the Bolsheviks were approaching; so two days later we were sent on to the *stanitza* of Baltapachinska. We left in the middle of the night and had a terrible passage across the steppe. There were no roads, and we had to guess where the paths were. We heard distant singing in the night, without being able to know if they were the voices of friends or enemies, and we went on, tossed from side to side and tormented by the constant fear of advancing towards the Reds.

We reached the *stanitza* at dawn. The sun was rising, one could just make out the world and recognise the track, and our surroundings seemed less dreadful now. Each of us had some wish that he hoped to satisfy when he arrived at the village; mine was to have a bath, Kube's one dream was a glass of cognac. We were able partly to satisfy these wishes. There was no bath, but we were able to get clean in a *bania*, a Russian steam-room, and Kube had his cognac.

Chkouro had seized Kislovodsk with a handful of Cossacks and would never have been able to resist a Bolshevik attack. He had to manœuvre constantly in order to avoid fighting. We were surrounded on all sides by Red detachments, which pressed us without daring to attack us, not knowing the exact size of our forces. Chkouro had laid hands at Kislovodsk on a country radio-telegraph station, by means of which he had been able to contact the main body of the White army and to learn that a large body of men under General Pokrovsky was marching on Baltapachinska to help us. The combined forces of Pokrovsky and Chkouro represented a powerful force, with which the Bolsheviks would have to reckon. This news filled us with joy.

We were all gathered in the main square, round the church, when

[1] Cossack village.

Pokrovsky's men arrived. They made a deep impression on us as they marched past. They were led by the *Sotnia* (a squadron of Cossacks from the Kouban of the Tsar's Escort) with their banner, whose golden eagle flashed in the sun. Many old Cossacks who had once been in the Escort wore their former uniform. The Bolsheviks had been driven from the *stanitza*, and the inhabitants were exultant. There even seemed to be hope of a return to the good old days! Many knelt down and weeping with joy, made the sign of the cross. . . .

To honour General Pokrovsky, a special committee formed by the refugees gave a dinner with music and speeches. The Grand Dukes Boris and André Wladimirovitch were among the guests. This was an important event in our nomadic life! We wanted to know how it was going, and Rodion Vostriakov, one of our great friends, made frequent trips from the room to give us detailed accounts.

We were quite safe at Baltapachinska and able to recover from our fears and suffering. But another question was beginning to arise: Where were we to stay until the whole of the southern Caucasus was quiet again? Some opted for Novorossisk; others for Ekaterinodar or Touapse. General Pokrovsky advised the Grand Duchess Marie Pavlovna and the Grand Dukes Boris and André Wladimirovitch to spend the winter in Anapa, where he said conditions were excellent and life completely calm. Also it was by the sea, which, in case of danger, would allow them to ship for safety. He arranged to organise the journey himself, and promised to provide an escort of Cossacks from his personal guard. Our route was almost carefully chosen: we were to go by waggon to the *stanitza* of Labinska, where we were to take the train to Touapse. From there a train would bring us to Anapa.

A whole group of refugees decided to take advantage of the escort of soldiers and leave with the Grand Duchess; some were making for Touapse, others for Novorossisk.

We had arrived at Baltapachinska on October 2nd, and we left again on the 19th, spending the first night at the *stanitza* of Popoutnaïa, which was in a region from which the Bolsheviks had just been driven out; the Reds had attacked the village the very day before we arrived, a threat which troubled our sleep. Next day we reached Labinska, a large *stanitza*, some of whose houses were made of stone and looked quite modern.

The train was not due to leave for another five hours, and so one of General Pokrovsky's officers undertook to lodge us in a house in the village. My sister and her husband, my son, Zina and I were thus lodged in a house inhabited by a large family who gave us a warm welcome, offering us tea and an appetising meal. To entertain me the daughter of the house showed me some magazines, and we came upon a photograph of my statuette sculptured by Prince Troubetzkoy. She began to explain that this was the famous dancer Kschessinska, and thought she was in a fairy tale when I told her who I was! Boris and André joined us late in the afternoon, but our hosts seemed troubled by their presence, fearing to be worried by the Bolsheviks if they ever returned.

Late in the evening the train was announced, and we went to the station. The carriages were in a terrible state after the knocks they had taken over the last few months; but these trifles did not worry us, and we settled in somehow, happy that we should soon be putting an end to our wanderings.

André, who had always served in the Horse Artillery of the Guard, being successively in command of the 5th and 6th batteries, had been put in command of the Brigade during the war, which included all the batteries of the Guard. Since the Revolution he had had to give up this post. His officers and men of the 6th Cossack battery had presented him with a sword which he treasured highly. It was somehow lost as we got into the train that day. Miraculously, it was later found on the line and brought to Anapa. It must have remained attached to the carriage.

At dawn on October 21st we arrived at Touapse. Nobody expected to see a policeman at the station wearing the old uniform, and many of our party rushed towards him to kiss him.

Since we had a few hours to spare, after a wash, which we needed badly, Zina and I went to the town market. We were both thinking of the happy days when we would walk together in Paris!

When we arrived at the quay, the boat, an old trawler, small and dirty, with the proud name of *Taifoun* (the Typhoon) was already under steam. Many of the refugees, convinced that the Grand Duchess Marie Pavlovna would refuse to embark on such a small boat, were waiting for her to arrive before accepting their lot. How was everybody to be accommodated in such a nutshell! But the Grand Duchess declared aloud, "What a wonderfully picturesque setting!" And, graciously acknowledging the Captain's welcome, she embarked without turning a hair! Sitting imperturbably in a deck-chair on the bridge, she began to look at the crestfallen refugees, who now hastened to follow her example.

The *Taifoun* had only three cabins, the Captain's and those of the officers, which were put at the Grand Duchess's disposal.

Lacking any other passenger space, we were ninety-six to share the bridge, and each managed as well as he could.

Luckily, the night was calm. There was neither wind nor rain, and our trawler, gently rocked by the waves, sailed in the deep, far from searches, arrests and ambushes. We were worn out and slept soundly until somebody, wanting to go to the lavatory, tried to step over the sleepers who lay flat on the bridge. This brought about a succession of exclamations, more of warning than anger, almost automatically spoken:

"Monsieur, you're crushing my fingers!"

"Be careful, monsieur, you're stepping on my nose!"

"My stomach, monsieur!"

And the cause of the trouble was full of apologies each time, pleading that he could see nothing.

There was nothing particularly funny about it, but after the nervous tension we had endured, this unexpected conversation, in the pitch dark, outside, and on the bridge of a boat, suddenly gave rise to general mirth which lasted until dawn.

Crossing then was very dangerous. None of the coastal lighthouses were working. This made it difficult to steer, and it was certainly out of the question to enter a port in the middle of the night. The greatest danger came from drifting mines, of which the Black Sea was full, and which were invisible at night. Since it was still too dark, the Captain avoided Novorossisk and decided to make for Anapa, which we sighted at five o'clock in the morning. But we had to wait for daybreak to put in. Immediately afterwards the *Taifoun* had to put to sea again to go to Novorossisk and land the remaining refugees.

CHAPTER XXIV

THE LAST YEAR IN RUSSIA

WE DISEMBARKED AT Anapa on October 22nd 1918 at about seven o'clock in the morning. The town was still asleep, and there was nobody on the jetty. We sat on our trunks while waiting for our fate to be decided. The situation was not the happiest. The town had been liberated, but, as often happened in the wake of the White Army, bands of partisans hidden in the forests or mountains sometimes attacked centres which could not be protected owing to the shortage of men. Miatch, the officer appointed by General Pokrovsky to escort the Grand Duchess, set out in reconnaissance to contact the local commander, establish the situation and, with the help of the local authorities, find somewhere for the Grand Duchess and all of us to live.

Anapa is an old dismantled fortress, twenty miles from the mouth of the Kouban, on the Eastern side of the Black Sea, just north of Novorossisk. The creation of this strong-point has been attributed to the Sultan Abdul Hamid, who had it constructed by French engineers in 1781. During the Russo-Turkish wars which followed, Anapa changed hands several times, but finally remained under Russian occupation and was dismantled in 1860. For several years it had been a bathing resort, and possessed a sanatorium.

Over an hour passed before Miatch finally returned, bearing encouraging news: order reigned in the town, and we were out of danger. We were advised, meanwhile, to put up at the Metropole, the only hotel in town. We set out accompanied by Captain Hanykov, an officer attached to the Grand Duke Boris Wladimirovitch. Apart from my son and myself, our party consisted of my sister and her husband, Baron Zeddeler, Zina Rachevska, and her French friend, Marie.

The Metropole Hotel proved modest and fairly primitive; it had been ransacked by the Bolsheviks, and the lavatories, in particular, had been turned into skating rinks by the frost and were in a pitiful state. The rooms, however, which were adequately furnished and not too dirty, were reasonable. We settled in as well as we could, glad to have a roof over our heads. The town was equipped with electricity, but the current was cut at about ten at night; so we had to use candles bought in church, the only place where they could be found. As I was very frightened of the dark, I let a candle burn all night, fixing it in the wash-basin for extra safety.

But a great trial was in store for me: Vova caught Spanish influenza. I was afraid I might not find a doctor in this small provincial town. Fortunately, Dr. Kouptchik, an excellent doctor from St. Petersburg, happened to be in Anapa.

Day began with breakfast, which we ate in a tiny Greek house whose walls were decorated with chromolithographs of the Greek Royal Family. On the way we bought *tchourekis*, Caucasian rolls, newly baked and warm, and were served "Greek coffee"—milk, sugar, and ground coffee all boiled together—quite a pleasant drink, in spite of the floating grains. On weekdays we each drank a single glass, but on Sundays we indulged in the luxury of two.

Next we normally made for the jetty to find out if a boat had arrived and to learn the latest news. Then we went to the market, where one could buy very pretty silver objects at bargain prices.

At first we lunched at an excellent restaurant, Chez Simon, which had a first-class chef. But, as we were not too well off, we soon took our meals in a little family *pension*, where we invariably ordered *bitki*, the cheapest and most substantial dish. Only Vova was allowed a larger and tastier dish.

A great many starving dogs roamed about town, looking so wretched that I tried to find them scraps. You should have seen them run towards me when I called them!

I had only been able to bring two dresses with me, one being a gala dress, which I kept for exceptional occasions! The other consisted of a bodice and skirt in black velvet, the same which Katia, the cow-hand, had stolen and then given back to me in the first days of the Revolution. This poor skirt had finally become worn and red at the knees.

The Grand Duchess and Grand Dukes lived in a house lent to them by a retired general, and André and Boris came to see us every day. Another frequent visitor was Vladimir Lazarev, whom Chkouro had appointed the Grand Duchess's bodyguard. We talked of the good old days, including the masked ball where we had first met. Our life was now sad and entertainments a thing of the past. Volodia Lazarev filled his time doing talented sketches of fantastic conception; I still have one today in remembrance of him.

I had always had excellent masseuses and it was a great hardship to go without one. By chance, however, I found an experienced masseuse in Anapa. Blum was Jewish. She had emigrated to America because of her political opinions, before returning, like so many others, to Russia after the Revolution. She began by making a very small charge, but later refused all payment. Although our political opinions were completely opposed, everything seemed to show that she liked me very much. During the massage sessions, we tried heatedly to convince each other of the rightness of our respective opinions. Finally, and after a long struggle, I won, and we became more friendly still. At first Blum absolutely refused to meet André. But later her attitude towards him completely altered. When we parted we were firm friends. When I returned to Kislovodsk, I received, among other telegrams, one from her congratulating me on the successes won by the White Army. All this was really extraordinary on the part of a political *emigrée*, a disciple of Lenin and Plekhanov, whom she knew personally.

We were overjoyed at the news that the war had ended. Now we were no longer cut off from the world and before long the English cruiser *Liverpool* and the French cruiser *Ernest Renan* arrived at Novorossisk.

Towards Christmas General Pool, commander of the English base in Russia, came to Anapa with General Boris Gartman, who had been attached to his staff. This unexpected visit greatly intrigued the whole town. The General had come to convey an invitation to the Grand Duchess Marie Pavlovna, in the name of the British Government, to take refuge abroad. Thinking that she was safe at Anapa, the Grand Duchess declined the offer. She had decided not to leave Russia until no other solution remained. General Pool was very impressed by this reply.

At the end of March Boris and Zina left us to go abroad. Boris Wladimirovitch tried to persuade the Grand Duchess to leave with him; but she was greatly distressed by her son's decision and refused.

On the 29th of the same month the story spread that a warship was approaching Anapa, and everybody hurried towards the jetty. Thick smoke could be seen rising on the horizon, but there was no way of telling whether it was a warship or a merchant vessel. Some Bolshevik sympathisers, thinking that they saw a red flag, soon began to exult. But their joy was short-lived: it was a British cruiser! The ship anchored in front of the harbour, and a motor launch with armed officers and sailors drew in to the jetty. Two sailors leaped out on to the quay, with guns at the ready, followed immediately by two officers, who began to cast circumspect looks about them. A lady who knew English fluently approached them and offered to serve as interpreter. We learnt through her that one of the two officers was Commander Goldschmidt of the cruiser *Montrose*, who had been sent by

Admiral Seymour, commander of the English Black Sea Squadron, to bring the Grand Duchess Marie Pavlovna and the Grand Duke André to Constantinople in case of danger. He was at once taken to the Grand Duchess, whom he informed of his mission. According to André, who was present, the Grand Duchess asked the Commander to convey her sincere thanks to Admiral Seymour for sending her a cruiser, but declined the offer, stating that she saw no reason at present for leaving Anapa, still less Russia. As she had already informed General Pool, she considered it her duty to remain in Russia and only to leave her country in case of absolute necessity. Visibly moved by such a sense of duty, the Commander replied, "You're right!" But it was arranged with him that in case of danger someone should telegraph straightaway to Novorossisk, where there would always be a British warship, which could be in wireless contact with him anywhere. Thus he could always be at Anapa in less than forty-eight hours.

Commander Goldschmidt invited the Grand Duchess to visit his ship and to have tea with him on board; but her legs were too weak for such an effort, and she was unable to accept. But André and the Grand Duchess's attendants went with the Commander to visit the cruiser. On the way he told André that when the Admiral had ordered him to make for Anapa, neither he nor the Admiral had known who held the port. This was why the ship had anchored some way out of the harbour and the Commander had landed with an armed escort; in addition, all the cruiser's guns had been trained on Anapa, so that they could immediately shell the port in case of necessity.

While tea was being made on board, Commander Goldschmidt drew André aside and asked him quietly if he thought that the Tsar had really died at Ekaterinburg. André replied that he had no information either way, but that he hoped the Imperial Family might have been saved. There were so many plausible and insistent rumours that the Tsar was safe and sound that one could not help believing them, and thinking that the Bolsheviks had a purpose in spreading the news of his death. We were in the same cruel uncertainty about the fate of the Grand Duke Serge Mikhailovitch, the first rumours of whose tragic end had reached us at Anapa on New Year's Eve. In that case, replied the Commander, would André allow him to drink to His Majesty's health? André saw no objection. His host then brought champagne and solemnly proposed a toast to the Tsar's health. In reply, André proposed a toast to the King's health. The Commander's gesture was later interpreted in a thousand different ways. André himself suspected that his host knew more than he was allowed to say.

Anyway, the Commander's toast showed clearly that at the time he did not personally believe in the Tsar's death and had no official confirmation. We later heard that the Bolsheviks, afraid of a general outcry, were trying to conceal the Emperor's assassination and continued to spread the rumour that he had been kidnapped by "white bandits".

Although the whole of the northern Caucasus had been liberated since February, we kept on putting off our return to Kislovodsk, where we had left all our possessions. The situation as a whole remained uncertain. In fact, the Bolsheviks were exerting fairly strong pressure, and they reoccupied the Crimea, compelling the Dowager Empress to leave Russia at the end of March.

I now decided to send for Ludmilla and Ivan, with clothing and linen, the few possessions which we had taken with us being by now in a sad state. Fortunately, our servants had succeeded in saving almost everything which remained in the villa, and brought us many essentials. I then lent Ivan to the Grand Duchess Marie Pavlovna, with whom he remained until she arrived in France.

Meanwhile, we had moved in to the house of a priest, Father Temnomerov, where we had two rooms, one for Vova and myself, the other for my sister and her husband. The Father had two charming daughters and a son, Volodia, who was Vova's age, a very nice and gifted boy. One day he treated us to a conjuring show, and for Easter he made a magnificent bust of the Tsar out of butter.

In May we decided to return to Kislovodsk.

As before, General Pokrovsky presided over the preparations for the journey. Once again he sent one of his officers and a detachment of his personal guard, not only to organise everything, but also to escort the Grand Duchess on the journey.

We left Anapa on May 24th, after a stay of seven months. We were brought by carriage to Tonnelnaïa Station, where two coaches had been reserved for us. The journey lasted two hours. At every station our Cossack escort got out on the platform, forbidding all unauthorised persons to approach our coaches. After all sorts of complications, which were overcome thanks to General Pokrovsky's officer, we arrived at Kislovodsk on May 26th at three o'clock in the morning. My sister and I moved back into the villa which we had occupied the year before.

Life had returned to normal in Kislovodsk. The White Army proceeded from victory to victory, and we were expecting any day to hear of the fall of Moscow: Bolshevism was to be stamped out and Russia would be once more what she had been before. The Allied help gave further food to our hopes. We lived like this until the end of the year. Then came a sudden reversal on the front, and the retreat began.

At the beginning of December André's aide-de-camp, Kube, was taken ill with typhus. In spite of the risk of infection, he was put to bed in the villa where the Grand Duchess and André were living, and died two weeks later, on the morning of December 20th. It was a cruel loss, especially for André, whose aide-de-camp he had been for many years. His friendship had been precious in difficult times, and all who knew him had felt sincere affection for him. Kube had proved his devotion when he chose freely to accompany André to prison. The funeral took place on December 22nd. He was buried with military honours in Kislovodsk cemetery. All we could raise on his tomb was a small white wooden cross bearing the two dates "29th October 1881—20th December 1919". He was only thirty-eight when he died.

CHAPTER XXV

EXILE

JUST BEFORE CHRISTMAS the position of the White Armies became critical. Everything seemed to show that they were no longer capable of stopping the Reds and saving the Caucasus from invasion. So as not to be caught in a trap, it was decided that we should leave Kislovodsk as soon as possible. We were to go to Novorossisk and wait to see what happened there, ready to go abroad in case of urgent necessity. The turn of events was a great surprise to us, so much had we believed in the military successes. Even the Grand Duchess Marie Pavlovna now felt that there was no alternative to leaving Russia.

I cannot describe our last days in Kislovodsk, our preparations to leave, our uncertainty about the date and details of the journey. We had reached the peak of nervous tension.

At last, on December 30th, at about eleven o'clock in the evening, we set out for the station, where two carriages awaited us: one first-class for the Grand Duchess and some of her friends who were ill or had children, and another, third-class, where Vova and I and other refugees got in. Ivan, my servant, had had the bright idea of bringing a small stove, on which his wife (whom I had lent with him to the Grand Duchess, and who served as her cook for six months) was able to prepare meals. My sister had been taken ill with typhoid the day before we left; she was laid in the first-class carriage, and André, who had given her his compartment, moved into our carriage.

The train remained all night at the station. We were only able to leave next morning at eleven o'clock. When the convoy was already in motion, some refugees were still clinging to the carriage, begging to be taken with us. We saw the same panic at every station. People were fighting to climb on to the train. Everybody had but one single idea—to flee, to flee from the Bolsheviks!

At about three o'clock in the afternoon, we finally reached Mineralnyi Vody Station, where for some unknown reason we remained until next day.

So we celebrated the New Year, 1920, in Mineralnyi Vody Station. At midnight the Chapochnikov family, who had moved into our carriage, brought out a bottle of champagne; and, dirty and exhausted, crammed on our wooden seats, we drank to the New Year, each trying to inspire the others with hopes of a better future, although we were all depressed.

The train left three hours later, and on January 4th, at nine o'clock in the morning, after a hundred endless delays and complications, we finally reached Novorossisk.

We spent six weeks in our railway carriage before succeeding in leaving town. One accident succeeded another. One moment there was no boat; next the boat was too small or only went to Constantinople; at another time there were cases of typhus on board; at another astronomical sums were being asked! . . . In addition, it was getting colder and colder, an icy wind swept through the station, and it proved almost impossible to heat the carriage. Our servants had to saw up old telegraph poles which littered the ground about us. Typhus was rampant, and there was great risk of infection, particularly in the station, where ambulance trains arrived, crammed with patients, several of whom had died on the journey. Every day we learned that one or other of our friends had just died. But one day General N. M. Tikhmenev, Inspector-General of the railways, discovering the dreadful conditions in which I had to live, put a saloon coach at my disposal, where we were able to live in comfort. Divan beds, a clean lavatory, electricity—it was like living in a palace! The food situation was proving increasingly difficult, for provisions were beginning to run out in town. André, however, sometimes managed to get supplies at the British canteen; he brought us marvellous biscuits and cocoa, things which were then looked upon as luxuries.

In Novorossisk we met many friends who were waiting, like us, for the opportunity of proceeding further; they were all going to Constantinople, where the visas needed for the rest of the journey could be obtained.

One day I went out into the town and came upon a sad procession: it was the burial of the young Count Illarion Ivanovitch Vorontzov-Dachkov, who had just died of typhus. He was laid in a simple coffin, placed on a cart. His widow, the beautiful Countess Irene, née Lazarev, followed the pathetic train. The bareness of the funeral and the Countess's grief made an unforgettable impression on me.

The postponement of our departure was chiefly due to the fact that there was no ship bound directly for France or Italy. All the boats leaving were only going as far as Constantinople, where we would have to land, find a hotel, obtain a visa and wait for another ship. The Grand Duchess did not want to stop in Constantinople, and the commander of the British base at Novorossisk shared her view. At last we heard of the arrival of the *Semiramisa*, an Italian liner of the Lloyd-Triestino Line, due to return to Venice. We could not have asked for anything better.

We embarked on February 13th 1920. This was the day we left Russian soil, since the ship, though anchored in a Russian port, was foreign. After so many hardships, a first-class cabin seemed a place of incredible luxury! But we really thought we were seeing a mirage at dinner: clean table-napkins, glasses, knives and forks! We uttered "ohs" and "ahs" of enchantment. We were rather embarrassed at having to sit at table in our shabby clothes; but when the impeccably dressed waiters began to serve us we felt as if we were in another world! Our state of mind can easily be imagined when it is realised that there was also the thought that we were at last safe, with nothing more to fear from the Bolsheviks!

We remained six days in Novorossisk Harbour. There was the continual loading of merchandise, and the steam winches worked day and night.

At last, on February 19th, the anniversary of the abolition of serfdom by the Emperor Alexander II in 1861, the *Semiramisa* weighed anchor. Our itinerary bound us to the coast: Novorossisk, Poti, Batum, Trebizond, Kerassoun, Orda, Samsoun, Inebeli and Constantinople.

Our feelings defy description. We were leaving part of ourselves in Russia, part of our lives, our hearts, and the wrench was the more intense for André because this was his last time in uniform. Of all the trials we had endured or had to endure, this was without doubt the bitterest and most painful.

We began to cast off towards evening. It was rather a complicated procedure owing to the large number of boats anchored in the harbour. All these ships with their lights made a dramatic sight, a poignant sight for us who saw it through our tears. We moved slowly out of harbour, passed the outer jetty and reached the sea. The lights of Novorossisk and the fleet slowly grew fainter before disappearing, and the *Semiramisa*, rocked by the gentle swell, plunged into the night.

As no one had any money, not even the Grand Duchess, the latter gave the Company as security a valuable brooch which covered all our passages. Most of the travellers, as far as I know, have never been able to pay back the cost. On board I soon made the acquaintance of the Captain, Gregory Brazzrvanovitch, a man of some age and apparently of Czech origin. He often asked me, as a special favour, on

35a. Strelna: the entrance to the park.

35c. Strelna: Vova dressed in his fireman's suit.

35b. Strelna: the mock Corregidor.

36a. The last garden fête at Strelna before the war.

36b. Strelna: a group of the wounded from my hospital.

to the bridge, where passengers were not admitted. When we were
approaching the Bosporus, he asked me again to join him for a better
view of the entry of the Straits, which he told me was a magnificent
sight at sunrise. It was still dark when I climbed on to the bridge. Then
day began to dawn . . . and I could not see much because we were
surrounded by fog. But suddenly the enormous silhouette of a British
dreadnought, also making for the Bosporus, loomed out of the mist.
She passed right by us, and the 5,000-ton *Semiramisa* seemed a tiny
craft compared to this sea-giant.

We entered the Bosporus on February 25th, and cast anchor in a
bay which was under quarantine. Passengers and their luggage were
brought to land in launches, and there, in groups of fifteen, we
were taken into decontamination rooms. We were asked to undress.
Not even the Grand Duchess was spared, though she refused. Each
of us had to do up his money and jewellery into a parcel. We
were allowed to keep this parcel with us, but all our effects were
sent to be fumigated (anything in leather was ruined) while we
went to the shower All this took some time, since there were many
of us, and it was five o'clock in the afternoon when we returned to
the ship.

Next day, towards evening, after inspection by the Health Department, we put in at Constantinople, but nobody was yet allowed to
land. The harbour was an impressive sight: we counted at least seven
Allied dreadnoughts, and there were other small squadrons of various
nationalities. It was like a fairy-tale at nightfall when thousands of
lights sprang up on the boats.

Next day, a Sunday, we were at last able to land and walk about
town. I was visited during the day by my old friend, Lilia Likhatcheva,
who was immobilised in Constantinople waiting for a visa; in the
evening we celebrated the eve of my birthday with champagne.

We took advantage of this three-day call to visit the Cathedral of
Santa Sophia, the tomb of the Soldier Makhmoud, the tomb
of Abdul-Hamid, the Mosque of Ahmet and Suliman, the market of
Constantinople, and the famous Onoup Cemetery, made famous by
Pierre Loti. Then, when we had received our French visas, we
immediately sent a telegram to Cap d'Ail announcing our arrival.

On Thursday, the *Semiramisa* left Constantinople for the Piraeus,
and the following day we passed the headland of Gallipoli, where we
had a distant view of the communal grave of five thousand French and
English soldiers. Just off the shore could be seen the half-sunk wreck
of a French cruiser which had made a heroic attempt to force the

Dardanelles; we also made out a number of grounded troop-carriers. "You can't imagine," said our Captain, "how many warships were sunk in the Narrows. There must be at least twenty-six under us."

We arrived at the Piraeus on March 7th, then moved into the narrow Corinth Canal and spent the night at Patras.

The crossing was uneventful, apart from the danger of hitting a stray mine. The Captain had warned us of this risk, and there was a sailor on watch day and night on the ship's prow.

At sunset on March 10th we saw the tall, distant outline of the Campanile and various churches. Soon the breeze brought us the sound of bells calling the faithful to evening office, and Venice appeared in all her glory. Who can remain untouched by the magic of that seductive city? We were all the more moved at seeing her, after so much anxiety and drama, gradually take shape in a vision of mist and old gold. At eight o'clock the *Semiramisa* cast anchor opposite the Doges' Palace.

André and I had been in Venice nineteen years before; young, carefree and in love. In memory of that happy time, we decided to have supper in the restaurant *Il Vapore*. After so many years, André had no difficulty in finding the way. But we first had to think of two things: the little money we had between the four of us—André, my sister and her husband, and myself—and our clothes, whose shabby appearance might get us turned away from the door. Taking our courage in both hands, we entered the restaurant. If some of the clients were elegantly dressed, others were scarcely smarter than ourselves. We had just chosen the most secluded table when we suddenly saw a notice asking guests to take off their coats. Only Vova firmly refused to remove his, since his suit was really in a very bad state. As a way of inspiring confidence and raising our credit in the eyes of the staff, André laid his gold cigarette-case prominently on the table. A careful study of the menu calmed our fears, and we were finally able, for thirty-eight lire, to enjoy a copious cold dinner with a bottle of asti spumante!

On the next day, March 11th, we finally left the *Semiramisa*, which had been our home for twenty-eight days. As a record of our passage, I gave the Captain some Fabergé cuff-links which André had somehow managed to save.

Thanks to the efforts of our Consul, the Grand Duchess was given a special train which left Venice just after one in the afternoon. Travelling via Milan and Ventimiglia, we finally crossed the French frontier and arrived at Cap d'Ail.

Vova, Ioulia, Baron Zeddeler, Ludmilla and Ivan got out with me. Although I had sent two telegrams announcing our return, nobody was there to meet us at the station. This made me very anxious, especially as all through the war I had remained without news of my villa. But Vova, who had been sent on to spy out the land, soon came back to tell us that all was well. He had found out from Antoinette, our old kitchen-maid, that the villa had been made ready as soon as our first telegram had arrived, but that the second had never come. Arnold, whom I was not expecting to find at Cap d'Ail, had managed, as a Swiss citizen, to leave Russia, and had also found employment with our neighbours while waiting for our return. He had succeeded in bringing from home a great many photographs and albums which I would henceforward find doubly precious. While Vova came to meet us, Antoinette ran to inform Margot and Arnold of our arrival. So I found them all together to greet me, delighted to see us again, but heartbroken not to have been able to get the villa properly ready.

André, who had accompanied the Grand Duchess to Cannes, where rooms had been reserved for her in the Grand Hotel, returned to Cap d'Ail for dinner.

Thus, on March 12th/25th 1920[1] after six years' absence, I was back in my dear villa Alam, amid a thousand familiar things. Margot and Arnold were to take up service with us again in a few days. Everything was as it had been and life seemed to start again as after a nightmare. But if we could only rejoice at being united and safe and having a home again, nothing could efface the piercing memory of so many dear ones who were absent or vanished for ever, nothing would ever wipe out the terrible reality of the ruins, losses and bereavements through which we had just lived.

Nevertheless, a tragic and painful page has been turned. Our life as *émigrés* was beginning.

[1] From now on all dates will be given by the Gregorian calendar.

CHAPTER XXVI

A NEW LIFE

Arriving penniless at Cap d'Ail, we had immediately to mortgage the villa, in order to pay my servants and my old gardener, Botin, who had looked after the estate while patiently waiting for my return. I also had to get some clothes, for all I had were my two old dresses, while Vova was so ragged that he could not show himself in public. The most fortunate was André, who had left his luggage in Cap d'Ail.

One of the first people we met was the Grand Duchess Anastasia Mikhailovna, Dowager Grand Duchess of Mechlemburg-Schwerin. She lived in the villa Fantasia at Èze, not far from us. She was a most wonderful woman. Unfailingly polite and kind, she had a heart of gold, loved life and knew how to enjoy it. She was very fond of our son. Before the war, when Vova had been ill at Cannes, she had often came to visit him and later had invited him to her home at the villa Wenden. She gave him delicious teas, and used to say with a laugh that he had not even left a crumb for the flies. Vova was eighteen, and the Grand Duchess wanted him to learn dancing; it was time for him to begin going out into the world, and his first outing was with her.

With the Grand Duchess we often speculated on the fate of the Grand Duke Serge Mikhailovitch, his brother and the other members of the Imperial Family who had been deported into the Urals. Had they been murdered? We had no more knowledge of their fate, as I have said, than of the fate of the Tsar's family. To avoid the shame of the truth, the Bolsheviks continued to spread the story that they were all safe, and we could not help believing this. Days of sorrow alternated with days of joy, according to the conflicting reports. It was heartbreaking to think that if Serge Mikhailovitch had given in to my entreaties and had left while there was still time, he would have been among us now!

We also met the Grand Duke Boris Wladimirovitch and Zina on the Riviera. They had been married at Genoa after their flight abroad, and had now come to settle provisionally in Nice. At Beaulieu lived Gabriel Constantinovitch, who had married Nina Nesterovska immediately after the Revolution. At Èze I also met Lina Cavalieri, whom Vova had once appointed commander of his regiment of monkeys! She had married Muratore the tenor and lived in a charming villa by the sea. Also, to my great delight, Tamara Karsavina, as elegant and beautiful as ever, paid me an unexpected visit. It was many years since we had met.

Soon after our arrival my faithful old friend Raoul Guinsbourg invited us to lunch at the Hôtel de Paris, with the famous writer Willy, and Serge de Diaghilev, who was living in the same hotel. It was a very gay luncheon: Guinsbourg was indefatigable and always full of anecdotes.

A few days later Diaghilev came and asked me to dance with his company during his coming Paris season. I was now forty-eight, but in perfect form and I could have danced with success. Though highly flattered by his offer, I felt that I had to decline it. Since the Imperial Theatres had ceased to exist, I no longer wanted to appear on the stage. For the same reason I turned down the equally flattering offer I received from Laloy, secretary to Rouché, the Director of the Paris Opéra, asking me to participate in the coming season.

The Empress Eugénie was then living at Cap-Martin in her villa Cyrnos. She had been very fond of André's late father, the Grand Duke Wladimir Alexandrovitch, ever since 1867 when, as a young man, he had accompanied Alexander II, his father, to the Exposition Universelle and narrowly escaped being killed by Berezovsky. They had often met at the Hôtel Continental in Paris, where the Empress Eugénie, the Grand Duke and the Grand Duchess all usually stayed. The Empress had known André since childhood. When she heard of the arrival of the Grand Duchess with her son, she immediately invited them to lunch in her villa. André told me he was dazzled by the Empress's youthfulness. She was so lively and gay that one could not believe she was ninety-four years old. She found a pleasant word for everybody and showed great interest in the Russian scene; she knew the names of the White generals and politicians, seemed fully informed about all that was happening, and had an astonishingly good memory. Her voice was firm and clear, and her hearing perfect. She complained that her doctors had put her on the strictest diet, and meanwhile cheerfully ate the same menu as her guests. She walked upright and firmly, and André learnt from her lady-in-waiting that after lunch, far from resting, the Empress would go for a drive. She spoke very animatedly of the journey she hoped to make to Spain, the welcome being prepared for her there, and of the King who would come in person to meet her. Yet she had certainly never lacked triumphal receptions! Nothing

pointed to her approaching death and she would no doubt have lived
for several more years, had it not been for the eye operation which she
decided, against her doctors' advice, to undergo. The doctors were
more afraid of post-operative shock than of the actual operation. The
operation proved successful, but the Empress did not survive it. She
died in Madrid towards the end of 1920.

Shortly afterwards Sima Astafieva, my brother Iouzia's first wife,
arrived from London. She moved into the villa Alam, and we often
spoke of our Italian journey of 1901 and her love for Petronius! Sima
had married Constantin Graves, but the marriage was unhappy and
ended in divorce. She lived in London now, where she had been the
first Russian dancer to open a dance studio, a project which had been
crowned with success. From her studio came two artists destined for
a brilliant career: Anton Dolin, whom Diaghilev immediately engaged, and Alicia Markova, who also made her début with Diaghilev.

During the summer of 1920, our first summer in France, André and
I went for ten days to Paris. We stayed at the Hotel d'Albe, a small
hotel on the corner of the Champs-Elysées and the Avenue Georges V,
since replaced by an enormous building several storeys high.

At Cap d'Ail as neighbour and friend we had the Italian Marquis
Passano, a very tall man made to appear even taller by a long black
beard. He was married to the daughter of Saltykov-Stchedrin, the
writer, and had lived for a long time in Russia.

The Marquis, who was in Paris at the time, one day invited us to
dinner in the Château de Madrid on the edge of the Bois de Boulogne,
where we had the joyful surprise of meeting the Grand Duke Dimitri
Pavlovitch, who had come to dine with friends. We had not seen each
other since the end of 1916, when he had been exiled from Petrograd
following Rasputin's murder. Moved to tears, he threw himself in my
arms and began to kiss me, regardless of the people about us.

Next day he asked us to lunch at the pavillon d'Armenonville, after
which we met him every day until we left Paris. He carefully avoided
the slightest reference to that night of destiny in the Youssoupov
Palace. But his exile, almost on the eve of the Revolution, may have
saved his life.

In summer we entertained Lilia Likhatcheva with her husband and
three children, and villa Alam became very gay.

But at the end of July André received a telegram from Contrexéville,
summoning him urgently to the Grand Duchess's bedside. He knew that
his mother was following a cure of the spa; but nothing led one to

expect a decline in her health. Overwhelmed, he left immediately for Contrexéville, where he stayed for almost a month. During this time —just twenty years after our first meeting—we embarked on a moving correspondence. André naturally gave me a detailed account of his mother's illness, but he also spoke of his feelings for me, and of our future life, which we must now plan. Reading these letters, which I have kept, one might think they were those of two young lovers: in a way we were indeed enjoying a second idyll. They are precious letters which I often re-read and over which I sometimes weep. Fortunately, his mother rallied. But André had only just returned to Cap d'Ail when a second telegram summoned him to Contrexéville. His brothers and sister were also sent for. This time I left with him, wanting to be by his side in these difficult days.

When we arrived the Grand Duchess was in a desperate state: her death was only a question of days and she was in great pain. Nevertheless, she was immensely happy to see André again, and kept on repeating his name, which she also murmured towards the end, when she began to lose consciousness. She also tried to say some words about Vova. She died peacefully, at dawn on September 6th 1920.

André felt the loss deeply. He alone of her three sons had spent the whole Revolution and the last three years of her life with her.

She lies in a chapel which she built herself not far from the Hôtel La Souveraine, where she used to stay. (A plaque above the door of her suite recording her visits was pulled down by the Germans during the Occupation.) The Mass for the dead was celebrated by Father Ostroounov, who had come from Cannes. Many famous people attended the funeral, including her half-brother, Prince Henry of the Netherlands, and the municipality of Contrexéville named one of its streets after her.

We left Contrexéville for Paris, where we remained for some time at the Hôtel Lotti.

During this time André was informed of the presence in Paris of Sokolov, the special magistrate entrusted by Admiral Koltchak with investigating the murder of the Tsar and his family at Ekaterinburg and that of the Imperial Family at Alapaievsk. Sokolov was the only man who could reveal for certain what had happened; and he was the only man who could say if there was any hope that some of the Imperial Family had been saved. So André asked Sokolov to call on him at the hotel. Gabriel Constantinovitch, whose three brothers had died at Alapaievsk, and his wife were present at the interview.

Sokolov told us all the details of his investigation, which put an end to the legends of survival. Without the evidence of eye-witnesses, and in the absence of the victims' bodies, which had not been found, the actual fact of the murder could not be formally and indisputably established. But the information taken as a whole left no doubt: all the prisoners in the Ipatiev house had undoubtedly perished and their corpses had been burnt in the forest. Sokolov's conclusions were later entirely confirmed.

Concerning Alapaievsk, the assassination of the Imperial Family had been proved: all the bodies had been found in a mine, examined and identified. Sokolov showed us photographs there and then. A careful list had also been drawn up of all the effects found on the victims.

We left this interview deeply afflicted. There was no hope left. All had perished! André had asked the magistrate to send him the file of the Alapaievsk investigation. Sokolov did so, and André and I spent a whole night making copies of the most important documents.

All the small belongings found on the victims had been given to the Grand Duchess Xenia Alexandrovna, who distributed them among various members of the family. I received what had been found on the body of the Grand Duke Serge Mikhailovitch: a little gold medallion with an emerald in the middle and a small gold pendant, representing a potato at the end of a chain. The medallion contains my photograph, and around it are engraved the dates: "August 21st—Mala—September 25th". There is also a ten-kopeck piece, minted in 1869, the year of the Grand Duke's birth. I had given him this medallion many years before. As for the pendant, I remember that in their youth the Grand Dukes had formed a club, with the Vorontzovs and Cheremetevs, called the Potato Club. The origin of the name is doubtful, but they had all adopted it, and there are frequent references to it in the Tsar's *Journal*, during the period when he was still Tsarevitch.

Now I could entertain no single doubt: the Grand Duke Serge Mikhailovitch had been assassinated at Alapaievsk.

André and I often discussed the question of our marriage. We had in mind not only our own happiness, but also Vova's, and above all his position. Unlike some, we wanted to marry with the consent of the Grand Duke Cyril, head of the Imperial Family.

André went to see his brother, who was then living in Cannes, in order to ask officially for his permission to marry. He had told the Grand Duke and Grand Duchess Cyril of his intention to marry me long before in the course of conversation. They had seen no objection to the plan, saying that they found his wish perfectly natural, since we

37a. (*left*) Dancing the mazurka with my father when he was eighty-three years old.

37b. (*right*) The Grand Duke Dimitri.

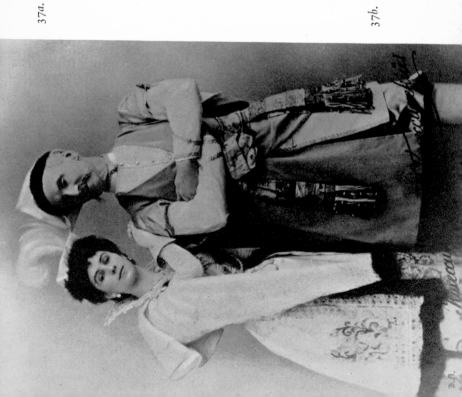

38. In the salon at my St. Petersburg House. (It was from this house that Lenin later addressed the masses.)

loved each other; and that they felt it their duty to help us in the matter, in order to make our life and Vova's easier.

The Grand Duke now gave his permission and bestowed on me the name of Krassinsky, with the title of Princess. Our son was similarly given the title Prince.

André next wrote to the Grand Duchess Olga Alexandrovna to announce our marriage and to ask her to inform the Empress Marie Feodorovna, who was living in Denmark. She replied with a charming letter, saying that the Empress was in favour of our union and wished us a great deal of happiness.

We therefore decided to be married on January 30th 1921, at the Russian Church in Cannes, for we wished to be blessed by Father Gregory Ostroounov, who had become André's spiritual director. The religious ceremony was fixed for four o'clock in the afternoon, and was attended only by my son and our witnesses: Baron Alexander Logguinovitch Zeddeler, my sister's husband, Count Serge Platono-vitch Zoubov, Colonel Constantin Wladimirovitch Molostrov and Colonel Wladimir Petrovitch Slovitsky.

Immediately after the religious ceremony we went, on their request, to visit the Grand Duke Cyril and the Grand Duchess Victoria Feo-dorovna, who received us most warmly and showed me a kindness which was soon to change into mutual affection. They were all in favour of our marriage, and never regretted giving their consent.

We then returned to Cap d'Ail, where a delightful table was waiting for us, with flower decorations by Arnold, a past master in the art. Apart from the witnesses, we had invited Marquis Passano and his wife, and Lilia Likhatcheva, her husband and Boris, her eldest son. It was an exceedingly gay dinner and André wrote in his journal: "We spent a marvellous evening. My dream has at last come true. I am infinitely happy."

Later, in 1935, in order to regularise the question of morganatic marriages, the Grand Duke Cyril decided to give morganatic wives and the children of such unions the name Romanovsky, to which they could add a second name of their own choice; with the title Prince would go the prefix "Serene Highness". We therefore decided to keep the name Krassinsky, which we added to that of Romanovsky.

Since most of the people concerned did not conform to this decree and continued to call themselves Romanoff, André did not want our son to be the only person without the family name to which he be-longs by blood; since the war he has therefore borne the name Romanoff.

H

After my marriage I was received by Queen Alexandrina of Denmark, daughter of the Grand Duchess Anastasia Mikhailovna and André's first cousin. She was living at Cannes, and, knowing her mother's love for me, she was extremely pleasant and kind.

We later visited Queen Marie of Roumania, who lived in the Château Fabron at Nice. When André and I arrived at the château the queen and her sister, the Grand Duchess Victoria Feodorovna, had gone out for a walk. Marie and Kyra Kyillovna, the Grand Duchess Victoria's daughters, received us most kindly. The Queen soon returned to the château. She was amazingly beautiful, a great lady, lively and energetic, who could lead the conversation with wit and success, and had the gift of immediately being liked. We also called on Queen Olga Constantinovna of Greece at the Ritz in Paris. She was old now, but still cheerful and affable, always staring at visitors through her eyeglass, for she was very shortsighted. After the uprising in Greece, Queen Olga had known persecution and exile, but now that the former Government had been restored, she would be able to return to Greece, which made her infinitely happy.

Our old friend, Paul Alexandrovitch Demidov, and his wife were the first of our Nice acquaintances to give a luncheon party in our honour. It would be impossible to name everybody who showed their affection on the occasion of our marriage.

For the anniversary of the Grand Duchess Marie Pavlovna's death, André, Vova and I went to Contrexéville, where we met the Grand Duke Cyril Wladimirovitch, Princess Tiouria (Catherine) Golitzin and A. A. Savinsky, who had come to France with the Grand Duchess and remained with her until her death.

Now that a year had passed since the Grand Duchess's death, we began to have parties in Cap d'Ail. The Grand Duchess Anastasia Mikhailovna, as gay and sparkling as ever, with whom we often went dancing at the Carlton in Monte Carlo, often came to the villa Alam. We invited our gayest friends and those she liked best. In this way we had some delightful evenings: Arnold surpassed himself and organised surprises. Once, for instance, as we were dancing in the drawing-room after dinner, the lights suddenly went out and the garden was illuminated with Bengal lights.

Nobody could have guessed then that the Grand Duchess Anastasia Milhailovna would so soon be taken from us. She died at Èze on March 11th 1922. We had seen her two days before her death, as gay and lively as ever. Olga, her devoted old servant, begged us to come at once, because the Grand Duchess was in a very serious condition. When we arrived at the villa Fantasia she had already lost consciousness. Her private secretary was holding a mirror up to her lips to make sure that she was still breathing. Suddenly she gave a deep sigh, and the end came. We all knelt round her bed and said a prayer. Then we closed her eyes. Vova could not believe that his beloved aunt, who had surrounded him with love from childhood, his great friend, was dead. During these last two years she had really filled our life with joy and tenderness.

Two hours later her niece, Princess Xenia (daughter of the Grand Duke George, the Grand Duchess's brother) arrived in haste from Cannes with her husband, M. Leeds, and Father Ostroounov. The Grand Duke Alexander Milhailovitch, the Grand Duchess's brother, arrived next day from Paris.

Her daughter, Queen Alexandrina of Denmark, arrived shortly afterwards in Nice, and we spent some days with her in the villa Fantasia, where I helped her sort her mother's small possessions and put aside what she wanted to take away with her. Very kindly, she gave André all the family miniatures and Russian books, and invited my son to choose whatever he wanted to keep in memory of the Grand Duchess.

Her remains were taken to the Russian Church in Cannes, where the funeral took place, and later to Mecklemburg to be laid in the family vault. Our son later had a bronze crown placed on her tomb.

Shortly before this, on February 15th 1922, Her Serene Highness Princess Yourievsky, morganatic widow of Tsar Alexander II, had died in her villa Georges at Nice, aged seventy-five. As soon as we heard this, we went with the Grand Duchess Anastasia to pay respects to the dead, and later attended the funeral together in Nice Cathedral.

CHAPTER XXVII

MEETINGS

ONE DAY, QUITE by chance, I met Virginia Zucchi in Monte Carlo. Over thirty years had gone by since I had last seen her in St. Petersburg. But I recognised her at once, and we threw ourselves into each other's arms. I have already related what a decisive influence this incomparable artist had had in forming me when I was just fourteen, and I had never forgotten it. Virginia Zucchi came to our villa, and we talked about the time long ago of her dazzling successes in Russia. Alas, it was our last meeting, for she died shortly afterwards.

Another unexpected meeting was with Isadora Duncan when I was lunching one day at Claridge's in Nice. She had changed so much that I should never have recognised her had I not been warned who it was. Our friendship remained unbroken, but Isadora was also to die soon afterwards, in tragic fashion, strangled by her own scarf, which had got caught in the wheel of a motor car.

In Monte Carlo lived a celebrity of the period—the beautiful Lady de Bathe, Lily Langtry. Queen Alexandra's lady-in-waiting and Edward VII's favourite, she left the Court ruined to become an actress and acquire immense fame in Shakespearian roles. Her villa was full of memories of her court and stage life, and her conversation was enthralling.

At Nice I also met the famous dramatist, Henri Cain, and his wife, *née* Girodon. A great connoisseur of food, he introduced me to *boeuf bourguignon*, and gave me the recipe. He also dedicated to me some lines of verse which he wrote in the villa guest-book.

We saw most of the famous tenor, Jean de Reszke, during these years. He and his brother Edward, who had a magnificent bass voice, had been the idols of St. Petersburg in the 'eighties; it would be hard to imagine a better performance of *Romeo and Juliet* than that in which they both appeared. I had often met Jean in the theatre in St. Petersburg.

The de Reszke brothers came of a wealthy noble Polish family. Jean de Reszke lived in a luxurious villa in Nice, where he gave large parties. He had long ago retired from the stage and gave singing lessons. He never failed, after lunch, to summon one of his pupils and make him sing for us. Then he would give him valuable advice, insisting above all on the singer's obligation really to understand the meaning of the music.

But there was a sad note in his family. Mme. de Reszke's son had been killed in the war, on the very day of the Armistice; she had been terribly affected by this cruel loss.

We were also frequent guests at the villa Olivetto in Nice, home of Princess Marie Radziwill, *née* Countess Branitzka,[1] known as "Bichette". Once when she left Nice for Rome she called on her way in most picturesque style, her car crammed with suitcases and her dogs yelping about her.

We celebrated my son's coming of age on July 1st 1923 with a dinner party at the Château de Madrid in Paris, to which we invited our closest friends: Count Michel Grabbe, Paul Demidov, Count Serge Zoulov and his wife. The party ended at the Château Caucasien, a famous Russian night club of the time, with *tzigane* music in private rooms overlooking the floor, and the Grand Duke Dimitri Pavlovitch joined us. The whole evening was a great success; all our friends shared in our happiness and took part in this family occasion.

During dinner my neighbour, Count Serge Zoubov, told me that he had just lost a highly prized cuff-link, which he treasured for sentimental reasons. He thought he had lost it near our table, but nobody could find it. So I advised him to have faith and give an offering to the poor of St. Antony of Padua. I myself, by such an offering, had been able one day at Strelna to find a brooch given to me by the Tsarevitch which I had lost while picking mushrooms in the park. I noticed my loss when I returned and had immediately promised to send an offering to St. Antony of Padua. I then returned to the place where I had been picking mushrooms, and suddenly remembered that Vova had leaped on to my shoulders the very moment I was bending down. I plunged my hand into the thick carpet of moss and found the brooch. Count Zoubov promised me that he would willingly make an offering. No sooner had he finished speaking than a waiter brought him the cuff-link. It had been found, not where he expected, but in a very busy path, where it might easily have disappeared in the gravel or the grass.

In the autumn of 1923 N. P. Karabtchevsky and his wife came to visit me. When they were announced I was, to say the least, very surprised. If he had come alone, I might perhaps have refused to receive him, but I could not refuse his wife. It grieved me to see

[1] The Branitzky estate near Kiev, *Bielaia Tzerkov* (White Church), was known for its size and remarkable historical monuments.

this old man, the former star of the Russian Bar, rushing towards me, almost kneeling, to implore me to forgive him for not helping me after the Revolution. His repentance was a little late, but pity won the day. . . .

To redeem himself, he begged me to allow him to write my biography, saying that he knew me so well. But I declined this suggestion.

During one of my trips to Paris at the time I attended a performance by Alexandre and Clotilde Sakharov; I was enchanted by their act, which was perfect of its kind, and sent them flowers with a few complimentary words. I received a touching letter in reply, in which they thanked me for the happiness which my praise gave them, adding: "The opinion of such a great and incomparable artist will be the best pledge of success in our search for new creations."

Later I saw the Sakharovs again at Aix-les-Bains. The taste and talent of their stylised dances, their attention to the smallest details of movement, attitude and costume were truly exceptional.

On Easter Eve, May 2nd 1926, I invited Serge de Diaghilev, Koribut-Dachkevitch, his uncle, Boris Kochno and the dancers in his company: Tamara Karsavina, Peter and Felia Vladimirov, Grigoriev and his wife, and Serge Lifar. I had hired cars which took us all to the Cathedral in Nice. After midnight Mass we returned to the villa for the *razgoveni* or traditional supper. A special Easter table had been arranged with *paskhas*, *koulitchs*, multi-coloured eggs, ham and other delicacies. I gave each guest a small token. After the meal people began to dance. Serge Lifar became rather gay and started to court Tamara Karsavina; but Diaghilev took this amiss and ended the flirtation by saying, "Young man, you seem to be rather too gay! It's time to go back home!" And they both returned to Monte Carlo. Serge Lifar has described this evening with great detail in his book.

During one of my first visits to Paris I was able to meet Anna Pavlova again at a charity performance at Claridge's, where she was dancing her enchanting solos. I went to kiss her after the performance. "Maletchka!" she said. "How happy I am to see you! We ought to put on the *grand pas* from *Paquita* together, like in the old days in St. Petersburg! Tata Karsavina, Vera Trefilova, Sedova, Egorova, Preobrajenska are in Paris. You'll have the main part, and we'll dance behind you. It will be lovely!" These words moved me deeply. Pavlova, then at the height of her glory, was ready to dance in second place behind me! She showed in this her great and beautiful nature both as a dancer and woman.

I saw her again at Monte Carlo, and she often came to have dinner or lunch at our villa. One day she invited us with some of her friends to the Sporting Club at Monte Carlo. We had a very gay dinner, speaking of the past which meant so much to us, of the Maryinsky Theatre, of our artistic careers. . . . Then we went to the gaming rooms. Pavlova dressed in a strange and original way. She did not really wear a dress at all, but merely pinned a large shawl to her petticoat; the shawl's long fringes fell from her shoulders like sleeves. Lively and nervous, she liked gambling, but had little confidence in her memory, and asked her friends to stay by her to remind her on what numbers she had laid her stakes. She placed her counters very quickly and all over the table: if the number was too far off for her to reach it she took the rake and pushed her stake across, knocking and displacing other people's counters in the process. At once cries of protest arose on all sides, but the gamblers calmed down as soon as they recognised her and merely whispered, "It's Pavlova! The famous Pavlova!" Meanwhile, embarrassed, Pavlova apologised, tried to replace the counters and knocked over others with the fringes of her shawl! This went on the whole evening, but the victims smiled and helped her. In the end Pavlova lost all the money she had on her and asked me to lend her a thousand francs, which she later returned in a lovely black silk purse with a gold fastening, which I have treasured in memory of that evening.

When she left the Riviera we all saw her off at the station. We had been told by friends that she always left in an atmosphere of nervous haste and commotion. First countless cases of varied size and appearance were brought into the compartment, which Pavlova counted, miscounted, re-counted, until she grew enervated; while everybody else, trying to help her, also counted, re-counted and miscounted, adding still further to the confusion. Whereupon Pavlova grew angry, but soon began to smile. In the end everything turned out all right and everybody grew calm . . . but not for long, for suddenly Pavlova was heard to cry, "Where is the cage with my little bird?" This was the spark which set the whole bonfire blazing again. Right and left all with one intent began to look for the bird. The cage with her bird in it, cried Pavlova, was the most precious thing in all her luggage! Fortunately the cage and its occupant were soon found, and Pavlova, her spirits restored, left for Paris, waving and calling goodbye through the window.

I saw her in Paris when she was dancing *Giselle* at the Théâtre des Champs-Elysées. She was clearly tired, but it was none the less a magnificent performance. She was unrivalled in this ballet. The impression she made in the second act when she crossed the stage diagonally on points, with a lily in her hand, was beyond description; she seemed to move without touching the ground, she floated, like an immaterial being.

The first friend I met in Paris was Vera Trefilova. I went to see her as soon as I had been given her address, a hotel in the Place des Pyramides. She had remained extraordinarily young, and Diaghilev immediately asked her to dance for him in Monte Carlo. She had not danced or worked for a long time. But she worked so well for this performance that in *Swan Lake* we were all struck by her stylish entry, her classical curtsy and the amazing ease of her movements, gestures and stage presence. The mark of our school was everywhere visible— in her noble movements, her elegant attitudes, all showing the class which had not been seen for a long time in Western Europe and which people had ceased to expect. Trefilova was exceptionally beautiful in *Swan Lake*, which was rightly considered her best role. None of the ballerinas who followed her in it came near rivalling her.

I had always been very fond of Liouba Egorova. She often came to visit me after completing her studies at the Theatre School; she sometimes spent several days at home with me and had even accompanied me to Vienna in 1908. After an unhappy first marriage to Mamontov, she had married one of the great friends of my youth, Prince Nikita Sergueevitch Troubetzkoy. During the emigration she opened a ballet studio which she ran admirably. I can assert unhesitatingly that her studio is the best in Paris; a judgment made from seeing her pupils who sometimes come to my classes. The stamp of an excellent school can be seen in all; the arm and leg positions are excellent, and the movements carried out in the truest spirit of our school. While she was dancing for Diaghilev in Monte Carlo, Egorova and her husband, Prince Troubetzkoy, were my guests.

At the same time Julie Nikolaïevna Sedova, another of our dancers, settled in the south and opened a studio at Cannes.

On April 28th 1928 Zoë Inkina came to visit me. The date has stuck in my memory, for it brought me a cruel blow. I was delighted to see Zoë, for I hoped that I would at last find out what had happened to the box containing the Tsarevitch's letters which I had entrusted to her mother before leaving Petrograd. Zoë now told me that their home had several times been searched and that her mother had even been arrested. To keep the letters would have been a mortal risk, and they had therefore had to burn them. This news was all the more cruel because I had been certain I had put my letters in safety.

The destruction of these letters affected me as much as any of my losses during those years. I had hoped so much to see them again, to hold them once more in my hands, to re-read them. . . .

My brother, Iouzia Kschessinsky, had remained in Petrograd. In the beginning I had been able to correspond freely with him, and to send him, through the excellent administration of the Hoover Committee, parcels of food and clothing. Iouzia had married Celine Sprechinska as his second wife and had two children: a boy, Romuald, and a girl Celine. He did not complain about conditions, but assured me that artists were well treated and that he was still living in his old apartment. But I was distressed to know that he was forced to live under Bolshevism and I wanted to bring him over to live with me in France. Serge de Diaghilev came to my help and gave me a letter inviting my brother to join his company. I was thus able to obtain a French visa for Iouzia and I sent him money for his travelling expenses through Finland. But he replied that he would rather stay in Petrograd, repeating that artists were in a privileged and exceptional position, deprived of nothing; his main reason was that he did not wish to leave a world to which he was bound by so many memories. Moreover, he had been allowed to celebrate his artistic jubilee, although he had retired from the stage, and this had given him great joy. His daughter Celine had finished her studies at the Ballet School and was already appearing at the Maryinsky Theatre. She greatly resembled me, he said, both in appearance and as a dancer; though after her marriage she gave up dancing. When the war came, in 1939, all correspondence with my brother ceased. For a long time I remained without news, and learnt only recently that he had died during the siege of Leningrad by the Germans. This was all I found out: no doubt he succumbed to hunger and cold. Poor dear Iouzia!

It had become traditional with us, since we lived in the South of France, to spend the last three days of Holy Week at Cannes, where, twice a day, we attended the services at the Orthodox Church and André and Vova received Communion on Easter Saturday.

Like all my family, I was a Catholic, but I felt the wish to be able to receive Communion in the same church as my husband and son. I therefore decided to become Orthodox. I had been familiar with the religion since childhood, since as children in the Theatre School we took part in Orthodox services. Father Ostroounov prepared me and celebrated the rite in our church at Cannes on December 9th 1925.

André, who was a patron of the Alexandrino Russian School in Nice, was in charge of collecting funds and once a year arranged galas at the Hotel de Paris. The school held an important place in our life at Cap d'Ail; and when we moved to Paris we twice returned to Monte Carlo to give dinner parties in its aid.

The late King Gustav V of Sweden, whom we often met, was very fond of us and treated our son with great warmth and kindness. We always invited him to our galas, which he adored. Iakovleva the singer took part, and Diaghilev kindly gave us the help of his company. We also organised a lottery, with prizes from the best firms: Chanel, Molyneux, Mappin and Webb, Cook, Maquet. At one of these galas King Gustav had the exceptional fortune to win the three first prizes: a magnificent coat from Molyneux, a case of champagne, and another valuable prize. He was delighted and insisted on carrying the whole lot away himself, so that he could give these wonderful gifts to his grand-daughters! At dinner I sat next to the King, opposite Capitoline Makarova and my husband.

Capitoline Nikolaïevna Makarova was another of the Russian colony in Nice who often came to our house. She was the widow of Admiral Makarov, who had died at Port Arthur, on April 13th 1904, on board the *Petropavlovsk*, which was sunk by a mine. The Grand Duke Cyril Wladimirovitch was one of the few survivors from the same warship: only three or four officers and a few dozen hands were saved from a crew of almost a thousand. Another guest was General Alexander Alexandrovitch Mossolov, for long Head of Chancery at the Imperial Court Ministry, and our Ambassador in Roumania during the last years of the War. Both of them were great friends of mine. In spite of their age, they were surprisingly youthful in mind and body. One day, after dinner, they decided to dance the mazurka, as in the good old days, and did in fact perform it with great class and brio.

There were endless stories about Capitoline Nikolaïevna Makarova, dating from the time when her husband commanded the port of Cronstadt. With her magnificent appearance, she was really the great Admiral's equal, but she always acted with perfect tact and presence. She was "a character", as everybody admitted without reservation. The anecdotes about her were always harmless and affectionate. Now, during the emigration, she remained wonderfully dignified, always appearing in the forefront of all religious or official ceremonies. Once, when invited by an English admiral to have tea with him on board his ship, she only accepted on condition she was paid the full military honours formerly due to her late husband. When she found a launch manned by an ordinary sailor waiting for her at the quay she refused to embark and informed the admiral that he was to send a launch manned by an officer; which he promptly did!

Among the old friends who often came to our house was W. Fonsivin, a descendant of our great national poet. He was a man of considerable taste and culture and a poet. He wrote a few lines to me, and I yield to the pleasure of quoting them:

Le Menuet[1]

Belle et noble dame, charmante,
Je voudrais vous voir danser,
La danse de l'époque enivrante,
Le Menuet des temps passés.
Je voudrais vous voir en marquise,
Dans des atours ensoleillés
Par votre grace toujours exquise,
Perle unique de nos ballets.
Je voudrais vous voir de roses enguirlandée
Dans un panier faisant la révérence
A Monseigneur émerveillé
De tant de grace et d'élégance.
Belle et noble dame, je voudrais vous voir danser
Charmante, le Menuet des temps passés.

Diaghilev had asked me to show Vera Nemchinova how *Swan Lake* was danced in St. Petersburg, and I often went to Monte Carlo to work with her. There I saw again my old friend, Raoul Guinsbourg, the famous impresario. We had met him a long time ago in St. Petersburg, at the time when he had brought French operetta to Russia. He later became impresario and finally Director of the Opéra in Monte Carlo. He had first appeared in operetta in Bucharest during the war

[1] *The Minuet:* Noble and beautiful lady, charming one, I should like to see you dance the dance of the enchanting years, the old-fashioned Minuet. I should like to see you dressed as a Marquise in a costume brightened by your exquisite grace, sole pearl of our ballet. I should like to see you, garlanded with roses, dressed in a hoop skirt, curtseying to Monseigneur who is amazed at such grace and elegance. Noble and beautiful lady, I should like to see you, charming one, dance the old-fashioned Minuet.

with Turkey. He describes in his own *Memoirs* how he was then engaged as a nurse in the Russian Red Cross and while rescuing wounded
near Nikopol he suddenly noticed that an enemy strongpoint was
weakly guarded. With other stretcher-bearers, he charged, uttering
terrifying cries of "Hurrah!" carried forward the whole front, and
Nikopol was captured! He himself stated that he had merely lent a
small hand in helping to capture the town. He now became a faithful
friend of Russia, and when Tsar Alexander III asked him how he could
thank him for the capture of Nikopol, Guinsbourg replied, "Become
friends with France, Your Majesty!" He liked to tell this story with
many details, whose truth nobody could guarantee, but he was always
listened to with delight. He was extremely grateful to the Grand Duke
Wladimir Alexandrovitch, who had spotted him when he was on the
stage, and he passed on this gratitude to his sons and in particular
André.

He had already asked me as early as 1895 to dance in several performances at Monte Carlo. He was then courting me assiduously and
I can still see him pacing up and down in front of my hotel.

He often invited us to lively luncheon parties at the Hôtel de Paris,
to which he invited the leading dancers of his company and various
personalities. He was a keen connoisseur of food and invented new
dishes whose cooking he would personally supervise. But when
rehearsal time came Guinsbourg would get up and leave straight for
the theatre in order to supervise everything and give his instructions.
He was a composer, and had several of his operas performed with
some success.

One remarkable thing about him, which all artists valued, was that
he rarely signed contracts, his word being worth more than any
written document: nobody ever had cause to complain of it.

When his daughter was being married he invited us to a family
dinner, some days before the wedding, to introduce the fiancé. We
thus discovered that the dining-room cupboards all contained not
china but the most select wines!

The Grand Duke Dimitri often came to spend a few days at the villa
Alam where we always had friends from Paris. We had gay times
together. After dinner we usually went to the Sporting Club at Monte
Carlo; André and I returned home early, but Dimitri and Vova, who
were young, often stayed late into the night.

Once in spring when we were in Paris we invited Dimitri and his
sister, the Grand Duchess Marie, to the pavilion of Armenonville with

39a. Act I of Fokine's ballet, *Eros*, in the Maryinsky Theatre.

39b. Act II of *Eros*: dancing with Vladimirov.

40a. The villa at Cap d'Ail.

40b. The Grand Duke and Grand
Duchess Cyril.

a few close friends. Afterwards we went to a famous cabaret of the time, in a cellar in the Palais-Royal, where the orchestra began to play Russian songs for us. Two English couples now came in and asked the musicians to play jazz, while we continued to ask for Russian songs. This displeased our neighbours, but when the Grand Duchess finally agreed to sing us the romance *Kalitka*, on condition I performed my Russian dance—which I did—the two Englishmen were so delighted that they came and knelt before us, begging us to accept a glass of wine. The ice was broken: we moved our tables together, and finished off this marvellous evening as friends.

A few years later, on November 21st 1926, Dimitri Pavlovitch married Miss Audrey Emmery at Biarritz; she was a lovely American girl, who soon won all our hearts. We often went to see them in Cannes, where they had rented a villa after their marriage, and later, when we were living in Paris, at the Château de l'Eure, which has left us with wonderful memories. At about the same time we met and went out several times with the Shah of Persia, who was a close friend of the Grand Duke Boris.

The question of money had come up in crucial fashion from the very first day of our life as *émigrés*. We had left Russia penniless, having lost all we had; all we had left was seven thousand francs in the bank at Monte Carlo. In the beginning we were able to make ends meet by mortgaging the villa. André received his share of the inheritance after the death of the Grand Duchess Marie Pavlovna, but the time for selling precious stones was over, and we received a much smaller sum than we expected.

André still had hopes of raising money from his real estate in Poland; but the final frontier arrangements restored that part of Poland to the U.S.S.R. and this last hope vanished.

I therefore decided to open a dance studio in Paris. But if I knew that I could dance well, could I also be sure that I could teach my art? Whatever doubts I might feel, however, I no longer had any choice.

The person who most encouraged me to make this decision was Tchaednev, a Russian lawyer and friend, who died soon afterwards and was not able to see the fulfilment of the plan.

Accordingly, in the autumn of 1928 we went to Paris to look for a studio and a flat. The agencies sent me all over town. I was determined to have a house with a garden, and it was also essential that the studio, while separate from the house, should nevertheless be fairly close to it. I finally discovered a studio in a building which was still under construction. Shortly afterwards we were found a small house in the

16ème arrondissement, No. 10 Villa Molitor, which is still our home today. The moment we saw the house with its little garden, we liked it.

When the arrangements had been settled we returned to Cap d'Ail to prepare what we wanted to send on to Paris. I meant to return towards the end of the year in order to open my studio and start work during the winter season. But we did not have enough money for the move and the repairs which our new house needed; after endless complications which I prefer not to mention we were finally able to leave Cap d'Ail on February 4th 1929. We settled in our house in Paris the next day.

A number of people spitefully claimed when I arrived that I had lost my fortune on the gambling tables. But one thing is certain: I have always enjoyed gambling, but I have never played for high stakes, especially at the Casino, neither after the Revolution nor even before, when I might have done so. I have lost a relatively small sum in gambling, certainly not the millions which some have spoken of and which I should have been very happy to possess!

CHAPTER XXVIII

A SECOND CAREER

THE FIRST THING to be done in Paris was to furnish the studio at No. 6 Avenue Vion-Whitcomb. This called for certain expenses which, in our straitened circumstances, I could not have met without the precious help of my friends. In particular I have to thank an Austrian Countess, whom I then met and who spontaneously offered to help me, and Ivan Ivanovitch Makhonin, an eminent engineer well known in Russia and France for his discoveries. He had married Nathalie Stepanova Ermolenko-Ioujina, a Wagnerian singer of the Imperial Theatre; he himself had a great love and knowledge of music, was an excellent violinist and a first-rate singer. He moved in theatrical circles, and knew all the leading artists and composers. He had known and admired me when I was dancing in the Maryinsky Theatre and did not hesitate to give me generous help.

The installation of the studio took more than two months: barres for exercises had to be ordered and put up, electricity installed, the walls painted and the most necessary furniture bought. It was ready only at the end of March, when we asked the Metropolitan Eulogius, Metropolitan of all the Russian churches in Western Europe, to celebrate a *Te Deum* and to bless the studio.

I had met the Metropolitan Eulogius the year before, when I had just hired the studio, at the entrance to the block, and we had both asked: "What are you doing here?" The Metropolitan replied that he had just been visiting a Russian family who lived in the house, and I explained why I was there. He thoroughly approved of my plan and asked me to invite him without fail to bless the studio. The ceremony took place on March 26th 1929 and was attended only by my closest friends who had helped me to find the studio and were interested in my enterprise.

As pianist I had taken Mme. Wasmoundt, whose husband and father-in-law, both generals, were respectively friends of my husband and the Grand Duke Wladimir. An excellent pianist, she is still my faithful helper.

I gave my first lesson on April 6th. My first pupil was Tatiana Lipkovska, sister of Lydia Lipkovska, our famous opera singer. Tania

Lipkovska, as we all called her, brought me luck, and her portrait still decorates my studio in the position it occupied on the first day.

It was scarcely a favourable time for opening a studio: the academic year was approaching its end, and all those who learned dancing took classes in two other studios. I had few pupils between April and July. But this gave me a chance of estimating my powers and judging whether I was capable of giving classes. Convinced that I should be able to fulfil my task, and do it well, I prepared for the autumn season, hoping for pupils to flock in with the new school year.

From May 22nd to June 12th 1929 Serge Pavlovitch Diaghilev gave his spring season at the Théâtre Sarah Bernhardt. We thus had the pleasure of meeting again and chatting, seated in my garden. His conversation, touching on Russia, the ballet, dancers and Paris society, was always most interesting: he had the gift of the happy, incisive phrase. He then left for London, where his company was to give a summer season at Covent Garden. We were at Royat when we heard the news, as unexpected as it was tragic, of his death. He had died in Venice, on August 19th 1929, aged only fifty-seven.[1]

I lost an old and trusted friend in Serge de Diaghilev. In spite of our short quarrel, he remained to the end what he had been to me from the beginning. He knew that I truly loved him and he valued my friendship.

Diaghilev was indisputably a unique figure, a true Russian *grand seigneur*, with innate talent. A real connoisseur of art and literature he understood and lived ballet with love. We had countless impassioned discussions on the subject. A conversation with him was a real treat, and one always left enriched by what he had to say.

His service to Russian ballet was enormous: one has only to remember that he introduced our Imperial ballet to Europe, as well as Russian music and our decorative artists.

At first Diaghilev brought to Paris a company exclusively composed of dancers from the Imperial Theatres, with Russian decorators and costume designers, and presented splendid productions. As principal maître de ballet he had the great Fokine, whose superb works will remain among the treasures of choreography. Gradually, however, Diaghilev's repertory visibly altered. Though he still put on classical works, he included Fokine's new creations in his programme, and began also to present ballets which would never have been produced on the Imperial stage, and which provoked discussions whose echoes

[1] Serge de Diaghilev was born on March 19th 1872, in Russia, in the province of Novgorod.

are still heard today. The proportion of Russian dancers began progressively to decrease after the First World War, and the company was completed by dancers of various nationalities, bearing Russian stage names. From this point the only Russian thing about the ballet was its name. Shortly before his death I asked Diaghilev how, with his taste and love for true Russian ballet, he could have so far gone astray as to present works in his last programmes which to my mind were revolting and ugly. I do not intend to publish his reply, since our conversation was private and intimate. But he made me understand, beyond any doubt, that in deciding to follow this path which led him away from the traditions of classical Russian ballet, he had been influenced neither by his tastes, which remained unchanged, nor by his own wishes, but by wholly other considerations. I was glad to learn that my old friend's artistic ideas had remained unaltered, and that circumstances alone compelled him to give other ballets.

In the autumn of 1929 I met Prince Serge Mikhailovitch Volkhonsky for the first time since the emigration. Twenty-eight years had passed since his resignation as Director of the Imperial Theatres, following our quarrel over the hoops of the costume for *La Carmargo*. We met during an interval at the Opéra; and it was if we had never had any misunderstanding. We almost kissed, so happy were we to see each other. After this we became great friends and began to see a lot of each other. He came quite informally to watch classes in my studio, and often lunched with us, always bringing me a small bouquet of flowers. At that time he was writing interesting theatre and film reviews in the newspapers, always written with intelligence and style. One day we mentioned the old hoops "affair". I explained quite honestly what had happened and assured him that I in no way blamed him: the true culprits were those who had reported the incident, distorting the facts for the sole purpose of arousing his hostility towards me. He would certainly have judged the matter differently if he had known the truth, and would have understood my position as the artist responsible for the ballet's success. I cited many instances in which I had always performed the management's orders in exemplary fashion. The Prince unreservedly admitted that my arguments were valid and that he had interpreted the affair in a wholly different light. He had been told that I had refused only in order to cross him, that my decision was a mere whim which must be totally disregarded. He told me that he was very sorry he had believed these allegations, instead of sending for me in his office, which would have been simpler and avoided all misunderstanding.

The Prince was a very cultured man, an informed musician, a very talented pianist and an excellent actor. He often successfully took part in amateur performances.

I still remember a conversation we had about mime. He thought that it was inadequately taught and that artists often made gestures which did not correspond to their words. Pupils, he said, should learn to use their arms so easily that they should not be put off by the movements accompanying declamation. I then asked him to give lectures in my studio on this subject, to which he willingly agreed. The first of these lectures, accompanied by practical demonstrations, took place on November 28th 1929 before my pupils and a few guests, and was entitled "Movement in dancing, mime and musical mime".

Prince Volkhonsky was a constant visitor to my studio, and approved of my method of teaching, which corresponded to his own ideas. He expressed this opinion a few years later in an article published after the appearance of my pupils for the International Dance Archives, on April 21st 1935.

The Directors of the International Dance Archives had asked me to give a public demonstration of my methods and results. I chose six pupils, from the youngest, who was just beginning her course, to the eldest, who was completing hers. Prince Volkonsky wrote: "When M. F. Kschessinska opened her studio in exile and from being a ballet star became a teacher and educationist, we were amazed by the sudden revelation of her teaching gifts. Those who undertake teaching in maturity, without practice, rarely succeed, since teaching is to some extent a new art, calling for a particular gift—a gift inherent in Kschessinska's nature. Moreover Kschessinska had danced less abroad than most of our other dancers; her name had crossed the frontier bearing the splendour of a glorious past. Europe had accepted her on trust, without direct proof. But her teaching and educational work are tangible facts, which have developed in full view of her contemporaries and have won her an undisputed highly personal place from which she can now speak with authority.

"Only those who have been able to visit Princess Krassinska's studio and to watch her classes can appreciate the educational importance of her work. I myself have been most of all delighted by seeing technique and the individual perception of beauty develop side by side. None of her exercises consists merely of gymnastic and technical figures aridly repeated; in what might appear to be the most soulless exercise a place is always reserved for feeling, grace and personal charm. Thus each pupil's particular gifts are free to blossom. Does not the art of execution lie in interpreting the same thing in different ways? The trade may be taught (we are no longer amazed by technique today); but to bring out each dancer's innate gifts and direct them in their own proper path, here lies the teacher's real talent, a talent which cannot be learnt!

"The performance was a great success and will no doubt fill one of the brightest pages in the chronicle of the International Dance Archives, in its chapter on 'Russia'."

Prince Volkhonsky then left for America, from where we heard of his death in October 1937. In reply to our letter of condolences his widow told us that shortly before his death her husband had again spoken warmly of us. It was a great comfort to know that he felt genuinely reconciled with me.

I began my second academic season on September 3rd 1929. The number of my pupils kept on increasing in spite of the lack of all publicity. I had realised, from the very first classes, that I could teach effectively and my enterprise soon took shape. The pupils understood perfectly what I wanted of them, while I felt that I had them well under control from the smallest to the oldest. What particularly fascinated me was working with the beginners, seeing them take note of my advice and a month or two later succeed in doing easily all that I had taught them.

A year after the opening of my studio Anna Pavlova, who was then dancing in Paris, told me she would like to come and see it. I immediately told all my pupils that she was coming, so that they should all be present on that day. We offered her flowers when she arrived; she then watched the class and at the end came up to me and kissed me, exclaiming, moved, "And I thought you were no teacher!"

This was to be our last meeting. She left shortly afterwards for a tour with her company. The following January, when André was seriously ill and in hospital, I learnt that Pavlova was also critically ill in The Hague. Dr. Zalevsky, her regular doctor, was also André's doctor, and Pavlova's husband sent me a telegram asking me, in view of her extremely grave condition, to let him come to her. I did not feel entitled to refuse, especially as André was being looked after by other doctors. So Dr. Zalevsky left Paris for The Hague on January 20th.

Alas! Anna Pavlova could not be saved. She died on January 23rd 1931.[1] André was very fond of her and we concealed the sad news

[1] Anna Matveavna Pavlova was born on January 31st 1882 in St. Petersburg, and graduated from the Imperial Theatre School in 1899.

from him, as we had concealed the reason for Zalevsky's hasty departure three days before. We even stopped him reading the newspapers in order not to upset him, and he only learnt of her death several months later when he found a paper which had been forgotten on his bed.

Anna Pavlova's body was brought to London, where her solemn funeral was celebrated in the Russian Church. Her body was then cremated, and the funeral urn laid in the Golders Green Cemetery.

Many years later I stayed for three weeks in London with friends[1] living in Golders Green, not far from Ivy House, where Pavlova had lived. I was thus able to go into the park and see the pond where Jack, her favourite swan, had grown up; I also visited the house before going to say a prayer by our dear Pavlova's ashes in the nearby cemetery. There was a white marble urn, as delicate and graceful as Pavlova herself, surrounded by white flowers alone. One could feel that these fresh flowers, so tastefully arranged, had been laid by an affectionate hand. I was also shown, in one of the London parks, a place surrounded by flowers and roses where a monument was to be raised to her.

When I think of Pavlova I must mention the article which Serge Makovsky wrote about her appearance in *Giselle*, on May 9th 1930, at the Théâtre des Champs-Elysées:

"Anna Pavlova—irresistible, as lithe as a flame, as light as a feather—is dancing *Giselle*. Nothing more needs to be said. Anna Pavlova never astonished one with her technique; she charmed one by her inspiration. Even in the past one never dissected her dancing (which was always full of faults): one only wanted to admire it, forgetting the rules of dancing in order to be farther carried away by her divine talent."

At the beginning of the autumn of 1930 I felt acute pains in my right hip. Dr. Zalevsky, my doctor, at once suspected sciatica; but the pain did not diminish in spite of all treatments, and I could scarcely move. I was then taken to a radiologist for a more exact diagnosis. After examining the X-rays, Dr. Zalevsky and M. Gattelier, the surgeon, whom he had consulted, were quite definite: I must without fail stop working and even abandon the studio, since any sudden movement could lead to very serious danger.

This was equivalent to a death sentence. I had opened my studio less than eighteen months ago, and put all our resources and hopes

[1] Eudoxia Iakovlevna Tongonogova and her daughter, Xenia Pavlovna, who had been my pupil from 1934 to 1936.

41a. The Grand Duchess Anastasia Mikhailovna.

41b. With my husband and the Grand Duchess Marie Pavlovna (1953).

42*a*. In our Paris garden with my husband, the Grand Duke André and our son, Prince Romanoff.

42*b*. Our house in Paris.

into it; and now, in a single moment, all was collapsing. I asked both doctors to think of the consequences which such a verdict entailed. But they were definite; they could not, in all conscience, allow me to go on.

I had grown accustomed during my life to enduring the blows of fate with courage, but never to admitting defeat. I immediately informed my son, who was in the South, of the doctors' diagnosis and my own despair. I also sent the X-ray photographs to Kojine, the surgeon, in Nice, who was an old friend of mine and had already looked after me in Russia, and begged him to give me his opinion.

I received the following telegram in reply from Vova, on September 29th 1930: "I have prayed fervently for you before Notre-Dame de Laghet—Vova."

Almost at once I received a moving letter from my son and another from Dr. Kojine. My son's letter, written from the Sanctuary of Notre-Dame de Laghet, was dated September 29th:

"Dear Mother and Father whom I love with all my heart. I have just prayed before the miraculous Image for both of you and for us all. I firmly believe that the Holy Virgin will grant my prayer and send us salvation, joy and happiness, that all will go well, and that you, dear Moussenka, will be cured. I have sprinkled this letter with holy water. When you receive it, take it and bless yourself with the sign of the cross. You will be immediately and completely cured, dear Moussenka. I bless you in my thoughts and make the sign of the cross over you.

"Holy Virgin, save us! May God keep you!

"Vova, who adores you."

Meanwhile, Dr. Kojine told me that after a close examination of the X-ray he had come to a radically different interpretation from the Paris doctors. He thought that complete rest could only harm me and that I should, on the contrary, continue working in spite of my pains. Knowing my energy and will-power, he was sure that I would soon get better.

These replies gave me new life and courage. I had been saved by my faith; a miracle had taken place. I went to the studio and began by putting my bad leg on the barre. The pain was terrible, but I gritted my teeth and endured it and soon afterwards resumed my classes.

I made such a complete recovery that six years later, in 1936, I danced at Covent Garden, where I performed my Russian dance with success.

But other trials were in store. In the same year, about Christmas, André fell seriously ill with purulent pleurisy and an abscess of the lung. After a consultation between Dr. Zalevsky, Professors I. P. Aleksinsky and Besançon, M. Gattelier the surgeon, and Drs. Clerc and Claude, it was decided to transport my husband at once to hospital. He struggled against death for three months.

These eminent practitioners, and particularly Drs. Clerc, Zalevsky and Gattelier, looked after him the whole time. Professor Duval was called in when a lung operation proved necessary, and the operation was performed by Dr. Gattelier. The doctors despaired of saving him and told me openly that the only hope lay in a miracle. At the same time Vova caught measles, and I was forbidden access to his room in case I gave the illness to André.

I therefore lived in André's room in the hospital, returning there in the evening after my work in the studio. How can I describe the torments I suffered during those months? When I saw the doctors powerless to save my husband I often gave way to despair. Through God's help, André was saved—but at the price of indescribable effort and suffering!

Everybody asked daily for news of his health, and I was surrounded by the most moving attention throughout this period of trial. The Grand Dukes Cyril and Boris Wladimirovitch came to visit André, as did their sister, the Grand Duchess Ellen Wladimirovna, with her husband and daughters. The Grand Duke Dimitri Pavlovitch was particularly kind; not only did he visit my husband every day, but he also took him whatever he was allowed to eat and drink by the doctors. His moral support was invaluable to André during his illness.

André was able to return home shortly before Easter but he was confined to bed for a long time still, and the Easter night service, followed by the traditional supper, was celebrated in his room. In summer we spent a month at Évian, in a small, attractive family *pension*, situated high up. The fresh air allowed André to make a rapid recovery and we were able to walk together in the surrounding forests and meadows.

On our return we went to Marly-le-Roi where Prince Gabriel Constantinovitch and his wife were living in Robert Bienaimé's villa. The Grand Duchess Xenia also paid us frequent visits.

In 1932 George Alexandrovitch Grammatikov and his wife, Elisabeth Pavlovna, entered our service as butler and cook respectively. George Alexandrovitch belongs to a noble family from the Crimea.

He had volunteered for the White Army in 1919, during the Civil War, obtained a commission and been awarded the Order of St. George, Fourth Class, for his bearing at the front. Evacuated to Gallipoli in 1920 among the very last detachments of Wrangel's army, he had then arrived in France. His respect and affection for André led him to seek employment with us. Circumstances had freed his wife to find a post, where she was so successful that she is now as good as the best *cordon bleu*. They have both continually shown us the most affectionate loyalty and are now part of our family.

At first I was able to run the studio alone, but I soon had to find someone to help me. I therefore engaged a Russian acquaintance, Anastasia Petrovna Iolkina, and her daughter. They came to live in the studio and saw to its upkeep and the secretarial work, duties which they always fulfilled most competently.

During the first years I accepted boys as well as girls; among these I am glad to mention Lichine, Kniazef, Dollinof, Eglevsky, Grand Mouradoff and Boris. There were many others, not always of Russian origin, such as Jean Lemoine, who is now among the foremost French dancers. After a time, however, I gave up accepting boys, except for private lessons, since many families did not like the idea of their daughters working together with boys. The high standard of my pupils led to frequent requests to lend them to charity performances or private parties. Thus they danced at the Russian Press Ball in Paris on New Year's Eve in 1930, and had a great success. At about the same time I arranged a performance with my pupils for the Egyptian Princess Chivekiar, who had a magnificent apartment with a stage. And until the war in 1939 I often arranged public performances of my pupils in dances which I composed.

The number of pupils went up every year, exceeding a hundred in 1933-34 and 1934-35. It became essential to enlarge my studio. Fortunately the flat next door fell vacant. I immediately rented it and had a connecting door built between the two. This gave me two dressing-rooms and a huge reception room. The reconstruction took all summer, and work was only completed for the beginning of the 1935-36 season.

I asked the Metropolitan Enlogius to bestow his blessing again on the enlarged studio. The celebration of the *Te Deum* was arranged for October 7th 1935 with the aid of the Afonsky Choir, and was followed by a buffet lunch. I invited Prince Serge Mikhailovitch Volkhonsky, Princess Tamara Eristov, Prince Nikita Troubetzkoy, all of whom had helped me to instal the studio, all my pupils and a few friends. After the *Te Deum* and the blessing, the Metropolitan gave a short address. He said that all art is pleasing to God, and told the legend of the poor dancer who, having nothing but his art to offer to the miraculous statue of the Virgin, resolved to dance before her. Knowing that he would never be allowed to dance in church, he slipped in secretly during the night. When the first monks entered the church to pray in the early morning they were amazed by the sight of the artist still dancing, lost to the world around him. The monks were indignant and on the point of ending this scandal, when, to their great confusion, they saw the Virgin stretch out her arms to the dancer and lean towards him, as if to thank him, while he bowed down at her feet. His offer, so pure and sincere, had been accepted.

CHAPTER XXIX

FAREWELL TO THE STAGE

ON MARCH 2ND 1936 the Grand Duchess Victoria Feodorovna died at Amorbach in Germany, where she had been to visit her daughter, Marie Kirillovna, Princess of Leiningen.

She had fallen ill on arrival at Amorbach, and the news of her health had been disturbing, but none of us imagined, until the very last days, that her end was near. Nothing led one to guess that her health and strength had been so undermined by hardships and cares that she would be unable to resist a serious illness.

It was a hard loss for us to bear, and I mourned her sincerely. She had given her consent to our marriage, with the Grand Duke Cyril Wladimirovitch, and since then had shown me great affection. We had often been to lunch or tea with her, and she took the greatest interest in the studio, where she had often visited me, sometimes with her daughters and Princess Beatrice, her sister. On her first visit she spoke these charming words to the pupils: "Be happy to work with such a famous artist as your teacher!"

A funeral service was held the same evening in the Russian Cathedral, rue Daru, by the Metropolitan Eulogius. The service was crowded, although there had been no time to tell the sad news to everybody.

Two days later André and Vova left for Coburg to attend the funeral on March 6th.

The Duke of Coburg gave a family dinner on the 6th in his old feudal castle. Vova had been very impressed by the appearance of the old castle: a steep, winding path led to the top of the mountain where the eagle's nest was situated; the way in was by a dark, vaulted doorway. The Duke's private rooms were intimately and comfortably furnished, but the dining-room, which had not been altered for hundreds of years, had bare stone walls, deep-set windows, and ancient trophies. This mediaeval room was oppressive in appearance.

After the funeral service and absolution, the coffin was taken down to the family vault of the Princes of Coburg. The mourners included Queen Marie of Roumania, her sister, Alexandra of Hohenlohe, with her husband, Queen Elizabeth of Greece, Queen Marie's daughter, the Grand Duke of Mecklemburg-Schwerin and the Leiningen family, King Ferdinand of Bulgaria, who lived at Coburg since his abdication in favour of his son, King Boris, was also there. Several of the German princes had put on their old uniforms.

After the funeral the Queen of Roumania invited the whole family and all the mourners to lunch. Next day King Ferdinand invited André and Vova to a lunch of all the family, at which the Grand Duke Dimitri was also present. The King had a charming thought for me: he took a small bunch of violets from the table, which he had just received from his family estate, and asked André to give them to me in memory of him. The King was much attached to André, who had twice visited him in Sofia, and had shown himself delighted at our marriage. He liked to shroud himself in mystery, and André kept notes which he had received from the King in answer to his letters: there were always several envelopes with strange addresses and various instructions where to bring the answer and what precautions to observe, etc. . . .

André knew King Boris well. He had accompanied him to Kiev at the time of Stolypin's murder, and the King often sent him large presents of Bulgarian cigarettes bearing his monogram.

The late King Alexander of Yugoslavia had also been a close friend of André's. They had met in Russia, when the King was studying at the Pages' Academy, but their friendship dated especially from André's visit to King Peter in Belgrade. They had exchanged cigarette cases (André managed to save his, but the King lost his during the War). King Alexander never failed to invite André when he came to Paris, and we deeply treasured this help during my husband's illness. We could not foresee the tragic end which fate had in store for him. Our son, who knew him, bears him in affectionate memory.

Of all my new artistic relations formed after my arrival in France, those I enjoyed with Arnold Haskell were among the most important. I had met him by chance at Monte Carlo in 1925.[1] He was a young ardent balletomane, short, thin, full of enthusiasm, and with intelligent eyes. Diaghilev was then trying to persuade me to return to the stage and appear in his Paris season, but I refused. "The loss was enormous," wrote Haskell. "Kschessinska would have dazzled us then, just as she could dazzle us today. She thought otherwise, and would not risk the memory of those days, when she stood, more than Pavlova even, for the Imperial Russian Ballet and its great traditions. I still feel sore at having lost that season; without it, my collection of memories is sadly incomplete."[2]

Our second meeting was in Paris after the opening of my studio.

[1] See Chapter XVIII, above.
[2] Arnold Haskell, *Balletomania* (London, Victor Gollancz Ltd., 1934), p. 325.

Prince Volkhonsky himself brought him to see me, which greatly pleased Haskell, since the Prince had left the Imperial Theatres "in one of the greatest balletic comedies in history and the happy ending was artistically correct in this case".[1]

After that we met frequently. Haskell often came over from Paris to attend the ballet performances given by the Blum and de Basil companies. We went to the theatre together and afterwards went to see the artists on stage before having supper with them and exchanging impressions. Our one regret was that these wonderful evenings had to come to an end.

Arnold Haskell also liked to watch classes in my studio, and followed my teaching method very closely. He has given his impressions of this in his book, *Balletomania*, where he also faithfully records one of our conversations:

". . . There is about her a harmony that is enhanced by something exciting—charm, intelligence, character—that breaks up the monotony of harmony, and makes her perfect, the complete artist. Kschessinska is the artist in life as well as on the stage. To watch her at ease, let alone dancing in her classroom, is to learn something new about the possibilities of movement. Beside her the word *graceful*, that we so often use, has absolutely no meaning.

"It is useless, I am completely defeated, I cannot translate Kschessinska into words. A small pupil in her class recently paid her a greater, simpler tribute.

"For two weeks the new arrival, an eight-year-old, would not attempt to make a movement or to join in with the others. She stood apart and watched. Then one day, coming up to the great ballerina, she said, 'I like your dancing. Now I will try.' And she tried with conspicuous success.

"The class is one of the finest I have ever seen: very personal, stimulating, and a definite artistic experience. Kschessinska has given herself to the work with intense enthusiasm, working and dancing with her pupils, sometimes for eight hours a day.

"The first dancer to gain supremacy for Russia over the Italian school, Kschessinska is teaching those who will maintain the Russian name. These ideas have already produced Riabouchinska, Rostova, Simeonova, Tarakanova, Lichine and others. That is a proof of their wisdom. When you applaud them, you applaud her."

Haskell has been an enthusiast of Russian ballet from his youth.

[1] Arnold Haskell, op. cit., p. 325.

The art of dancing, whose technique he studied by attending classes, scenic art, backstage and artistic life have no more secrets for him. I rate him today among the greatest connoisseurs of ballet. Sincere, conscientious and impartial, he did not hesitate to accompany de Basil's company round the world, in order to study on the spot the conditions in which artists worked.

Ballet owes him several works of basic importance, including *Balletomania*, *Diaghileff* and *Dancing Round the World*, whose exactness and precision are enhanced by a complete mastery of the subject, by penetrating observations and a true writer's talent. But apart from these and so many other works, Arnold Haskell has played an enormous role, especially in England, in the development of the art of ballet. There was no English ballet when he began. There was need of hard work and great tenacity to alter public opinion and prove that ballet had the same rights as drama and opera, that it too was an art and not merely an entertainment.

The credit for this is also due to Serge de Diaghilev who organised ballet seasons in London, where he scored brilliant successes.

Dame Ninette de Valois (who had danced with Diaghilev), convinced by the example of our Imperial Schools that national teaching was essential if a real ballet was to be built on a solid basis, determined to found a national school in London. After several years' work, Dame Ninette de Valois and Arnold Haskell were thus able to assure ballet an honourable and universally recognised position at the Royal Opera House, Covent Garden.

The traditions of our Imperial ballet maintain a visible influence in English ballet. Arnold Haskell and Ninette de Valois have now had practical experience of the prime importance of a single school for the company.

Having visited the School twice, in 1936 when it was first begun, and in 1915, I have been able to measure and appreciate the distance covered.

At first it was merely a timid project, backed by limited funds. But one could already see that Ninette de Valois had founded her teaching on true principles. Arnold Haskell was her active supporter, and it was he who asked me to come to London to visit the School and to give the company a demonstration on the stage of the Vic-Wells Theatre.

Arnold Haskell wrote at the time that the idea was "to inaugurate a five-year plan for the Vic-Wells ballet with the idea of creating a national school by Russian methods". And he added: "The great ballerina is keenly interested in the plan, especially as many of the artists have worked under her. She and her husband, the Grand Duke André Wladimirovitch, have agreed to be Vice-Presidents of this plan, and will closely follow its working out." Unfortunately, circumstances prevented me from taking a more active part in this great work.

Later, when I paid my second visit to the School, in 1951, it had developed so much that it reminded me a little of our Imperial School. Pupils of all ages were accepted, which meant that the company could always be reinforced with new strength. The teachers, who were chosen from among the dancers, assured that ballet traditions would be maintained. There was, of course, much discussion on the matter, some saying that new tendencies called for new methods, while others, including Arnold Haskell, Ninette de Valois and myself, clung to the old ideas, experience having shown that a classical training, unlike new methods, would allow the dancer to tackle both the classical repertoire and modern dance. The Sadler's Wells School chose the right path and its efforts have been crowned with brilliant success. Two permanent companies have been formed, one of which appears at Covent Garden, while the other undertakes tours in England and abroad, where it meets with enormous success.

My friendship with Arnold Haskell has never stopped growing since our first meeting. Not only has he shown me the most flattering attention in his books and in life, but he has sent me the best dancers who wished to perfect themselves in ballet.[1] Many English and American pupils have come to take classes with me, and several of them later opened dance studios. I shall mention only Lipkovska, my first pupil, Shirley Bridge, Adrianova in Canada, Semenova in Texas, O'Connor and Tarassova (Henry Troyat's sister) in New York. Georgia Hiden my former pupil, is now head of the ballet at the Vienna Opera. Others formed small companies.

It is a curious fact that this unshakable friendship came about through the offices of Serge de Diaghilev and Prince Volkhonsky, with whom I had formerly had the severest conflicts in my career. It is true, however, that these later gave way to the truest friendship.

After Diaghilev's death, Colonel de Basil had formed a company of charming young artists, the chief of whom were Toumanova and Baronova, Preobrajenska's pupils, Riabouchinska, Semenova, Shirley Bridge (Adrianova) and Loulou Kilberg (Rostova), my own pupils.

[1] The following members of the Sadler's Wells Ballet attended my studio between 1935 and 1937: Pearl Argyle, Andrée Howard, June Brae, Margot Fonteyn, Pamela May, Elizabeth Miller, Molly Brown, Laurel Gill, Mary Honer, Gwyneth Matthews, Anne Spicer and Harold Turner.

The Company had great success in London, and there is no doubt that de Basil helped greatly to develop English ballet along Russian traditions.

During his ballet season at Covent Garden, Colonel de Basil formed the idea of organising a kind of jubilee performance bringing together Kschessinska, Preobrajenska, Egorova and Volinine. Preobrajenska and Egorova refused, Volinine was unable to attend, and in the long run I was the only one to take part.

For my programme I chose the Russian Boyar dance, which I had last performed at Krasnoïe Selo before the Tsar, on the eve of war. The *sarafan* and *kokochnik* (traditional costumes and head-dress) designed by Salomko were re-designed from memory by Ludmilla, my maid. Karinska arranged to have my costume (to be ready for my arrival) made partly in London and partly in Paris.

On July 13th André, Vova and I left for London. Just as we were leaving we saw Serge Lifar arrive out of breath and leap into the train: at the last moment he had decided to attend the performance. Crossing by Calais, we ran into a heavy swell which made us arrive almost an hour late in London. I was greeted at Victoria Station by de Basil, Tania Riabouchinska, and David Lichine, with armfuls of flowers, while the reporters and photographers pressed round. I was then taken to the Savoy to meet the Press, while André and Vova went to the Waldorf Hotel. In the evening we all went to the Alhambra to see Blum's company, which was performing Fokine's ballets, and the day ended with supper at the Savoy, given by Arnold Haskell.

Covent Garden was packed with a very smart audience. Following English custom, a red notice signified that all tickets had been sold. The whole Press had been writing of my appearance.

The Grand Duke Dimitri Pavlovitch sat in a box with André, Vova and Serge Lifar. He seemed more anxious than anybody, and at the last moment turned away, asking Lifar to tell him if he could look at me or not. I was given a wonderful reception. I received eighteen curtain calls, a rare event in England, where the public is more reserved than in Russia and France. The stage was buried in flowers. It was my last appearance in the theatre. I was almost sixty-four.

Two days later André received a letter from Queen Marie of Roumania, expressing her joy at my great success and saying how sorry she was to have been unable to attend. The mourning ordered after George V's death had not yet been raised at the English Court.

After the performance Colonel Bruce Ottley gave a supper party

to which were invited the leading balletomanes and many members of
English society.

Arnold Haskell gave a party at his mother's house, followed by a
magnificent Russian dinner. He presented me with a silver vodka set,
made by Russian silversmiths. When I returned home I noticed that
there was a letter engraved on each glass, the whole forming the word
"souvenir". Haskell told me later that he had not noticed this and was
delighted by the surprise.

Eudoxia Iakovlevna Tonkonogova asked me to dinner at the Savoy.
We were also invited to visit Marie Rambert's and Mrs. Koon's
studios, and to have tea in a women's club, the Forum Club, where
Mrs. Henry Villiers welcomed me with these flattering words: "Yester-
day I had the honour of having tea with the Queen, and today with
the Queen of Russian ballet."

We often had supper with Fokine and his wife after attending the
performances of de Blum's[1] excellent company, in which were many
of my former pupils.

It would be impossible to name all the friends who surrounded us
with friendship and affection during this delightful visit. I was able,
after twenty years, to see my nephew Slavouchka Kschessinsky, my
brother Iouzia's son by his first wife, who had married an English-
woman and settled in London. We returned with many regrets to
Paris on July 22nd.

Shortly afterwards a book was published dealing with the ballet
companies of Colonel de Basil, René Blum, the Ballets Jooss, and
Alicia Markova and Anton Dolin's company. It was illustrated by the
famous London photographer, Gordon Anthony. Although I was not
a member of any of these companies, my photograph in Russian costume on the stage at Covent Garden figured on the first page.

The following year, during the Exposition Universelle, the Sadler's
Wells Ballet gave a series of performances at the Théâtre des Champs-
Elysées. Led by Ninette de Valois and Frederick Ashton, the pioneers
of English ballet, the excellent, strong company already had a large
repertoire.

The first performance took place on June 15th, and was attended by
the President of the French Republic, the British Ambassador and the
whole English colony. The theatre was packed with the smartest Paris
audience.

I was able to invite home some thirty members of the company,

[1] De Blum was murdered by the Germans during the war.

including several who had worked in my studio. Serge Lifar also came to this gay supper party, which was served on small tables.

I cannot remember when nor how I first met Lifar. I must have seen him dance in Diaghilev's company soon after his arrival from Russia, in January 1923. But I think I met him at Easter 1926, when he came to my villa with Diaghilev.

Later, when I was living in Paris and Lifar was maître de ballet at the Opéra, he often came to see me and I grew very attached to him for his kindness, intelligence and talent both as dancer and choreographer. In fact, he became a member of the family. He on his side swore great affection for me. In memory of the first Easter supper at Cap d'Ail, I invited him every year, and if he happened to be away from Paris on that night, he never failed to give me his good wishes by telephone. He often told me that the Grand Duke and I took the place of his parents, and one day he even introduced us as such to one of his friends.

When he had a stable position at the Opéra, Serge Lifar often invited me to ballet performances and to his new works. Afterwards we went to find him on stage or in his dressing-room, which was always full of admirers, before supping together in the nearest restaurant.

Lifar had arrived to join Diaghilev without any preparation; nevertheless, by determined, hard work, he succeeded very soon in becoming an excellent dancer. Two years later he was already the Company's leading male dancer.

I thought him an artist with a rich personality and an excellent dancer. He was outstanding in *Giselle*, which he had rehearsed with P. Vladimirov. Spessivtseva, his partner, was also very beautiful in this ballet.

Many of Lifar's creations at the Opéra were enormously successful and I would have been glad to see them again. Others, however, sometimes suffered from hasty production, while the scenario and music did not always suit Lifar's taste but had been imposed upon him.

Serge Lifar has attained an eminent position at the Opéra, becoming one of the best-known maîtres de ballet This is the reward of an exceptional career, especially when one remembers that Lifar is a foreigner. Furthermore, one of the things most to his credit is that he has been able to raise ballet to its due rank, on a level with opera, whereas before it was relegated to second place: ballets, in fact, were only performed at the end of the performance. The Administration would not believe Lifar when he claimed that the public would equally

43*a*. My Paris studio before it was enlarged.

43*b*. A Christmas party in the studio, 1954. Lifar is standing just behind me.

44. In the studio with my pupil, Tatiana Riabouchinska.

come to performances exclusively devoted to ballet. It was thought that the box office receipts would fall. In fact not only did the public begin to frequent ballet, but the theatre was full and people were fighting for tickets. Lifar began by giving several one-act ballets, and later a full-length work. Today a performance at the Opéra is devoted exclusively to ballet, as in Russia. Dancing is no longer treated as a poor relation.

CHAPTER XXX

BLACK YEARS

At 5.30 p.m. on April 12th 1938 died the great, incomparable Feodor Ivanovitch Chaliapin. We all attended the service in his flat at eight o'clock, and in the Church, rue Daru, the following day. But we could not attend the funeral, because we were due to leave for Antibes on the 14th.

In spite of his apparent good health, Feodor Ivanovitch suffered from diabetes. People said that he should have kept from over-indulgence at table, but he was too fond of good living to deprive himself. He was often ill during his last years, and a final crisis carried him off.

I had known Chaliapin in Russia, when we were both appearing on the Imperial stage. He always called me "*ma petite*" in a friendly way, but we did not meet in private life. During the emigration, however, when his daughters Marina and Dassia[1] began to take classes with me, he sometimes came with Marie Valentinova, his wife, to the studio.

I remember a dinner party which Feodor Ivanovitch gave on February 1st 1930, when he asked me to dance my Russian dance. I had never liked dancing on private occasions, but Chaliapin knew how to ask so that one could not refuse. I accepted on one condition, however: that he should sing! The compromise was accepted. Marina also promised to dance the waltz which I had arranged for her. Mme. Wasmundt, my accompanist, was among the guests, who included MM. Paul Boncour and Philippe Berthelot, then Secretary-General in the Foreign Ministry.

Chaliapin started the concert by singing a romance. After that I danced my Russian dance and Marina her waltz. Feodor Ivanovitch was enchanted and could not thank me enough, while Paul Boncour paid me the highest compliments; we remained very good friends afterwards.

We were often Chaliapin's guests, especially after he had sung in opera. When we went to congratulate him in his dressing-room he

[1] Marina began to take classes on October 10th 1929, and Dassia on November 8th 1930. Dassia, Chaliapin's youngest child, was also his favourite. My pupils also included the granddaughter of Broussan, the former Director of the Paris Opéra, and Sophie Volkhonsky, the granddaughter of Rachmaninoff, who came several times to my studio.

immediately invited us, without ceremony, to have supper with him. His home was always full of people, and stocked with excellent food and wines. Chaliapin was a marvellous story-teller, and he held everybody's attention with his anecdotes. He liked recalling his beginnings in a church choir and his first provincial recitals; his life was like a novel He used to tell us that when he drank in gay company in taverns he used to ask for a new bottle by rolling an empty one down to the innkeeper's feet; and then, to tease his wife, who did not like practical demonstrations of this kind, he rolled an empty bottle into the corner of the dining-room and said, "Macha! Let's have another bottle!" Marie Valentinovna protested, half angrily, half imploringly, "Fedia, aren't you ashamed?"

One day Marina and Dassia invited us home, in their parents' absence, to celebrate the arrival of their elder sister, Marfoucha, who had married an Englishman. The three sisters proved excellent hostesses and treated us to *blinys*. We had a very jolly time; Marfoucha particularly kept us in fits of laughter. Feodor Ivanovitch later told me that she was already famous for her gaiety and originality.

Although the Grand Duke Cyril Wladimirovitch felt the effects of what he had endured in the Russo-Japanese War, his health during the last years had not caused any major anxiety. He suffered, however, from pains in the right foot, due to bad circulation, which the doctors hoped to be able to relieve. He had been deeply affected and weakened by his wife's death, but had insisted on attending the marriage of his daughter, the Grand Duchess Kyra Kirillovna, to Prince Louis-Ferdinand of Prussia, on May 12th at Potsdam. He then returned to his estate at Saint-Briac, where André and Vova had often visited him.

He felt fairly well all summer, and we went, as the year before, to Cauterets, where André went for the sake of his bronchial tubes. Suddenly, on September 19th, the Grand Duke's secretary told us on the telephone that his health had deteriorated: symptoms of gangrene had appeared, calling possibly for an operation. He asked Boris and André to come with all speed to Saint-Briac; the Grand Duke's eldest daughter, the Grand Duchess Marie Kyrillovna, Princess of Leiningen, and his son, the Grand Duke Wladimir Kyrillovitch, who was on a visit to London, had already been sent for.

Two days later Boris Wladimirovitch drove André and the Russian surgeon Owen to Saint-Briac. They found their brother in such a serious state that they decided to move him immediately to Paris, where he could be best looked after.

On the following day he was admitted to the American Hospital, where his sister, the Grand Duchess Ellen, who was in Paris, spent days at his bedside with her daughter, Princess Olga of Yugoslavia.

The famous surgeon de Martel confirmed the symptoms of gangrene; but did not dare operate for fear of cardiac complications and a spreading of the illness. The doctors hoped to be able to use less radical treatment than amputation.

With our fears for the Grand Duke's health came political anxieties: Hitler was threatening war, the city was plunged in darkness, reservists had been recalled, news which oppressed the poor patient. Fortunately, war was avoided, but the Grand Duke's health kept on deteriorating, and he died peacefully on October 12th, the eve of his sixty-second birthday.

Almost the whole Imperial Family came to the funeral, and the French President was also represented. There was ample proof of the affection in which the Grand Duke had been held: people of all classes kept vigil over his body, and a crowd passed day and night to pay its last respects.

After a solemn church service in the rue Boileau, the coffin was taken in a hearse to Coburg, where the Grand Duke Cyril Wladimirovitch was buried in the family vault next to his wife, the Grand Duchess Victoria Feodorovna.

His death was a terrible blow to us all. We had known each other for over forty years. I had first met him in 1896 in Moscow, during the Coronation, when he was not yet twenty, and had just been promoted to sub-lieutenant. His brother Boris and he used to visit me almost every day in my hotel, and later in St. Petersburg and Strelna. We had remained on the best terms since then, though meeting less often, owing to his naval duties. After the loss of the *Petropavlovsk* in Port Arthur, he went abroad; in 1905 he married the Grand Duchess Victoria Feodorovna, and stayed abroad for several years. Then came the emigration, and I have already mentioned the affectionate ties which bound me to him and the Grand Duchess after my marriage with André.

After the end of the 1938-1939 school year, particularly happy with the number of my pupils, now a hundred and fifty, I decided to take a cure at Aix-les-Bains. After this André and I went to stay with the parents of one of my pupils, on Lake Geneva, near Évian. But we could not stay long. War was threatening again. In France the reservists were called up on August 24th, and this seemed the prelude to general mobilisation. There was great anxiety, hotel-workers were called up, and people on holiday began to leave. We also decided to return without delay to Paris. At every station a crowd of passengers stormed the already overfilled carriages.

The atmosphere in Paris was still more alarming. The blackout, siren practices, the distribution of gas-masks, advice to the public what to do in case of air attacks—all last year's defence measures had been re-established. Life in the capital was thrown out by the recall of reservists; among other things, the buses came almost to a halt. People were advised to leave the city, which would probably be the first place to be bombed.

On September 1st Poland was invaded. War had begun. Two days later France entered the struggle. We decided to move temporarily to Le Vésinet, where we found a villa for ourselves and a few friends. The very next day the sirens wailed and we had to spend three hours in the cellar. This was the first air raid warning, and we soon had to get used to these sinister shocks in the middle of the night.

Meanwhile, I had to think of my studio, which enabled us to live. At first most of my pupils had left Paris, but they gradually returned. So I had to travel by train and underground between Le Vésinet and Paris. The cold winter did not help things; however, our villa was comfortable and well heated, and we lived in relatively good conditions. Friends often came to see us from Paris. The apprehension of the first days of war was passing; all was quiet at the front and the phoney war seemed likely to go on for ever.

We returned therefore to Paris on January 19th 1940 after four and a half months at Le Vésinet. But events came quickly to a head in spring, and once more anxiety seized us all. The Grand Duke Boris Wladimirovitch now invited us to share his villa in Biarritz in order to await the outcome of the situation.

I do not intend to write of the all too familiar nightmare of that exodus; thank Heaven we were spared it. The station was truly hell. We were able somehow to leave Paris on June 11th. Three days later the Germans occupied the city. On the 17th Marshal Pétain asked for an armistice. On the 26th the German forces reached Biarritz, where the refugees had never stopped pouring in. The sight of families forced to leave their homes, carrying a few belongings, sleeping in cars, was heartrending. Their faces were pale and worn, full of exhaustion and the general anxiety which reminded us all too well of the similar scenes we had lived through almost twenty years before.

We stayed for three and a half months with the Grand Duke Boris and his wife, Zina, before returning to Paris. Officially the war was over in France, and life somehow started up again. But it was heartbreaking to see France invaded and occupied, France which we loved and which had offered us its generous hospitality. I reopened my studio, and the number of my pupils began to grow rapidly, in spite of the Occupation. True, I had many fewer than before the war; but this was a small matter.

The situation remained fairly quiet until the summer of 1941. But on June 22nd 1941 the Germans invaded Russia. The overwhelming news reached us at breakfast. What would happen to our poor country? What would become of us? Vova had been under no illusions about the coming invasion, nor of the consequences for Russia of a German victory, nor of the fate which awaited him. He did not conceal his thoughts from us, but courageously determined to endure this new test.

He went as arranged to church before going to spend the day at Le Vésinet with friends. No sooner had he left than the German police arrived at our house to arrest him. I explained that he was out for the day, and they departed. One of them returned, however, to make sure that our son had not come back, and informed us that he was to report on the following day without fail to the German police in Place Beauvau.

Vova telephoned us when he left church. Learning what had happened, he decided to return for fuller details. But it was now fairly late, and he went first to have lunch at the restaurant kept by Mme. Griffon, our neighbour; she gave him a delicious meal, with the best wines, to celebrate Russia's entry into the war. After seeing a few friends, to whom he gave his last instructions in case of his imminent arrest, he spent the evening at Le Vésinet and did not return until midnight. He would not allow us to run any danger, since the German police had come to us, and told us that he would attend the summons.

Accordingly on the following day, the 23rd, he went to Police Headquarters. In agony of mind, we gazed after him, and I repeated the sign of the cross over him until he disappeared into rue Molitor. We waited for him all day in terrible anxiety, telephoning everywhere for news of him: the only thing we learned was that many Russians had been arrested in Paris. People said, however, that it was merely a census. We were also told that the prisoners had been put into trains for an unknown destination; there was no means of verifying the truth of this story. We lived through a terrible time, and the worst thoughts passed through my mind. It was not until four days later that a Russian released by the Germans informed us that our son and the other prisoners had been taken to Compiègne and imprisoned in an Army camp surrounded by barbed wire. This Russian was fairly reassuring: he said that the prisoners were well treated and fed. Vova sent us an urgent request for linen and toilet accessories, having taken nothing with him. Visits were not allowed, but parcels could be delivered to the guard-room. Accordingly André and I used a friend's car to go to Compiègne on the day before Vova's birthday. He thus received his first parcel and we sent him one almost every week.

Later visits were allowed, and we were able to see him several times. He showed great courage and tried to reassure me. All who returned from the camp told us that Vova's behaviour was praise-worthy, and that he raised his fellow prisoners' morale. Meanwhile, time was passing, many prisoners had been set free, but in spite of all our efforts and repeated promises Vova was still a captive. Nobody could tell us the reason for this discrimination. We learnt later that the arrest of the Russians at the time of the outbreak of war with Russia was due to the German fear that the well-organised *émigré* groups might join the Resistance.

In the course of our visits to Compiègne we made the acquaintance of the Camp Commandant, Captain Nachtigall, an officer of the old Imperial German Army, who treated the prisoners in a decent, humane way. This noble man did his best to improve their lot, and saved a great many Jews. All the prisoners were grateful to him. He also tried to help us, and allowed us to meet Vova several times in his office, where we could speak without witnesses. Later, at the time of the Liberation, Nachtigall was taken prisoner, and all the former prisoners from Compiègne sent a detailed request to the Americans for his liberation. And, as justice demanded, Nachtigall was set free.

Four months, however, had now gone by and Vova was still detained. André and I did our best to cheer each other, although, as we afterwards confessed, we lived in the fear of being arrested our-selves. Then, one evening, the telephone rang. It was Vova! We thought at first that he was speaking from Compiègne, but no, he was free! He was at the Gare du Nord; in a few minutes we should have him in our arms! Infinite joy suddenly took the place of despair. Weeping with happiness, we rushed to the nearby Métro station. We could only guess the cause of his sudden liberation.

We suffered three family bereavements in 1942 and 1943. In March 1942 André heard by an indirect source of the Grand Duke

Dimitri Pavlovitch's death at Davos. He had been admitted to a sanatorium, where he died on March 5th. We later heard that before his death his health had so much improved that he had celebrated his recovery. He was only just over fifty, and we lamented his premature end. Life at first seemed to smile upon him; he had found a beautiful and wealthy wife, who had given him a charming son. Then all was lost: he divorced, his health suffered, and he ended his days in Davos, far from those who loved him. A few mourners followed the hearse to the little village cemetery. Poor, dear Dimitri!

Six months later, on September 28th, my husband's cousin, Prince Alexander Gueorguievitch Romanovsky, Duke of Leuchtenberg, died at Salles-de-Béarn. He had been ill for a long time and we were all prepared for his death. I knew him very well, and in the old days had sold him my house in St. Petersburg.

We suffered a severer loss in 1943 with the sudden death, on November 8th, of the Grand Duke Boris Wladimirovitch, André's brother. His wife Zina had telephoned us to say that Boris was in a critical condition. We hastened to him, but it was too late: he was already dead. André, who thus saw the last of his brothers vanish, sadly said, "It's my turn now."

In spite of the Occupation difficulties, an imposing crowd, which included most of the leading Paris personalities, attended the funeral. The moving of his body to Contrexéville was, however, put off in the hope of less troubled times.

Boris was one of the most noble and delightful of men, always full of life and high spirits, and he was mourned by many.

We also lost some dear friends during these two years. In 1942 we heard of the death in America of Michel Mikhailovitch Fokine.[1] Before 1939, Fokine had often come from the United States, where he lived, to Paris to put on various ballets for René Blum, Ida Rubinstein and other companies. He had also arranged dances in my studio, in particular one for Maroussia Kapnist, one of my pupils. I was always happy to receive him and to listen to his gripping conversation. Before leaving for America he gave me, as a souvenir, some crystal liqueur glasses in an old case. I have already spoken of my admiration for this great choreographer from his earliest creations. Time will never spoil the brilliance of such ballets as *Eros*, *Pas-de-Deux*, *Rondo Capriccioso*, *La Valse de Kreisler*, and *Le Papillon*, all of which he created for me; nor of *Schéhérazade*, *Petrouchka*, *Les Sylphides*, *Le Carnaval*, *Le Spectre de la*

[1] Fokine was born in 1880, and graduated from the Imperial School in 1898.

45. My last appearance on the stage at the age of sixty-four: the Russian
Dance in London, July 14th, 1936.

46b. The Grand Duke Wladimir, Head of the Imperial Family, with the Grand Duchess and their daughter, the Grand Duchess Marie, 1955.

46a. My son, Prince Wladimir Romanoff, in 1942.

Rose, *Les Danses Polovtziennes du Prince Igor*, Glazounov's *La Bacchanale*, and Saint-Saëns' *La Mort du Cygne*, created for Pavlova. These immortal works will go on triumphantly wherever they are performed.

Although Fokine reformed ballet, he remained faithful to classicism. He never resorted to acrobatic movements, nor forced his dancers to roll on the ground and leap on each other's backs. All his works had the stamp of nobility, but some of his isolated dances cannot be reproduced without him, and have died with him.

In 1943 one of my dear friends, Vera Trefilova,[1] died. During her last years she had been constantly ill, but continued to give dancing classes, although her temperature in the evening went up to almost 104° F. One day I learned that she had been taken to hospital. Although I found climbing stairs very painful—I suffered from acute pains in the joints of one leg because the studio could not be heated— I visited her almost every day, bringing her flowers which she loved. She had altered so much that when I first visited the hospital I had difficulty in finding her, and looked for her through all the wards.

The day before leaving for Dax, where I was going to cure my leg, I went to say goodbye to Vera and brought her a bunch of roses, which she drew up to her face, deeply breathing in their scent. When we parted Vera put her poor, thin arms round my neck and thanked me for my affection; she said that none of her old friends from the theatre had been so kind to her. I knew that I should never see her again, but I tried to cheer her, telling her that by the time I returned from Dax she would be recovered and we would then have a gay time. This was on Wednesday, July 7th 1943. I left for Dax on the next day. On the 11th Vera Trefilova breathed her last. I could not attend her funeral, which was on July 14th, and begged Serge Lifar to lay a wreath for me on her coffin.

Next year, in 1944, Vova had to undergo a serious operation in a nursing-home at Neuilly. The operation, performed by Professor Bergeret, was completely successful. But Vova had to spend almost a month in the nursing-home, and the difficulties of visiting him may be imagined. Life in Paris was becoming harder and harder. Then events rapidly came to a head.

On June 6th the Allies landed in Normandy. The Russians were advancing towards the frontiers of the Reich. Rome fell. Hitler narrowly escaped a bomb plot. . . . The Germans, more and more alarmed and harassed by the Resistance, undertook mass arrests and the

[1] Vera Trefilova had graduated from the Imperial School on June 1st 1894.

execution of hostages; we were terrified that our son might be re-arrested.

As the Allied armies advanced, air-raids became increasingly frequent and the sirens wailed ceaselessly.

On August 11th the wireless announced that the Allies were drawing near Paris. We were in perpetual anxiety. Would the Germans blow up the monuments and principal buildings, as people said, or fight before Paris, or draw back to their own frontier? Apparently they were preparing to defend the city, which was already fortified in several quarters. It was a terrible prospect. From August 17th, how-ever, the occupying forces began to withdraw, evacuating their offices and taking their possessions with them. The banks and post offices closed. Life was entirely suspended. Soon rioting broke out, and there were summary executions in many districts. We spent the whole of August 24th waiting for the Allied armies, but the wireless did not announce their arrival until 10 p.m. Then came an unforgettable time. All the church bells rang out and a delirious crowd poured into the streets. From a nearby villa, all lit up, a gramophone at full blast sounded the triumphant tones of the *Marseillaise*. Next day we all ran out to see General Leclerc's tanks passing through our district by the rue Michel-Ange. People threw flowers to the soldiers and offered them champagne; women climbed up on to the tanks to kiss our liberators. Occasionally, however, shots rang out from the rooftops, and we did not know if they came from German sympathisers or soldiers who had stayed behind. The tanks fired back, and there were several casualties.

On August 26th came General de Gaulle's triumphal entry into Paris. Finally, on the 29th, the American Army also came in. The war was not yet over, but the fighting was now far from Paris and would soon be outside France altogether. Our life immediately became more normal.

As soon as we were liberated we received from all over the world parcels, telegrams and letters from countless friends worried about our fate and anxious to show their affection.

Work at once began again in the studio, and the number of pupils rapidly increased. In December Diana Gould, Yehudi Menuhin's wife, arrived from London, and I was very happy to see one of my favourite pupils again. She was in charge of a small company of dancers, all in the Forces, which was going round to provide entertainment.

On February 27th 1945 I had another happy surprise: an Army lorry

brought the whole Sadler's Wells Company to my studio, including
Ninette de Valois and my old pupils, Margot Fonteyn and Pamela
May, who took me out to lunch in a British military club in Rue
du Faubourg Saint-Honoré. They too were in uniform and part of the
Army! The company gave a few performances at the Théâtre des
Champs-Elysées.

I was also visited at about this time by my old pupil, Shirley Bridge,
who was passing through Paris and whom I had not seen for seven or
eight years.

The war was drawing to a close. On May 2nd Berlin was captured
by the Russians, who joined up with the Allies on the Elbe. We
celebrated Russian Easter in the gayest spirits. On May 8th the sirens
wailed for the last time: Germany had surrendered. The nightmare
was over.

CHAPTER XXXI

AFTER THE WAR

THE GRAND DUKE WLADIMIR, head of the Imperial Family since the Grand Duke Cyril's death, had grown more and more attached to André, who himself had grown increasingly fond of his nephew. In 1948 the Grand Duke married Princess Bagration-Moukhransky, a descendant of the old ruling family of Georgia, and in 1953 they had a daughter, the Grand Duchess Marie, an adorable and lively child. André stood as godfather, but, to his great distress, he was unable because of his health to attend the baptism. Soon after the war, however, my husband and son visited the Grand Duke Wladimir and his wife in Madrid, and in 1950 we spent a week in their villa at San Sebastian, which has left me with wonderful memories.

In 1950 Serge Lifar sent me his book, *A History of the Russian Ballet*.[1] If this book had had a different title, I should not have taken such exception to certain statements. So much is written about ballet that one would have no time to correct all the inaccuracies. But *A History of the Russian Ballet* calls for a detailed criticism.

I cannot therefore refrain from protesting against certain passages in this book. Otherwise time will pass and we shall all disappear, we who were members of the Imperial Ballet and who played a large part in the glorious flowering of our art. Then there will be no answer to a *History* which might appear objective, but in fact reflects a mere personal opinion.

As far as I am concerned, my name is constantly linked from the very beginning with that of another dancer who graduated from the Theatre School long before me, but only became famous much later. I have great respect for this dancer, who proved herself through hard work; but to place our two names side by side in this way provides a distorted picture of reality, since each of us had individual qualities which do not lend themselves to comparison.

Furthermore, the author twice insinuates that Pavlova and Karsavina threatened to eclipse or replace me at the start of their career. Neither Pavlova nor Karsavina nor any other artist eclipsed or replaced me

[1] Serge Lifar, *Histoire du Ballet russe des origines jusqu'à nos jours* (Paris, 1950).

during my career as an artist. Each had her own way to follow; none stood in the way of the others.

I occupied a prominent position in our ballet from the moment of my graduation, a fact which can be easily verified from the contemporary chroniclers.

This *History* later states that I was less successful abroad than another dancer. Arnold Haskell is perfectly correct in writing in one of his books that Anna Pavalova was better known than I abroad; but I appeared much less abroad than she did. Pavlova appeared outside Russia and began to undertake tours soon after her graduation; she told us herself the price she paid for her glory. I on the other hand preferred my life in Russia. As has been seen, in 1903 I even turned down a very profitable American offer, and soon after the Coronation one from the Kaiser to dance in Berlin; when I accepted offers abroad, I always enjoyed the greatest success, as in Vienna in 1903 and at the Opéra in Paris in 1908 and 1909. (Many years afterwards Gaubert, the Director of the Opéra, who had played a flute solo at the time, still talked of my triumph in Paris in *La Korrigane* and my solo from *La Fille du Pharaon*.) Beyond this, there is my London appearance with Diaghilev, as well as the flattering invitations I received both from him and the Paris Opéra when I arrived in France in 1920 and was already forty-eight years old! I am thus justly proud of these appearances, which won me the most favourable reviews in the international Press. All this, however, is passed over in silence in *A History of Russian Ballet*, where it is even implied that if I had greater success in Russia than some other dancer it was solely because I was all-powerful on the stage: a fairly offensive remark, it will be agreed!

To reach a high position in the theatre and make a name not only in Russia, but throughout the world, calls for far more than an all-powerful position; it calls for the gift that distinguishes one artist among so many and raises her on a pedestal for all to envy.

To back my remarks, I should like to quote an extract from an article by A. Plestscheev which I recently received from America, written on the eve of my benefit performance on February 4th 1904. Plestscheev witnessed my whole career from its very beginnings, and could therefore give an impartial judgment of my contribution to ballet:

"Kschessinska, with her great natural gifts, holds an exceptional place on the contemporary Russian stage, and even in Europe as a whole, where Zambelli is perhaps the only outstanding dancer today. Closest to Kschessinska in talent and affinities is the Moscow ballerina

L. A. Roslavleva, also a star of the first order. None of the others can be compared to Kschessinska. We have gifted ballerinas and soloists, but each with her own qualities; in general their talents lie either in dancing or in mime, and not in both. Mlle. Pavlova II has more natural gifts than the others; but her time has not yet come" (*Diary of a Balletomane in St. Petersburg*, February 1st 1904).

In his article Plestscheev does not even mention the dancer whom Lifar, in his *History of the Russian Ballet*, places on a level with me, and who, according to him, might have eclipsed me.

One further detail: the author did not think me worth a full-page photograph. Was this a pin-prick aimed at me?

My reason for correcting these inaccuracies is my desire to restore my name to its true position in the history of the Imperial Ballet.

The ballet world is like the rest of the Russian émigré world, in which the titles of Count, Prince and Colonel are appropriated without any right at all.

In *Balletomania* Arnold Haskell points out the way in which people misuse the names "ballerina" and "prima ballerina" which had in Russia a distinct and definite meaning, and which were only awarded to a limited number of dancers. If generals were common in Russia there were only five or six ballerinas, and one prima ballerina alone, M. F. Kschessinska.

All this is quite true. The dancers were strictly graded according to the decisions of the Imperial Theatres Administration into certain classes: corps de ballet, coryphées, second and first-class dancers, soloists and finally ballerinas. After several years as a ballerina, and having been honoured with the title "Artist Emeritus of the Imperial Theatres", became a prima ballerina. I write all this not from pride, but for the sake of accuracy. I cannot help being distressed by the unjust remarks in a book written by a friend whom I always treated with the greatest affection.

On the other hand, I was deeply moved by a manuscript sent to me by a friend, describing the memoirs of Henri Marre, a former Lieutenant in the 6th Regiment of the Gloukhov Dragoons, invited by an uncle for his first visit to St. Petersburg. He relates how he met me at a masked ball in the Maryinsky Theatre, and I cannot refrain from quoting a few extracts:

"Towards the end of January 1900 I arrived in St. Petersburg, where there was no shortage of entertainment—theatre, opera, ballet, operetta, comedy and of course music-hall. I saw the two celebrities of the time:

Lina Cavalieri and the beautiful Otero, 'the diamond queen'. I heard
Battistini and the incomparable Masini sing. But it was ballet which
thrilled me most. Russian ballet, as every critic and connoisseur agrees,
was the best in the world. I was able to admire the greatest stars in
their finest roles: the divine Mathilde Kschessinska in *La Fille du
Pharaon*, the ethereal O. O. Preobrajenska in *La Flûte Enchantée*, and
Legnani the Italian in *Le Petit Cheval Bossu*. There were two ballet
performances a week, on Wednesday and Sunday. . . .

"As I was walking alone between the ballroom and the foyer, a
masked figure came up to me. 'My poor fellow,' she said. 'I can see
that you're horribly bored. You're alone, of course, and from your
uniform I'm sure you're from the provinces.'

"She took my arm. I offered her a glass of champagne, but she said
she preferred orangeade. We talked about ballet, opera and other
things; then I said, 'A masked ball is fun for those who have many
friends. But who can I flirt with? Nobody knows me, and I know
nobody.'

" 'Are you so sure that you don't know me?'

" 'You're beginning to fascinate me! But I'm sure I've never seen
you and don't know you.'

" 'Well, you're wrong. You've seen me several times—here, in
fact.'

" 'I know! You're a ballet dancer. But I've seen lots: that doesn't
mean I know you!'

" 'You can't fail to know me,' she exclaimed, laughing. And she
vanished as abruptly as she had first appeared.

"Meanwhile, I remained where I was, thinking, imagining a hundred
possibilities, more intrigued than ever.

"I began to wander alone again. From the foyer to the ballroom,
then back to the foyer. And suddenly I met her again. But this time I
went up to her boldly. 'Listen,' I said. 'You intrigued me and then you
vanished. Was that fair? At least tell me in what ballet and what role
I might have seen you?'

"She looked at me with an air of astonishment under her mask.
'You're wrong,' she said. 'I've never seen you before and I've never
formed an intrigue with you. But I can see what's happened. There
are two of us here in the same domino and the same ribbon. We're
trying to form an intrigue with a friend. Do you like ballet? Are you
interested in it?'

" 'How could I fail to like it? It's my first visit to St. Petersburg
and my first sight of ballet. Kschessinska and Preobrajenska are divine.

I shall dream of them in the wilds. You're a dancer too, aren't you? And what about your friend? You must be happy to dance with them, even if you're only their attendants!'

" 'Have I really charmed you so much? Very well. I believe you. Shall I show them to you? No, not today—on Wednesday, after the ballet. Come to the stage door. Walk up to the second door. You'll find me there. You'll recognise me by the blue ribbon on my cape. Then I'll show them to you when they get into their carriages. You've only seen them on the stage, I'll show them to you in real life. . . . Meanwhile, will you do something for me. You see the Colonel there? Well, will you tell him that "the black domino with the little blue ribbon" is waiting for him in the Prefect's box? What's wrong? You look appalled! That isn't such a hard thing to do. And remember —Wednesday!'

" 'All right! But it means infringing orders, and I'm sure to be arrested. That Colonel is the Grand Duke Serge Mikhailovitch. I'm not allowed to go up to him. But I'll do it for you. I'd have done anything for the Goddess of ballet! See you on Wednesday, then—if I'm not arrested.'

" 'Go on! Don't be afraid! Nobody will touch you!'

"The 'Colonel' stood head and shoulders over everybody else. He was looking about him as if seeking someone. I went up to him. I clinked my spurs. I made a small bow.

" 'Colonel,' I said.

"He looked at me in surprise and leaned towards me. I seemed so small next to him.

" 'Colonel, the black domino with the little blue ribbon is waiting for you in the Prefect's box.'

"He smiled pleasantly. 'Thank you, Lieutenant. I've been looking for her for some time.'

"He held out his hand, which I took. I bowed again, then took a step backwards. When I turned round, an officer was already coming towards me! But the young lady in the black domino rushed forwards and blocked his way. She stopped him and whispered a few words in his ear. The officer listened respectfully, gave a polite salute and moved off.

"The fateful Wednesday came. It was *La Fille du Pharaon*. As I watched the corps de ballet and the *premières danseuses* I kept on wondering, 'Which one?' Kschessinska, as always, danced divinely. No, it was not dancing, but something more, something indescribable.

Her plastique, her mime, the charm of every gesture and movement!
The theatre rang with applause.

"The curtain fell for the last time. I made for the stage door, wondering if it had all been a joke. In front of the stage door were the
sledges, coaches and enormous carriages for the dancers and pupils.
I entered, and went up to the second door. There were people waiting
for the dancers on all sides: civilians, soldiers, officers, pupils from the
Pages' Academy, from High School, from the Law School. . . . The
dancers were beginning to leave. Their admirers rushed towards
them and carried them off. They all passed by me, but none was wearing the little blue ribbon! I took out a cigarette, meaning to light it
when I left the theatre. At that moment one of the theatre staff came
down towards the stage door which he opened and called out, 'Kschessinska's carriage!'

" 'That's all right,' I thought. 'My little stranger from Sunday isn't
here, but I'll be able to see the Queen of ballet close to!'

"The door opened. Applause rang out. I saw a charming little face
wrapped in a scarf. Then, suddenly, on her cape I saw a blue ribbon.
She stopped, smiling, and gracefully acknowledged the applause.
Then she turned towards me and said, 'I've kept my word. Thank you
for what you did for me. Here's your reward.' And she handed me
her blue ribbon, adding, 'In memory of me.'

"I managed to stammer, 'So it was you.' And I kissed her finger-tips.

" 'Yes, it was me. Will you see me home? We can talk in my
carriage.'

"Can I describe my feelings! She went on, 'I live quite near here.
We won't have much time to talk. But the Grand Duke thought
highly of your presence of mind, and he asked me to thank you, on
behalf of the Colonel! . . . Here we are! Come and have tea with me
tomorrow afternoon at five o'clock.'

"Her words remained for ever engraved in my memory. I can still
hear her voice today.

"The next day, at five o'clock exactly, the maid showed me into
the drawing-room. Mathilde Felixovna soon appeared. She gave me
her hand and I bowed. A superb black poodle ran in; she showed me
how he could remain on guard and how he could jump over the
chairs. Then she asked me about my family and regiment. Tea was
served. After two cups I accepted her invitation to smoke and took out
my cigarette case. She appeared interested in it and said, 'Please show
it to me. I see it's covered in monograms and designs.'

"Officers traditionally engraved their monograms on friends' cigarette cases, as well as spurs, stirrups and epaulettes.

" 'How interesting,' said Kschessinska. 'But there's one space still free. Will you keep it for me? I'll have my name engraved on it. You're staying this week? Good. Then I'll take your cigarette case to Fabergé today, and when it's ready I'll send it you. Give me your address.'

"I was in ecstasy. I was going to have Kschessinska's signature! But that was not all.

" 'Have you seen me in *La Fille du Pharaon*?' she asked. She rose and disappeared into the next room. A minute later she returned with a parcel.

"Your name and Christian name?"

"She sat at a small table and signed photographs of herself in different poses.

"Two or three days later her maid brought me a large parcel, so big that I was amazed. In it was my cigarette case with the facsimile of her signature, and also a book, *Our Ballet*, a history of Russian ballet by Plestscheev. It was a large folio, magnificently bound in purple leather, with a medallion of Kschessinska on the top heft-hand corner. The fly-leaf bore the dedication, *To Henri Ludvigovitch Marre, in memory of the ballet. M. Kschessinska.*

"I went to thank her the same day. She gave me a warm welcome and said:

" 'If ever you need anything, let me know, however far away you may be. I'll do my best for you, whatever it is.' "

Almost two years went by. Henri Marre was in the Far East. One day, in Vladivostok, he heard that an officer he knew called Luman had been condemned to two and a half years' imprisonment for killing another officer. The details of the affair were given to Marre by Luman's wife.

The officers of a Siberian sharpshooters' regiment had organised a dance to which they invited the officers of a Cossack regiment, including Luman, with their wives.

One of the officers, a Captain Afanassiev, was particularly importunate and tactless towards Mme. Luman. A quarrel broke out between the two officers. The Commander of the regiment, instead of settling the incident, took Afanassiev's side and asked Luman to leave.

On the way out Luman and his wife ran into Afanassiev on the front steps, and he gave them a mocking salute. Luman, enraged, cried out, "You're a coward!" Afanassiev slapped him, Luman pulled out his revolver and shot him dead.

Luman was condemned to death. However, the President of the Court tried to obtain a free pardon for him from the superior authorities, in view of Afanassiev's provocation and the Commander's inexcusable behaviour. But all he could obtain was a commutation of the death sentence to two and a half years' imprisonment.

Luman's wife framed a petition to the Tsar, but the commission charged with delivering the petition decided, for unknown reasons, that it was impossible to submit it to the Emperor. Luman, his wife and the President of the Court were in despair: they could no nothing more.

After listening to Mme. Luman's story, Marre asked her the President of the Court's name, and asked her permission to see him. This is how he describes their conversation:

"I arrived at the President's house towards evening. After apologising for disturbing him so late, I said:

" 'Your Excellency, I have to come to see you about a matter in which you are interested. It is about Luman, for whom you have been good enough to appeal. I know a certain way of getting the petition to His Majesty the Tsar.' And I mentioned a certain name.

" 'You know her personally?' exclaimed the President. 'You're sure she'll deliver the petition?'

" 'Yes, your Excellency, I have the great honour of knowing her personally. Look at my cigarette case. But she won't deliver it herself. Someone else will do it, who will not refuse if she asks him and can do it without trouble to himself. She herself will be happy to do a good deed and will hand over the petition to the gentleman in question. My reason for bothering Your Excellency is that I do not know how the petition should be framed.'

"When the petition had been made out, Mme. Luman signed it and sent it by registered post to Mathilde Kschessinska, enclosing a letter to this effect:

" 'You were kind enough to allow me to write to you in case of need. The suffering undergone by two people (you will understand when you read this petition) compels me to ask you to deliver the petition to the Grand Duke Serge Mikhailovitch so that he may give it to His Majesy the Tsar. If this is possible, please wire me the single word, *Delivered*.'

"About a month later I received the following telegram: 'Delivered. Mathilde.'

"Luman later told me that the prison commander had received a telegram from St. Petersburg ordering him immediately to free Luman and to tell him that the Tsar had given him an unconditional pardon.

"I have never seen Kschessinska again. I have heard that she is now living in Paris.

"To end this chapter I think it my duty to say that Mathilde Kschessinska was not only the guardian angel of the poor, the unhappy and the oppressed, but also of the powerful.

"She was so pure that no scandal could touch her. Scandal is repelled by her beautiful personality just as grains of dust are repelled by pure crystal."

I was deeply moved by reading these memoirs, which Henri Marre had written for himself alone, never suspecting that I might one day see them.

I decided at once to write to him:

12th September 1949.

MY DEAR HENRI LUDVIGOVITCH,—You will be surprised to receive a letter from "the black mask with the blue ribbon".

Quite unexpectedly I have been given part of your *Memoirs*, in which you describe our meeting at the masked ball.

These impressions, written in such a simple but vivid style, took me back to a distant happy past.

I should be delighted to meet you. If you come to Paris, come and see me. Nobody cries "Kschessinska's carriage" now! I take the Métro, and for the last twenty years I have been working from morning till evening in my studio!

Once again, I should be delighted to see you.

Sincerely yours,
PRINCESS M. KRASSINSKY.

In reply I received the following letter:

The Seminary,
Faverney (Haute-Saône).
13th September 1949.

YOUR SERENE HIGHNESS,—I have been deeply moved and overjoyed to receive your warm and friendly letter, which I have read over and over again. Like so many others, I know your goodness which all treasure, and whose rays have again warmed me in my old age. Your radiant image has never left my memory. I am too moved to say more, but I shall write again without fail in a few days. I bow to you, I kiss your hands with deep respect and send you my sincere gratitude for your kindness. I remain the devoted and respectful admirer of your genius and infinite goodness.

H. MARRE.

PS.—On Sunday, September 18th, at 7 a.m., I shall have Mass said for you in the Seminary Chapel. I shall serve it.

Henri Marre lived at the Seminary at Faverney, not far from Plombières, where my husband, my son and I went for our annual cure. We invited him to lunch at Plombières.

When I came down to the lounge before lunch, a man at once rose from a corner and advanced towards me. It was Henri Ludvigovitch Marre. Small, old, with old-fashioned side-whiskers, and simply but carefully dressed, he drew near, plainly moved. He greeted me and kissed my hand with the deepest respect. He was so moved that he could hardly speak. He looked at me with tenderness, thinking no doubt of our first meeting at the masked ball, fifty years ago!

After lunch I walked with him to the station. I said goodbye and started to walk back. When I turned, I saw that he had not moved, and he began then to make the sign of the cross over me.

I then received several moving letters from him for various festivals, and I resolved to see him again in Plombières the following year.

In his last letters, however, he complained of his health. He said that he was too weak now to distribute the heavy parcels which came to the Seminary, and found it difficult to serve Mass. At the beginning of summer he told me that he was too ill to come and see us at Plombières this year. He feared that he might not see me again.

In August 1951 we visited him at Faverney. I found him greatly altered and he did not conceal that he felt increasingly weak. I visited his room, a real monk's cell, where I saw my photo, which I had sent him the year before from Paris. He asked me to sit down for a moment in the one armchair in order that later he might call my presence to mind. Then he accompanied us to the car, proud, he said, to hold my arm. I was happy that everybody greeted him with respect as we passed. We said goodbye, and never met again.

On returning to Paris I was informed that Marre had been moved to a hospital in Vesoul, and shortly afterwards the Director of the hospital, in accordance with the former Lieutenant of Dragoons' last wishes, informed me of his death on September 21st 1951. The news gave me great sorrow. My dear Henri Ludvigovitch Marre was no more. But Fortune had allowed me to see him twice before his death. May his soul rest in peace!

On March 1st 1951 I had the grief of losing a faithful friend, Ludmilla Roumiantzeva, my last maid and confidant. She had shared thirty-nine years of happiness and sorrow with me. She had been a dressmaker in the Imperial Theatres wardrobe department before entering my service, and was considered one of the most experienced dressers. I made her my official dresser. Her work was by no means light, especially when I had to change costumes for each act, but Ludmilla was particularly skilful. I became very attached to her and engaged her as my maid. An extremely hard worker, an experienced dressmaker and wardrobe-mistress, she could do anything, and do it admirably well. I have already related how she proved her devotion during the Revolution, and later did not hesitate to choose exile with us. She died suddenly at the age of sixty-seven. We accompanied her to her last resting-place, the Russian cemetery of Sainte-Geneviève-des-Bois, near Paris. Many of her friends attended the funeral and I had a Russian cross erected on her grave, with a small ikon in it which she had loved.

I should like here to say a few words about my servants, who served me with unfailing devotion for so many years. They all stayed with me for a long time, and none was ever dismissed. I had fourteen servants in St. Petersburg, four in my *datcha* (not counting the extra summer staff) and three at Cap d'Ail. Some of these will always remain in my mind with gratitude and love.

I have already spoken of Ludmilla, Arnold and Denissov, my porter. I have also mentioned Ivan Kournossov, who entered my service as butler in 1909. Ivan was demobilised when the Revolution broke out, at once returned and shared the trials of those terrible years with us. He behaved admirably, followed us into exile, and only left us in Paris after his marriage. But we never severed our ties, and Ivan, who now rests in the Russian cemetery at Nice, left my son, as a last gesture, a little house he had in Nice and all the presents we had given him. In recalling the unswerving loyalty of those who served me I pay my respects to Ludmilla and Ivan for their devotion.

There was also Ivan Kajourkin, porter in my first house and later in charge of the heating, who remained in my employment for twenty-five years. He had had his foot amputated for frost-bite, which he suffered when rescuing furniture during a flood of the Neva; he felt the deepest gratitude towards me for the attention with which he was surrounded.

I cannot omit Larion, my coachman for more than ten years, who left me when cars arrived and would not take other employment, preferring to retire to his home village. Nor can I leave out Denis, my French chef, who for twelve years displayed his masterly talents. We met him again in Paris after the Revolution; he often came to see us and never failed to bring Vova, in memory of the past, a *krendel*, the traditional birthday cake, which he made himself.

In May 1950 the Federation of Russian Classical Ballet was founded in London. Twelve studios were included in it with the aim of preserving the fundamental principles of Russian ballet and teaching the dance according to the methods of the Imperial Schools.

The Federation asked me, through one of my former pupils, Barbara Vernon, to be a patron, to which I willingly agreed. I approved of giving the cause of ballet a trump card by the application of our tradition to the English schools. In May 1951 the organisers asked me to spend a week in London in order to attend the first General Meeting of the Federation's members, to give a few demonstration lessons, to preside over the graduation exam and to distribute the diplomas, which bore my signature. I went with André.

We were welcomed at Victoria Station by Barbara Vernon and her husband, John Gregory, by a group of pupils with flowers, and by photographers. Victoria Dubitt, aged five, the youngest pupil in the St. Luke Street School of Russian Ballet, gave me a beautiful statuette by Michael Morris.

We were taken to the De Vere Hotel, opposite Kensington Palace and the Park, an old-style but very agreeable hotel. In the evening we received journalists and photographers. My room was full of flowers, which never stopped arriving, and Tamara Karsavina thoughtfully sent me a bunch of lilac, which I am very fond of, for it always reminds me of Russia. Next morning we attended the first set of exams, and I was most happy to meet my one-time favourite pupil, Nina Tarakanova, now Mrs. Maclean. I was then asked to give a character dance class, and I asked Nina, who had been one of my best character dancers, to help me. She succeeded admirably, and could not help joining in the final dance!

We had been invited to lunch, with Tamara Karsavina, by Arnold Haskell in his charming house. There is no need to describe my pleasure in seeing dear Tamara and talking over the past with her.

We also had the pleasure of meeting Mr. Bruce, her husband.

In the evening we went to the Stoll Theatre to see the Festival Ballet Company of Anton Dolin and Alicia Markova. In the first interval my box was invaded by journalists and friends. One lady journalist wanted to know about my size in shoes and what diet I followed. Meanwhile, Arnold Haskell introduced the famous English ballet critic, Cyril Beaumont, into my box. When Beaumont heard this journalist's questions about my London appearances, he said, "Don't ask Mme. Kschessinska. I'll tell you!" This is what she wrote, after describing my last visit to London in 1936, when I performed my Russian Boyar dance at Covent Garden: "Cyril Beaumont tells me that he can still vividly remember the elegance and nobility of her dancing and gestures, two qualities which only dancers brought up in the atmosphere of the Russian Imperial Court can perfectly achieve."

After the performance I was taken on to the stage and photographed with Anton Dolin, Alicia Markova and others dancers of the company. The evening came to an end with supper at the Savoy, to which Arnold Haskell invited us, with Markova.

On May 23rd the General Assembly of the Federation, composed almost exclusively of women, met at our hotel. John Gregory made a long speech, dealing partly with the Federation's activities, and ended with a few kind words about me. In reply I read a speech in French which André proceeded to translate into English. Then tea was served, and I was able to talk with most of the Federation's members, Barbara Vernon acting as interpreter.

Next day we were shown round the Sadler's Wells Ballet School by Arnold Haskell, the Director, who then invited us, with Choura Danilova and Alicia Markova, to partake of the School lunch. On May 26th we went to the French Institute to see a performance arranged by Barbara Vernon and John Gregory, the Directors of the Russian ballet school. We were received on arrival by Miss Flora Fairbairn, who gave me flowers and conducted me into the theatre. The audience immediately rose, greeting me with a volley of applause, which only died down when I had reached my place in the front row and had turned to thank the public for its warm welcome. All this had been so unexpected and spontaneous that I was moved to tears.

The performance was extremely interesting. Pupils of both sexes and all ages danced classical and character dances. There was quite a lot

47.   The funeral of the Grand Duke André: at the church in the rue Daru, Paris.

48a. The lying in state, at home.

48b. The church at Contrexéville where the Grand Duke André will rest by the side of his mother and his brother, the Grand Duke Boris.

that was naïve, certainly, but some pupils showed promise. I then mounted the stage and distributed diplomas. We stayed on in the theatre after the performance. While the parents asked me for my impressions, the little dancers surrounded me like a swarm of little bees! I was so touched by this welcome that the thought of it still moves me. I had not expected London to remember me and my two appearances in 1911 and 1936, nor to receive such a warm and enthusiastic reception. After such a greeting, I did not feel like going home, and André and I decided to go and have supper at the Savoy, as in the old days of 1911. There, to our great surprise, we met David Lichine having a lonely supper at the next table. Delighted to see us, he invited us to join him and we all three finished off the evening in wonderful style before going to see Tania Riabouchinska, Lichine's wife, who had stayed in her room with her daughter. From her room we telephoned to Vova in Paris to let him share in our enormous happiness.

We left London next day, happy and loaded with flowers, after being seen off at the station by Nina Tarakanova, Barbara Vernon and John Gregory.

Two years later, on June 3rd 1953, Vaslav Nijinsky's body was transferred to the Montmartre-Nord Cemetery.

In the autumn of 1939, when I had spent two weeks near Évian and visited Geneva, I had determined to go and see Nijinsky, who was then in a sanatorium in Switzerland. Every attempt to restore his memory had failed, including that of Diaghilev, who took him to the theatre where *Petrouchka* was being performed and even brought him on stage, where he met Karsavina. Nijinsky recognised nobody and seemed unaware of his surroundings. I had hopes, however, that he would recognise me, for I had been the first to choose him as partner when he had just graduated from the Theatre School. He had never forgotten this, and had always shown himself most affectionate towards me. But I was prevented by circumstances from seeing him then and had to return in haste to Paris.

Nijinsky died in London. Many years later Romola, his widow, told me that shortly before his death Vaslav had become almost completely normal: he spoke of the past, remembered me and often repeated my name, which made me bitterly regret to have been unable to see him in Switzerland.

I could not attend his funeral in London, but it was a great comfort to me to be present when his body was transferred to the Montmartre

Cemetery, where the famous dancer Vestris is also laid. Many people came to pay him a final tribute, and several speakers recalled his appearances at the Paris Opéra, where he had won immense fame.

When the ceremony was over I approached the grave and laid my flowers on it, praying ardently for the eternal rest of one who had been among the most gifted of my partners and one of my warmest friends.

Nijinsky's memory leads me to an analysis of what separates us from the new generations. Modern dancers, I am happy to say, greatly surpass their predecessors in technique. It is only natural that technique should advance. But few of these dancers are comparable with Rosita Mauri, Anna Pavlova, Tamara Karsavina, Vera Trefilova, Olga Preobrajenska, Olga Spessivtseva. Their acting is not as powerful as that of the ballerinas of old.

One of the reasons for this development, I think, is that there are so few ballets today—except *Giselle*—like those which used to be danced in Russia, *La Fille du Pharaon*, *La Bayadère*, *Le Corsaire*, *Esmeralda*, *Raymonda*, where, in a mimed scene, the artist could express her dramatic gifts. What is there left for her to do today? To beat the records of technique?

Another reason is that some dancers take lessons or practise, not to mention those who call themselves teachers without right, with teachers who are inferior to them; no doubt the modern dancer thinks it beneath herself to work with someone better than herself!

Moreover, I consider the constant move from studio to studio, in search of technical novelty, to be a major error.

When I was invited to dance at the Paris Opéra, though I was a ballerina in Russia, I was not ashamed to go and work with Rosita Mauri, whose fame rang out to the four corners of Europe; I did not see anything undignified in rehearsing under her my role in *La Korrigane*, in which she had proved incomparable.

Anna Pavlova worked with E. P. Sokolova, our eminent ballerina, when she herself already had an important position in the Ballet Company.

Today's dancers, ready to sacrifice everything on the altar of a frenzied technique, seem to forget that virtuosity without soul is dead art. Their technique is so extraordinary that one wonders how they achieved such results; but these feats leave us cold and cannot give the spectator the least feeling or emotion.

This leads to unforgivable faults of taste. One day, for instance, I was stupefied by a request made to me by one of the young *premières danseuses* from the Paris Opéra (which she left soon afterwards). She came with M. L. Vaillat to ask me to arrange her a few dances from the ballet *Esmeralda*. I was perplexed and not entirely sure what she wanted. She replied that she did not know herself and did not mind —she clearly hoped that I would help her to choose. But I did not understand what her request meant. Was she wholly unaware of the subject-matter of *Esmeralda*, which is drawn from Victor Hugo's famous novel and has a complicated, dramatic plot? Or was she lacking in artistic sense and taste? Could she not understand that it is impossible, for instance, to extract the mad scene in *Giselle* from its context without making it incomprehensible to the public? The same thing applies to *Esmeralda*.

I tried to explain all this calmly, and to show her the difficulty of the problem she had brought me. Did she understand? I do not think so.

For my part I was horrified and indignant to have been asked such a thing, especially about *Esmeralda*, my favourite ballet, into which I had put my whole soul. How could anyone suggest that I should mutilate it? It would have been to tear out a portion of myself. I concealed the strength of my feelings, however; I pleaded overwork and put off my decision until later—till the blue moon. She did not come back, however.

It is not for me to launch into criticism of French ballet and French dancers. But I may be allowed to express my personal preference and to say how much I appreciate Yvette Chauviré's grace, in the true sense of the word, which makes her live her roles, give herself heart and soul to her art and bring that emotion to the stage in which she most resembles the traditions of our School. I can only say that such great artists as Chauviré, Lycette Darsonval, Jeanmaire and others, from all over the world, have come to me, both to ask for advice and to improve in a particular dance.

In 1957 I was moved to learn that, despite events, politics and time, my name was not forgotten in Russia, and that a collection of facts and memories about me was being made at the Tchaikovsky Museum at Klin, near Moscow. The Director of the Museum wrote to ask me for photos and personal accounts of the way in which I had danced Tchaikovsky's ballets. He wished to know how I had thought out and prepared these parts. I was congratulated on the thirtieth anniversary of my ballet school and asked for my impressions of my best pupils, as well as the secret of my teaching methods. "You occupy," he wrote, "in the history of Russian ballet, and now in the history of world ballet, such a high position that posterity will reproach you if you do not write your memoirs. You must give us living portraits of your contemporaries and your colleagues. Interest in the development of Russian art is still enormous in our country, and it would be extremely valuable if you told our young people how you perfected your art. . . . The museum would be profoundly grateful if you sent us the shoes which you wore on your last stage appearance."

I loved and still love my art, and am never indifferent to anything concerning Russian ballet. Ballet shaped my life and gave me happiness.

In 1958 the Bolshoi Theatre Ballet Company came to Paris. Although I no longer go out since my husband's death, and divide my time between my house and the dancing school, where I work for my living I made an exception and went to the Opéra to see them.

I cried with happiness. This was the same ballet which I had last seen over forty years ago, with the same spirit and the same tradition. Technique, of course, has made enormous strides and deserves our respect, provided it does not seek to dazzle, but to charm and transport. Russia has been able, as nowhere else, to reconcile technique and art.

CHAPTER XXXII

A DREAM

WHILE DECORATING THE Christmas tree in 1951 I had the misfortune to fall and break my leg. I was taken to the American Hospital where I had an operation. Two or three days later, while I was still in hospital, I had the following dream:

I dreamed that with my pupils I was entering our Theatre School in St. Petersburg. I could not see my pupils, but, as often in dreams, I felt their presence and knew that they were near me. I showed them where things were: over there on the right, I said, are two large rooms where we had rehearsals and classes; and that was where, on the day of our graduation performance, we greeted the Tsar, the Tsarina and the Imperial Family. The classrooms are on the left, off this long corridor. At the very end of the passage, over there, is the little School theatre where I danced at graduation. That was where the Imperial Family later left.

While I was explaining all this to my pupils, suddenly someone cried out, "They're coming! They're coming!" And when I asked, "Who is coming?" the reply came, "The Imperial Family." "But how can they come? They're all dead?" "Their souls are coming," the voice replied. At that moment everybody began to sing in chorus:

> Christ is risen from the dead.
> By His death He has conquered death.
> To those who lay in the grave He has given back life.

This prayer was sung three times. Then everybody hurried down to meet them, and stood before the outside door, which was wide open. Outside the storm was raging, the wind howling and torrential rain falling. Somebody cried out that they could not come in. Then everybody hurried back up to the first floor and sang, "Christ is risen . . ." three more times, before waiting again, this time at the end of the passage, hoping to see them appear. But again somebody cried, "They cannot come in!" Then we all rushed up to the second floor and again sang "Christ is risen . . .". While I ran with the others I thought how when Tsar Alexander III appeared I would fall on my knees before him and kiss his hands, for I had really adored him! After our third "Christ is risen" we stopped, still waiting for the

Imperial Family to appear. Then I awoke, in tears, and continued to weep for a long time.

Next day I saw my past so vividly, so clearly, before my eyes, that I resolved to write these memoirs, which I had for long refused to do, fearing to evoke such distant memories and to revive old wounds.

On Easter night, with my broken leg, I could not go to midnight Mass celebrated by the Metropolitan Wladimir in the Church in the rue Daru; and so we decided to listen to it on the wireless.

The Easter table, loaded with *koulitchs, paskha,* Easter eggs and cold food, had been prepared in my room, where I sat in an armchair, surrounded by André, Vova, who had returned from the church in the rue Michel-Ange, where the Easter service had finished early, my sister Julie, Felia Doubrovska-Vladimirova who had recently come from America, and George Alexandrovitch and Elizabeth Pavlovna Grammatikov.

As soon as the broadcast began we lit candles. The speaker described what was happening outside the Cathedral: a large crowd had invaded not only the precincts, but also the adjacent streets. Then he announced that the procession, led by the choir, was about to leave the church. We soon heard indistinct singing, gradually growing louder. Behind the choir, continued the announcer, were people carrying banners, icons, a cross; finally the Metropolitan, surrounded by priests, came out of the Cathedral. The singing became fainter, then gradually louder, as the choir and procession moved round the Church. At one moment we were able distinctly to hear every single word. While the procession entered the Cathedral and the priests assembled under the porch, there was utter silence, an expectant silence. Then came the Metropolitan Wladimir's voice, "Christ is risen!" Immediately all the faithful and we ourselves replied in chorus, "He is truly risen!"

With tears in our eyes, we were filled with such an intense feeling of piety that, in spirit, we felt one with the faithful. And thousands and millions of Orthodox scattered all over the world, spiritually united now, were praying with us.

I remembered my dream. And, as in my dream, I could not see the speaker. I heard the Metropolitan chant, "Christ is risen!" but I could not see him. I heard the faithful reply, "He is risen indeed!" but I could not see them. I heard the hymn "Christ is risen!" but I could not see the singers. Yes, it was all as in my dream! And once again I began to weep, as after my dream. . . .

Paris, March 17th 1954.

POSTSCRIPT

On October 30th 1956 my husband suddenly died. His health was precarious, and we had always to be ready for the worst, but there was no sign on that day of a fatal end. He was just recovering from influenza, which had left him rather weak; and the doctor who examined him the day before thought that there were no complications to be feared in the immediate future. When he awoke on the day of his death, André said that he felt perfectly all right. He talked to Vova from twelve to half-past, then went to his study to type a letter. At a quarter to one he suddenly left the study, and, passing rapidly through my room to reach his, he murmured, "I feel dizzy." These were his last words. He just had time to lie on his bed when he breathed his last.

The beloved companion of my life was no more. . . . My whole being refused to believe it. My son had run in on hearing me call, and all we could do was weep and pray together.

There had scarcely ever been any septuagenarians in the whole line of the Imperial Family. Field-Marshal the Grand Duke Michel, Alexander II's brother and my husband's great-uncle, was the only one to reach the age of seventy. Thanks, no doubt, to the care with which he was surrounded, André beat his uncle by almost six months: he was so proud and happy at beating this old-age record!

God granted him an end free from suffering. He was a fine man, and I had the consolation, in my distress, of seeing the esteem and affection in which everybody, Russians, French and strangers, held him.

For three days his body, devoutly watched by officers of the old Russian Army, my son and myself, remained exposed in his room, and later in the drawing-room, transformed into a mortuary chapel; during all this time there was a constant stream of people who came to pay him their last respects, and hundreds of people attended the services which took place twice a day in the house. On the day of his death work in the district had left us without electricity, and we spent forty-eight painful hours by the light of candles alone. I remember the first night in particular; I was alone by André's body, not yet embalmed, but still untouched by death. He might have been asleep, he might have been as he always was, except for his deep silence.

During the funeral a crowd as big as or bigger than the Easter night crowds filled the church, the court-yard and the neighbouring streets.

The Grand Duke and Grand Duchess Wladimir had arrived in Paris the moment they heard that André, who was so fond of them, was dead; once again they gave me their infinitely treasured love.

The Grand Duchess Marie Pavlovna and Princess Irene Alexandrovna, Prince Youssoupov's wife, also attended the funeral. The messages from the Grand Duchesses Xenia and Olga, Nicholas II's sisters, and Ellen Wladimirovna,[1] André's sister, moved me to tears, especially the Grand Duchess Olga's letter.

After the funeral, performed in the Russian Church, rue Daru, by the Metropolitan Wladimir and almost all the Russian clergy in Paris, the coffin was taken into the small church, where it remained for two months before being moved into the crypt. There it remains until it is moved to the chapel built in 1912 by André's mother at Contrexéville, where she is laid, together with the Grand Duke Boris, her son. I am constantly delaying this time, for it is an immense comfort to visit the coffin, and it would not be easy for me often to go to Contrexéville.

With André's death my fairy-tale life came to an end. But I still have our son, whom I adore and who is my sole reason for living. For him I am still a mother, but also the truest and most faithful friend.

When I see the Grand Duke Wladimir, the living symbol of the Imperial Dynasty and heir of the Tsars, I seem to be looking at the Emperor Alexander III, whom he resembles so much in height and majesty: I hear once more the words which the Tsar spoke to me at the Theatre School: "Be the glory and the adornment of our ballet!" And I live again through those distant and moving hours. In offering a devout and grateful tribute to Tsar Alexander III, whose generous approval and encouragement had such a decisive effect on my life and career, I end this book.

Paris, June 1959.

---

[1] The Grand Duchess Ellen died on March 14th 1957.